INSIDE
WALL
STREET

SID MITTRA

INSIDE
WALL
STREET

1971
DOW JONES–IRWIN, INC.
HOMEWOOD, ILLINOIS 60430

Library of Congress Catalog Card No. 76–158050

Printed in the United States of America

For
BANI
for whom the book was written
and for
RITA and AJIT
for no reason

Preface

Three years ago I was invited to teach a course on the stock market by the Continuing Education for Adults of Oakland University. I spent a great amount of time searching for a book for the course that explained the major stock market theories without employing high-powered mathematics, statistics, or technical jargon, but I found none. Left with no other alternative, I began drafting one for the students in the course. *Inside Wall Street* is an expanded and improved version of that draft. In this book, besides explaining the basic investment theories, I have pointed out the different ways in which you can approach investing in the market and the various safeguards that offer protection to the investor from the market risks.

While I attempted to adopt a lucid style of writing because of the technical nature of the subject matter, I am sure I did not always succeed in my objective. Some portions of the book are understandably difficult; therefore, it may be necessary for you to reread these portions. But I assure you that when you are through reading the book you will have developed the self-confidence and knowledge which are prerequisites to successful investing on Wall Street.

Welcome aboard!

Oakland University
Rochester, Michigan
June, 1971

SID MITTRA

Acknowledgments

I wish to thank:

Mr. H. H. Bingham for using his blue pencil ruthlessly on several drafts of my manuscript and doing a superb job of editing.

Messrs. Hichael Fabrikant and Robert Wilds for providing encouragement, for supplying much valuable information, and for criticizing several versions of the manuscript.

Miss Helen Vlastos (now Mrs. Helen Ranney) and Robert Werschky for acting as most trusted student assistants.

Mrs. Marian Wilson for typing and retyping the manuscript several times and for her editorial work.

Mrs. Mary Isbell and Mrs. Lynette Lincoln for their secretarial assistance.

A Note About
Notes and Sources

The author's sources of quotations and other information from published sources identified by "superior" numbers (numbers placed above the line) in the text appear in numerical order in the footnote section at the end of the text.

The bibliography is arranged by chapters and lists books and articles containing material beyond the scope of this book which may be of use to those who wish to pursue the subject matter in greater depth.

Contents

ACT II
CRAFT, NOT WITCHCRAFT

ACT III
PUGWASH OR HOGWASH

ACT IV
THE ELUSIVE BONANZA

ACT V
BEHIND THE SCENES

ACT VI
THE HORIZON

YIPD

Your Investment Personality Detector

I have devised the following quiz so that you may determine your investor personality and *NOT to test your knowledge of the market or investment theories and practices.* In devising this quiz, I have assumed that you have some knowledge of the stock market world. I have also assumed that in the past you have bought and sold securities through a stockbroker. However, even if you have no knowledge of the market and have never contacted a broker, you still should be able to answer all the questions because, as I said above, it is your attitude toward the market that counts. You may therefore relax as you take the quiz.

One further comment: If you come across a question which in your opinion is not appropriately answered by any of the five alternatives, you should pick the one which you think *best* answers the question.

Let me now tell you about the system which is especially designed to grade the quiz. There are *no right or wrong* answers to any question. Rather, each of the five alternatives associated with every question has been assigned a numerical value (between 1 and 5). Please answer every question by selecting the alternative which best describes your attitude toward investing in the stock market.

Now that you understand what this quiz is all about, proceed to answer questions A through Z.

1

A. I consider myself the following kind of investor:
1. cautious
2. subjective
3. action-oriented (that is, anxious to buy and sell frequently)
4. sound
5. objective

B. I like to think of the stock market as a place:
1. where I can make a lot of money within a relatively short time
2. where I can build a sound investment portfolio
3. where I can invest all my savings safely
4. where I can gamble
5. which is a never-never land

C. I am a person who:
1. likes action in the market
2. takes a cautious but optimistic approach to investing
3. acts on intuition in the market
4. feels comfortable when I blindly carry out my broker's recommendations
5. knows so little about the market that I should not operate in it

D. I would consider myself a successful investor if I were to:
1. make money every time I sell a stock
2. realize a *net* gain from my investment every year
3. double my money every two years
4. make 25 percent on my investment every year
5. gain on an average 10–15 percent a year in the long run (that is, over 5 to 10 year period)

E. If my past investment record were a shameful one, this would suggest that:
1. I had a very bad broker
2. I failed to do my investment homework properly
3. I lost money only because the market in general was bad
4. big traders fixed the prices and made money at my expense
5. I should have sold my losing stocks and switched to some that were getting ready for major moves

F. If I ever need information about a stock, I would obtain it:
1. from a broker
2. from a successful investor
3. from a number of reliable sources
4. from the company
5. from an advisory service

G. When I look at the price of a stock, I like to think of this price as being:
1. synonymous with the value of that stock
2. somehow related to the value of the stock but not necessarily equal to it
3. too low, too high, or just right, depending upon the amount of money I have
4. an index of popularity of the stock
5. of little consequence, since the ruling price can be totally out of line with what it should be

H. I would consider a stock worth buying if:
1. its price has been going up consistently

  2. it is low-priced
  3. I had read something good about the company that issued the stock
  4. some advisory service has recommended it
  5. some of my successful investor friends own the stock

I. Before making a decision to buy or sell a stock, I would like to:
  1. investigate the stock as long as possible because I am never in a hurry to buy stocks
  2. spend very little time for fear I might lose the buying opportunity forever
  3. get as many views on the stock as possible
  4. reevaluate my investment objectives
  5. first decide whether the market situation is ideal for making such a move

J. If my broker recommends I sell a stock I am holding, I should:
  1. ignore his recommendation on the grounds that he is trying to make money for himself
  2. investigate his reasons for giving me this advice
  3. find out whether or not I could put my money in a better stock before deciding whether or not I should sell my stock
  4. sell the stock right away
  5. sell it if I could make a profit, but hold it if I would have to take a loss

K. If I were forced to take a loss in the stock market, I would:
  1. consider my misfortune as part of the game
  2. get terribly upset
  3. check to see if I have made any profits recently to offset the loss
  4. make a serious attempt to learn from my misfortune
  5. try to take my loss philosophically

L. If my broker phoned to recommend that I buy a certain stock, I should:
  1. buy the stock without delay
  2. ask the broker if he has his interest or mine at heart
  3. request the broker to send me all the relevant information he has on the stock
  4. tell the broker I am going to think about his recommendation so as not to hurt his feelings and then do nothing about it
  5. examine all the facts dispassionately and then make a decision

M. If the price of a stock were to decline sharply after I purchased it, I should:
  1. be critical of myself for failing to get rid of the stock earlier
  2. sell the stock at a loss and charge the loss to my bad luck
  3. hold the stock until its price goes up so I may recover my loss
  4. buy more of that stock to bring my average purchase price down
  5. investigate the stock thoroughly before making another move

N. Buying at the low and selling at the high:
  1. is the only way to invest in the stock market
  2. is the best investment objective
  3. is a worthwhile goal to pursue
  4. can rarely be attained
  5. should always be seriously attempted, even if it is difficult

O. If a stock I didn't own were to make a major move, I would:
  1. not touch it with a 10-foot pole
  2. grab it before the price advances even further
  3. investigate the company which issued the stock before buying the stock
  4. watch the stock closely
  5. try to buy it on a short-term dip

P. I prefer to treat the past performance of a stock as:
  1. of no consequence
  2. of some importance
  3. of utmost importance in a bull (rising) market, but of little importance in a bear (falling) market
  4. only one factor to consider
  5. of significance when the price of that stock is declining

Q. If the price of a stock I had purchased were to go up substantially, I would:
  1. sell it
  2. hold it in the hope I might make more money
  3. buy more shares of it hoping the price would continue to rise
  4. watch the price action on it carefully for a while
  5. investigate the company thoroughly before making up my mind about selling the stock

R. I consider the study of some leading stock market averages (for instance, the Dow Jones Industrial Average):
  1. to be of little value
  2. of great importance in making investment decisions
  3. of importance only for the chartists (those who graph fluctuations in market averages)
  4. useless, because what good is it to know where the market has been
  5. important only for buying and selling stocks but not for holding them

S. If the price of a stock I had purchased were to go down substantially, I should:
  1. buy more of it to average my buying price
  2. sell it immediately
  3. switch to a stock that is performing better
  4. ask my broker for advice
  5. hold that stock for my children

T. If I were to meet someone who boasted of his great success in the stock market, I would:
  1. take his story with a grain of salt
  2. ask him what his secret of success is and try to follow his method religiously
  3. compare his method with mine in the hope of benefiting from the comparison
  4. give his broker my business
  5. tell the successful investor my story and ask for his suggestions

U. I believe that a successful winner in the stock market, however defined, concentrates on:
  1. acting defensively
  2. outperforming the market

    3. learning new and better market techniques and perfecting the ones he already has

    4. trading, that is, buying and selling stocks frequently

    5. putting all his eggs into one basket and watching that basket carefully

V. The words "puts" and "calls":

    1. mean nothing to me

    2. say something about how to make lots of money cheaply

    3. are something too technical for me to comprehend

    4. are concepts I know I must understand before I can act intelligently

    5. are terms used by big professionals

W. During the 1969–70 bear market when stock prices declined sharply, I:

    1. took substantial losses

    2. did nothing thereby losing most of investment values

    3. bought several stocks very cheaply and came out a winner

    4. stayed away from the market completely

    5. got out of the market with huge losses and then got back into it when prices of most stocks had already reached their recent highs

X. Investing in the market is good for those who:

    1. want to make a lot of money in a short time

    2. wish to play the game defensively

    3. like to have a fixed monthly income

    4. have lots of money to play with

    5. possess technical knowledge about the market

Y. I have heard that every investor should attempt to buy different kinds (such as, speculative, income, growth) of stocks so that his twin objectives of safety and appreciation in investment are simultaneously met. I think that this idea:

    1. is a sound one

    2. is basically bad

    3. should not be treated as a universal investment concept since each investor must buy stocks according to his own needs

    4. is an excellent one only for those who are wealthy and can purchase lots of stocks

    5. can work successfully in a bull (rising) market but not in a bear (falling) market

Z. During the next three years or so, I expect to:

    1. make a lot of money on the stock market

    2. become a professional investor

    3. stay in the market and try to break even

    4. do better than the average investor

    5. learn a lot about the market and become an intelligent investor

    Congratulations! You have just finished taking the investment quiz. You may now determine your investment personality by following the procedure explained below.

    But wait just a minute. Let me first point out here that depending upon your score you will fall into one of the following three investor categories; namely, 1) aggressive and speculative, 2) cautious and uncertain, and 3) sound and confident. However, it should be clearly understood that your falling in group #3 by no means assures your grand success in the stock market. Similarly, if you are placed in the first category, that does not imply that your investment future is bleak. All your score measures is your attitude toward the stock market.

Now about grading the quiz. On page 268 you will find a table entitled *Answers to Investor Personality Detector Quiz*. At the top are marked questions A through Z, while on the left side are numbers 1 through 5 indicating the five possible alternatives to each question. On this table, for each question, please mark the number associated with the alternative you have chosen. For instance, if you have chosen A (5) and B (3), then the numbers to mark on the first and second columns are, respectively, 5 and 2. When you have marked all the columns, add up all the (twenty-six) marked numbers and then match your total grade against your investment personality column.

Now that you know the kind of an investor you are, may I urge you to have some fun reading *Inside Wall Street*.

ACT I

EYE ON THE "DOUGH" NUT, NOT ON THE HOLE

1

Room to Roam

As early as the seventh century B.C., men developed one of their most fascinating inventions—money coined by the state. Paper money has been in use for the past 300 years. Men worked hard for their money and naturally they wanted to make sure that it was well protected at all times. Before 1781, when the first U.S. bank, the Bank of North America, was chartered in Philadelphia, people could not put their money in banks because there were no such institutions in existence anywhere. And, of course, even when banks did appear on the scene charters were hard to come by and frequently were not renewed. Banks were widespread throughout the United States by the end of the Civil War, but some were of the "wildcat" variety and all were potentially unsafe for the depositor because of early state and federal laws. Naturally people were quite reluctant to put their money in banks because of the general distrust of bankers. So in order to reduce the risk of loss of their money holdings, many people buried their treasure in their backyards. And, in most instances, it worked insofar as keeping the money intact was concerned. But it wouldn't be a wise procedure today, even if anyone were eccentric enough to try it.

Why not?

Because some money may be lost today even if it remains intact. In our economy, even if money is physically protected, there is always the risk that, over time, money may lose some of its purchasing power.

Let's say that in 1960 you embarked upon an austerity program which enabled you to save $1,000. You did not feel it was safe to put the money

9

in a bank, so you buried it under your favorite yew tree. Now suppose you dug it up in 1970—10 years later. It looks beautiful, doesn't it? You look at the dollars, caress them, and count them; they are all there. But wait just a minute. They *look* just the same, but they are *not* the same. An invisible thief has robbed you of part of your money. That thief, in case you haven't guessed yet, is inflation. Your $1,000 in 1970 will not buy as much as it would have bought in 1960. As a matter of fact, prices during these 10 years have gone up so much that to buy the things you could have bought in 1960 you would, on the average, need an extra $300 by 1970. For instance, you paid $60 for your suit in 1960; today you would have to pay $78 for that same suit. A pair of shoes which cost $10 in 1960 now costs over $13. In 1960 you rented your apartment for $200; today your landlord won't accept a rent of less than $260. Similarly, you pay more for a quart of milk, a bus ride, education, an automobile, and your living room furniture.

If you've been wondering where your dollars went, take a quick look at Table 1–1. It shows how your dollar has shrunk between 1945 and 1970. In constructing this table I have used the average 1957–59 dollars as the basis for comparison.

TABLE 1–1

SHRINKING VALUE OF THE DOLLAR

Year	Value	Year	Value
1945	$1.59	1958	$0.99
1946	$1.47	1959	$0.98
1947	$1.28	1960	$0.97
1948	$1.19	1961	$0.96
1949	$1.20	1962	$0.94
1950	$1.19	1963	$0.93
1951	$1.10	1964	$0.92
1952	$1.08	1965	$0.91
1953	$1.07	1966	$0.88
1954	$1.06	1967	$0.86
1955	$1.07	1968	$0.82
1956	$1.05	1969	$0.78
1957	$1.02	1970	$0.74

It is not just your bad luck that you have *lost* part of your hard-earned savings. This steady price increase, or inflation, has been with us virtually since the country began, and it is going to stay with us as our permanent, unwanted guest. That price increases have become a part of our lives is evidenced by the following item from *Time* magazine:

. . . it now takes three to tango, four's a crowd, and that favorite song of a few years back has become *Four Coins in a Fountain*. Similarly, the number 14 is bad luck, and so is four on a match. A stitch in time saves ten, cats have ten lives, two birds in the hand are worth three in the bush, a bluffer is a fiveflusher, and that soft drink should really be called Eight-Up. Life these days begins at 41, girls are Sweet 17 and never been kissed, and inescapably, the American consumer is behind the nine ball.[1]

Since it seems that we will not be able to get rid of inflation in the foreseeable future, we had better ask if there is anything we can do to protect ourselves against substantial and continuing inflation. The answer is: There *is* something we can do. We can *use* our money to make more money than is lost in the inflationary process. Notice, I said "use," not abuse. One way to use our money and avoid its abuse is to invest it in the stock market. Now this by itself cannot guarantee absolute protection against erosion of the value of the dollar one owns. But consider the fact that while, since 1946, the dollar has lost over one-third of its purchasing power, the Standard and Poor's Index of Common Stocks has shown a five-fold *increase* by 1965. And despite current and past ups and downs of the market, the secular rise of stock prices has been consistent.

This book is about making money by investing it in the stock market. There are other ways of making money, of course, but we will confine ourselves to the stock market. To do a good job of investing—and not merely speculate about how to strike it rich in two weeks—one must embark upon a course of wise venturing. After all, Lord Fairfax once said:

> Wise venturing
> is the most
> commendable part of
> human prudence.

Happy wise venturing.

October. This is one of the peculiarly dangerous months to speculate in stocks. The others are July, January, September, April, November, May, March, June, December, August, and February.
—MARK TWAIN

2

Taking Stock of Stocks

ARE YOU A SLEEPER OR AN EATER?

Let me assume you are not one of those idealistic and altruistic persons who believes in a profitless society and the possibility of a utopia. You are probably interested in making a modest amount of money honestly, or perhaps you even aspire to become very rich someday.

If you wish to try your luck via the stock market, you have two clear-cut choices: either you sleep well or you eat well. You will find it difficult to do both. Here's why. If it is your desire, through investing in stocks, to create or maintain a high standard of living in our inflated, materialistic economy, you must make *substantial* profits your investment goal. In doing so, you are likely to, or in fact must, take speculative risks. As a general rule, high-risk stocks bring high returns, but investment in these stocks also increases one's blood pressure and aggravates insomnia. So, you see, you have to decide for yourself which you prefer—eating or sleeping.

WELCOME ABOARD

Let me begin by explaining what stocks are, who buys them, and why they are traded. When you buy stock in a company, you don't lend your money to the company; instead, you buy an actual ownership share of that company. If you bought 0.5 percent of the stock of Computer Sciences, you would *own* 0.5 percent of that company: its plants, its equipment, its products, its inventory. In short, you would own 0.5 percent of everything

12

in Computer Sciences. Also, whenever the company declares a dividend, you would be entitled to a 0.5 percent share in that dividend. If the company makes money, the value of your stock holdings is likely to rise. Conversely, if it loses money, the price of the stock will most likely decline.

The type of stock of Computer Sciences, or IBM, or Itek Corporation, that you are most likely to be interested in is known as *common stock*. When you buy the common stock of a company, you receive a stock certificate which is tangible evidence that a certain number of shares are registered in your name or your broker's name on the books of the corporation. As a stockholder, you have become part owner of the company. Now you may participate in its growth through increases in the value of the stock. You are entitled to share in its earnings through dividends. Yet your liability to the creditors of that company is limited to the amount you have invested in the stock.

Though you as a stockholder own part of the company, you could not possibly operate it. So you consent to having your corporation elect an administrative staff to run the show. However, even though you agree to having the company managed by elected staff, you do have a voice in the management of the corporation you partly own, assuming that your stock is classified as voting rather than nonvoting. Even large corporations, such as General Motors, or IBM, or American Telephone and Telegraph (AT&T), with millions of shares of stock outstanding and thousands of stockholders, hold annual meetings at which shareholders may vote on various propositions. Each one has votes proportionate to the number of shares of stock he owns. Those who are not able to attend stockholders' meetings may vote by proxy.

Not all shareholders have the same interest in a corporation, however. Those who would not be satisfied with the status conferred by common stock may purchase *preferred stock*. Preferred stockholders have prior claims on the company's assets and in case of liquidation are entitled to full payment before common stockholders receive anything. Furthermore, preferred stockholders are entitled to a fixed dividend each year, and it must be paid before any dividends are paid to common shareholders. If the preferred stock is *cumulative*, the claim to dividends may be carried over from one year to the next; if the company falls behind in its dividend payments, it must make up the entire amount before giving anything to the common stockholders. Remember, though, that as a general rule preferred stockholders do not participate in company management as do common stockholders with their voting rights.

There is a variety called *convertible preferred stock* which should be of special interest. Such a stock carries a contractual clause entitling the holder to exchange it for a number of shares of common stock of the same company within a specified period of time. For instance, shares of the 5 ⅛ percent convertible preferred stock of Texas Eastern Transmission Corporation are convertible at $22.50 per share through August 1, 1976. Convertible preferred stocks are generally more popular than preferred stocks without this feature.

Another type of preferred stock, *participating preferred stock*, is a popular form of investment. As a general rule, preferred stockholders surrender any claim to the residual earnings of their company after the dividends have been distributed. However, the holder of a participating preferred stock not only receives the dividend but also shares additional earnings with the common stockholder.

If you do not wish to own part of the corporation but still want to invest your savings in it instead of putting them in a bank, you may lend a fixed amount of money to a company for a fixed term. This you may do by buying a bond in the market. A bond is a beautifully designed, officially stamped IOU, which is the company's way of acknowledging its indebtedness to you for lending the money. On that bond, the company will commit itself to paying you a specified rate of interest until the money is returned to you at some specified future date. For most bonds, you can collect this interest when it is due by clipping your coupons and redeeming them at a bank. If you hold a bond till maturity, the company promises to return the principal to you. Should you need the money before the due date, you may sell the bond at any time in the market. Of course, you may get less or more money than you originally paid for it, depending upon the prevailing price of that bond in the market. But the important thing to remember about bonds is that their prices do not fluctuate as much as stock prices. Remember, too, that the price of bonds is not so much related to general business conditions as it is related to the general level of interest rates.

There are many types of bonds, such as mortgage bonds, debenture bonds, convertible bonds, collateral-trust bonds, callable bonds, bearer bonds, and income or adjustment bonds. While each of these types of bond has some special feature associated with it, all of them have one feature in common: A bondholder does not become a direct owner of that corporation; he becomes merely a creditor and, in case of liquidation, he is paid in full along with other creditors before the owners receive a share of the pie.

THE CORPORATION'S BALL PARK

Imagine for a moment, if you will, that you are the president of a corporation wanting to raise money. Your corporation was originally chartered by the state, and it is a separate legal entity apart from the individuals who started it and who run it. It can sue and be sued, it can sign contracts, and it does not cease to exist when any of its personnel die. Your corporation is legally empowered to issue common stocks, preferred stocks, and bonds. Once these stocks and bonds are issued, they can be traded on

the market. All or part of the profits can be ploughed back and the remainder distributed as dividends to the stockholders.

The funds your company obtains by issuing stocks and bonds are its
sources of equity or debt *capital*. This capital, which is the company's
liability, is employed to purchase various types of assets, such as buildings,
equipment, materials, and labor.

What are assets? The all-purpose definition of assets includes everything that a corporation owns or that is owed to it. Assets range from
liquid cash to multistory buildings. Since it seems implausible to put cash
and buildings in the same category of assets, it is customary to differentiate
between *fixed* assets and *current* assets. The former includes land, buildings, and equipment; the latter consists of labor, material, services, and
cash. Let me clarify this by a flow-of-funds chart (Figure 2–1).

FIGURE 2–1

SOURCES AND USES OF FUNDS

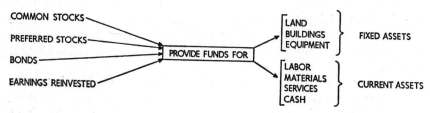

Necessarily, every company has to keep elaborate bookkeeping records
and establish effective data processing systems in order to assure clarity and
efficiency in its complicated operations. Actually the bookkeeping, the
principles of which are fairly simple, is based upon a set of easily understood concepts.

The resources of a company at any point in time may be shown on a
balance sheet. The balance sheet shows the company's resources from two
points of view: where they originate (the equities) and the form they take
(the assets). A familiar accounting equation is:

$$\text{Assets} = \text{Liabilities} + \text{Owners' Equity}$$

The following hypothetical balance sheet of Britts Company (Table
2–1) shows the assets, liabilities, and owners' equity of the company.

WHY STOCKS? WHICH STOCKS?

Now that you have been introduced to the major sources and uses of the
capital of a corporation, you may ponder two related but different questions. The first question has to do with deciding whether to put your
money into common stocks or into a savings account in a bank. After all,

TABLE 2–1

BALANCE SHEET OF BRITTS COMPANY

ASSETS (CAPITAL EMPLOYED)			LIABILITIES AND OWNERSHIP (EQUITIES)		
Current Assets		$ 32,000	Current Liabilities		$ 15,000
Cash	$ 5,000		Insurance	$ 5,000	
Labor	10,000		Rent	5,000	
Material	7,500		Payables	5,000	
Services	9,500		Owners' Equity		157,000
Fixed Assets		150,000	Preferred stocks	$50,000	
Land	$20,000		Common stocks	90,000	
Buildings	80,000		Surplus	17,000	
Equipment	50,000		Long-Term Liabilities		10,000
Total		$182,000	Total		$182,000

you may argue, these institutions guarantee a fixed rate of return on your savings, currently at least 4½ percent, whereas the corporation does not guarantee any return on its stock. Furthermore, your money in a bank is protected against loss up to $20,000 for each account by agencies of the federal government; a corporation never assures you that the value of your original investment will not depreciate or indeed that you will not lose it entirely.

The second question is: If you invest your money in stocks, what stocks should you select? Why, you may ask, should you buy the common stock of International Business Machines (IBM) when you know nothing about the computers it produces? After all, you are not sure whether or not this company will make money on its computers or whether or not this country will continue to value computers in the future.

Let me first weigh carefully the relative advantages of putting your money into savings accounts or into stocks. It is true that commercial banks and savings and loan associations guarantee a fixed rate of interest on savings or certificates of deposit. But it is also true that in case they make more money by using your savings, commercial or savings banks do not offer to pay more than they guaranteed you. Therefore, the fixed return on your savings can be viewed as both an advantage and a disadvantage. A corporation does not guarantee any rate of return, but it does offer the opportunity for an appreciable increase in your funds should the price of the stock increase at some future time. Another advantage to making money on stocks is that you are taxed at the lower capital gains rate under certain qualifying conditions, rather than at the regular income tax rate. And you can, under certain conditions, write off losses on stocks against your income tax. Of course, it is true that there is a certain amount of risk involved in the venture of buying stock. But then, taking some risk is assumed by anyone who wants to make money in the stock market.

In order to answer the second question, that of deciding what stock to buy, you must recognize that not all stocks are attractive to all persons at all times. Basically, each investor has a set of objectives that is short term, medium term, or long term in nature. Each investor has the natural desire to see his money grow. However, he must decide for himself how much risk he cares to take and how long he is prepared to wait before he measures the rate of growth of his money. Some investors would want to take account of the growth in the value of their money on a daily or a weekly basis. Others might look forward to a *reasonable* growth of their money over a period of 10 years or more. Depending upon your investment objective, you must decide what type of stock is most consistent with your personal aims. For instance, for long-term investment gains you might decide to buy AT&T, General Motors, Xerox Corporation, or Detroit Edison, even though you might not expect any of these stocks to serve your short-term objectives. On the other hand, stocks of Burma Mines, or Crestmont Oil and Gas, or Simmonds Precision might shoot up several hundred percent over a period of two weeks, whereas over a long-term period these stocks might not appreciate in value. As a matter of fact, some stocks are doomed in the long run to become worthless. Thus, the answer to the question of why one stock is better than another for you lies unequivocally in the objectives which you as an investor have in mind.

In this context I should like to point out that, as a general rule, a preferred stock commands a higher price than its common stock counterpart. However, preferred stocks do not move in price as sharply as common stocks. The reasons are simple. As mentioned earlier, holders of preferred stock are entitled to "preferred" treatment in the distribution of a company's dividends. In addition, in the case of liquidation the holder of preferred stock has prior claim over the common stockholder to the assets of the company. It would pay you to recognize these differences before you make your stock selection.

MORE INVESTMENT CHOICES

In addition to common stocks, preferred stocks, and bonds, you can buy a number of other types of paper, the more important of which I shall discuss.

One mysterious type of share which appears on the market in the form of an appendage "wi" to some securities is known as *when-issued shares*. Ordinarily the exchanges list "when-issued" shares after a listed company declares a stock dividend or split or announces it will issue new shares for exchange in a merger or acquisition. Once these decisions are made, corporations are obliged to give their transfer agents orders to do the paper work to get the new shares into the hands of their owners. Meanwhile, the new shares (for instance, shares after the split) are listed as "wi" as a convenience to investors. This means that the old stock, or any portion of it, can be sold "when issued" as if the split had already been put into effect. Thus, as a result of the willingness on the part of investors to trade in "when-issued" shares, a ready market is created for them, and you may buy and sell them as if they were another type of stock.

Another instrument of investment, which is often not well understood by investors, is known as a *warrant*. A warrant is neither a stock nor a bond. It does not represent ownership in a company; it is not a loan like a bond. Instead, it is a pledge by the issuing company to sell a share of its common stock at a specified price.

Warrants are frequently issued in connection with reorganizations of companies or along with initial sale of new securities which otherwise might not sell rapidly. Most warrants have a date of expiry tagged onto them but are generally good for a period of years. If not exercised by that due date, the warrants become worthless. In the terminology of investors, the word *exercise* means making use of the market instrument in question. In this case, you would exercise your warrants when you exchange them for stocks.

When you purchase a warrant in the market, you can do one of three things with it. You may turn it in on or before the specified date and buy the company's common stock at the price specified on the warrant; you can sell it; or you can do nothing with it and let it expire.

As a general rule, warrants have a much greater appeal for investors than the stocks which they "sweeten." The reason is that they are more volatile than the stock on which they are a claim. They normally rise faster than the related stocks in bull markets and hence find their way into inflation-protected portfolios. Of course, warrants become much more vulnerable in bear markets; therefore, in falling markets you should handle them with much greater care.

The third trading instrument is *rights*. Often a corporation raises capital by offering rights to its shareholders to subscribe for additional shares at a price below the current market. For instance, with its stock selling at $150 a share, a company might offer rights to one new share at $100 for every five shares held. This implies that the holder of 100 shares of the related stock would be able to purchase 20 additional full shares at the lower price. Like warrants, rights may be exercised or sold in the market by the stockholder. The value of a right is based on the difference, or premium, between the market price ($150) and the subscription price ($100).

Most rights are issued on a short-run basis, and, as you might expect, they become worthless after the date of expiration. Another point worth noting is that if you sell your rights, you reduce your percentage of ownership in the company since, through the rights offering, the corporation is increasing its total outstanding shares.

A Further Sophistication

Now that you have learned some basic facts about stocks, bonds, and other investment instruments, it might interest you to become familiar with some of the standard terminology of the market.

One of the terms frequently used by Wall Streeters is *blue chip*. Blue-chip stocks are high-grade investment-quality issues of major companies which have long and unbroken records of earnings and dividend payments. The term was originally derived from poker, where blue chips (in contrast to white and red) have the highest money value. Shares of AT&T, General Motors, Du Pont, United States Steel, and so forth, are called blue chips. I should point out here that the list of blue-chip stocks changes periodically. Some stocks which were considered blue chips in the past are no longer considered so; similarly, some new stocks are sure to be placed on the blue-chip list in the future.

The names of these large corporations mentioned in connection with blue chips might give you the idea that all blue-chip stocks are growth stocks. That is not always the case. A *growth stock* is one issued by a company whose sales and earnings are expanding faster than the general economy and faster than the average for the industry. The company is usually aggressive, research-minded, and ploughs back a large portion of its earnings to facilitate expansion. Only those blue chips which meet the above criteria can be called growth stocks.

Along with blue chips and growth stocks, you should also become familiar with *speculative stocks*. According to *Webster's Third New International Dictionary*, the word *speculate* means to "enter a business transaction or other venture from which the profits, return on invested capital, or other good are conjectural. . . ." In this sense all common stocks are speculative stocks. However, in stock market jargon, only high-flying glamour stocks are considered speculative stocks. These stocks sell at very high prices relative to their earnings. Another important characteristic of these stocks is that when the market is very strong, these stocks can quickly appreciate in price; conversely, their prices tumble much more rapidly in a down market.

Now that you have been moved into the stock market arena, let me take you on a conducted grand tour of the market.

The stock market is an ideal place for bulls, bears,
hogs, turtles, billygoats, eagles, and tadpoles.
—Growth Stock Outlook

3

"The" Stock Market: Nineteen in All

IN THE BEGINNING

Wall Street—the place where fortunes have been made and bankruptcies recorded—has had a long and venerable history. In 1789 and 1790, New York was the first political capital of the United States under the new Constitution, signed in 1787 and ratified by 1788, just as it is the financial center of the world today. Here the New York State Chamber of Commerce, established April 5, 1768, pressed the fight on the Stamp Act and the tax on tea. Here Washington was inaugurated as the first President on April 30, 1789. Here the first Congress gathered, its executive departments were organized and the system of federal government first began to function. Here, on July 21, 1789, the first 10 amendments to the Constitution, known as the Bill of Rights, were proposed to the states for ratification.

It was here on May 17, 1792, that 24 men representing a group of merchants and auctioneers met "under the buttonwood tree" and established a *regular market*. These 24 men were the original members of the exchange. They managed the trading of government stock which was floated to pay the costs of the Revolutionary War, as well as shares of insurance companies, Alexander Hamilton's First United States Bank, the Bank of North America, and the Bank of New York.

As time went on, it became increasingly apparent that a formalization of

20

market activities was necessary. In 1793 the group constructed for its trading arena the most pretentious building on Wall Street, the Tontine Coffee House and on March 8, 1817, the first formal constitution of the New York Stock and Exchange Board was adopted.

Although a formal constitution was adopted in 1817, by later standards the volume of trade continued to be small. The exchange did not make a continuous market in securities but continued to operate during periodic call periods. On Tuesday, March 16, 1830, only 31 shares passed hands: 5 shares of Morris Canal and Banking Company were traded at 75¼, and 26 shares of the United States Bank were exchanged at 119. On that day anyone with $3,470.25 could have bought up all the stock being offered for sale. Another indication of the small size of the operation was the fact that not until 1870 would a seat on the exchange cost anyone a cent. In 1871 one could buy a seat for $2,000. By 1929 the price of a seat would be over $625,000.

And so Wall Street grew, sometimes at a leisurely pace, sometimes by leaps and bounds. In 1863 the name *New York Stock Exchange* was adopted. Four years later the first stock tickers were installed and in the following year, membership was made salable. In 1871 the call market gave way to a continuous market. In 1879 the first telephones were installed in the exchange; in 1886, for the first time, a day's volume spilled over the 1 million mark.

The Great Depression of the 1930's shook the very foundation of the New York Stock Exchange as most stocks plunged to disastrous new lows. Many astute investors and speculators took advantage of the panic by hiding behind the loose regulations and laws and resorting to questionable practices. One such practice was known as a "washed sale." A speculator would ask his broker to sell, say, 5,000 shares of ABC Corporation to another broker, who in turn would sell these shares to a third broker. Thus, 10,000 shares would change hands fictitiously, giving the general public the impression that the stock was highly active. Another popular practice of the speculators was to use the spiral method for driving up the prices of worthless stocks in order to make quick profits for themselves. These manipulators would first activate trades in worthless stocks by buying them at successively higher prices, thus driving up their prices to the highest possible level. As these rapid price hikes induced the uninformed public to grab them as excellent buys, these speculators would quietly sell out, thereby locking up substantial profits for themselves. When the support for these stocks was withdrawn, the prices would collapse; then the specu-lators would return to the scene and repeat the performance.

Other devices were also used by many speculators to cheat the general public. At one stage the situation worsened to the point where the stock market authorities felt compelled to act. On the economic front, one of the most notable actions was taken in 1934 when the Securities Exchange

Act was passed giving the Board of Governors of the Federal Reserve System the power to prescribe the margin that must be required on loans for purchasing or carrying securities. The importance of this regulation is demonstrated by the following passage.

Before the regulation was authorized, a person having, say, $1,000 to put in the market could arrange with a broker, if the broker was willing to accept the risk, for the purchase of 100 shares of stock at $100 a share—that is, $10,000 worth—the stock being held by the broker as collateral for the $9,000 he was lending and giving him a margin of 10 per cent. If the stock rose or fell $5 a share, the borrower would have a profit or loss of $500. Customary margins in per-regulation days ranged from 10 to 25 per cent. Under the present requirement of a 75 per cent margin, the buyer could arrange to purchase only about 13 shares at $100 each, and a rise or fall of $5 a share would bring him a profit or loss of only $65.[2]

While the granting of the power to the Federal Reserve System in 1934 to impose margin requirements on investors was a giant leap toward controlling the financial side of the stock market, adequate steps were not taken at that time to safeguard the average investor from the malpractices of speculators and traders. However, as time passed the character of Wall Street changed slowly and operations in it were progressively strengthened. Today membership in the exchange is strictly regulated. The rules and regulations governing the conduct of members and allied members are set by the Board of Governors which is elected by the members. The Board exercises broad policy-making functions and is vested with wide disciplinary powers.

The administration of policies made by the board rests in the hands of the staff, headed by the president. The exchange has 2,920 employees, 675 of whom work on the trading floor. The exchange's revenues come mainly from members in dues and charges for services and facilities and from fees paid by corporations whose securities are listed on the exchange.

The exchange employs an amazingly swift and efficient network of communications. It uses "900" ticker systems which print at 500, 600, 700, 800, and 900 characters a minute. The "900" ticker systems are linked to the exchange's IBM-designed computer system. In short, the New York Stock Exchange is one of the wonders of the financial world.

How the NYSE Pendulum Swings

However preposterous it may appear, trading activities on the NYSE can be profitably compared with the transactions that take place on such primitive markets as, say, the Floating Market of Bangkok. Most Orientals would agree that Bangkok is the Paris of the Eastern world. Yet the Floating Market, which is basically a market for all kinds of consumer goods sold by floating boatmen, is the most unsophisticated bazaar ever encountered. To someone unfamiliar with it, this market appears to be a jungle of assorted goods of every conceivable quality. But incredibly enough, there is order in this market and goods do get exchanged to the satisfaction of both buyers and sellers.

Now think of a commodity, say, coconuts, which you may be interested in buying in this market. First, you try to identify and signal the boat carrying coconuts. When it approaches, the first thing you do is evaluate the product and estimate its true value. Then you ask the seller his price and, no matter what he demands, you make a lower counteroffer. You now have laid the foundation for a bargaining process which, through the feelings of mutual strengths and weaknesses, will eventually lead to an amicable setting of a fair price for the coconuts. Notice that the product is not a standard one and that you and the seller are not compelled to make the exchange. And yet, when the exchange does take place, both you and the seller are satisfied that a bargain has been struck.

The operations in a stock market are very similar to those which take place in the Floating Market. On the NYSE, for instance, there are some 2,800 listed issues of stocks and bonds. Each of these stocks is unique, since no two companies are alike. The "true value" of each is a matter of personal evaluation of individual buyers and sellers, and the market never sets its own price for any stock. The NYSE is equipped to handle a trading volume of 15 to 20 million shares a day. The companies whose stocks are traded on the market command great financial resources. They earn about 70 percent of all net profits after taxes reported by all U.S. companies, and they pay their stockholders about 60 percent of all dividends disbursed. Roughly 90 percent of these companies have paid cash dividends in the last 12 months, and some 600 have paid dividends every quarter for a period ranging from 20 to 100 years. These companies provide jobs for about 17 million people, and on the average, total assets per employee amount to over $25,000. They produce practically all automobiles and trucks made in this country, more than 90 percent of all steel, nearly 90 percent of all electric power, and over 95 percent of all aluminum; they handle 95 percent of all railroad traffic and air passenger travel. During 1970 alone, these companies paid over $15 billion in federal, state, and foreign income taxes. And yet a market sufficiently sophisticated to handle all the stocks of these industrial giants permits "crude bargaining" as a means for determining trading prices of stocks and bonds.

The New York Stock Exchange's 1970 *Fact Book* contains some interesting historical data on the exchange. The exchange appointed its first paid president in 1938. Not until 1952 did it drop Saturday mornings and settle on a five-day trading week. In 1953, the exchange first permitted a member to incorporate. Stock tickers were not installed abroad until 1964. Quotes became automatic in 1965. The five-day settlement was adopted in 1968. Central certificate service was established in 1969.

The *Fact Book*[3] illustrates certain developments by comparing the conditions that existed on the New York Stock Exchange in 1935 with those in 1969. In 1935, the Big Board did 78 percent and the American Stock Exchange 13 percent of the listed share volume. By 1969, the figures read 64 percent and 27 percent, respectively. In terms of dollars, in 1935 the Big Board accounted for 87 percent against the American Stock Exchange's 8 percent, the remainder being traded on the regional exchanges. By 1969, respective figures were 74 and 17 percent.

Most investors prefer receiving some income from their common stock holdings. Back in 1936, when 776 issues were listed, only half paid dividends totaling $1.3 billion. In 1969, out of 1,300 issues, 1,100 paid dividends totaling $19.4 billion. By industry, utilities paid dividends totaling $4.0 billion, oils $3.0 billion, autos $1.7 billion, chemicals $1.5 billion, and electronics $1.1 billion. The total number of listed shares increased from 1.3 billion to over 15 billion, while their aggregate market value grew from $47 billion to over $629 billion. Yet the average price per share rose only from $36 to $42.

The story is somewhat different in the case of bonds. In 1935, some 1,500 bond issues worth around $39 billion sold, on average, at 92 percent of par. In 1969, the 1,500 bond issues listed were worth $100 billion, but the price per bond averaged only 78 percent of par. Despite their unpopularity, bonds still make up about 16 percent of the value of all listed securities.

You will, I am sure, find it informative to follow step-by-step one NYSE exchange operation. Let us assume that a Mr. Bill Wild of Detroit has sold his house. After talking things over with his wife, who is very much interested in making money in the stock market, he calls up a broker associated with Meddalion & Company, and asks him to gather information about common shares in AT&T. The broker, Mr. Kay, employs an electronic interrogation device to get the necessary up-to-the-second information, and he reports that Telephone is quoted at "50 to a quarter, last at 50¼." This implies that at that moment the highest bid to buy AT&T stock is $50 a share, the lowest offer to sell is $50¼ a share, and the last transaction in that stock was at $50¼. The broker also explains to Wild that 100 shares of AT&T will cost him approximately $5,000, plus a commission of about $112.

After consulting with his wife, Wild decides to buy 100 common shares of AT&T. He calls up Kay and puts in an order for the stock. Kay writes out an order to buy 100 shares of T "at the market" and has it wired to his New York office, where it is phoned or wired to his firm's partner on the floor of the exchange. Each stock is assigned a specific location at one of the 18 trading posts, and all exchanges in that stock must take place at that location. In this particular case, the floor partner moves over to Post 15 where T is traded.

At this time, Mr. Stan, a business executive and a devoted husband, decides to sell 100 shares of AT&T to get funds to buy his wife a diamond ring for their anniversary. He calls his broker at Creek & Company, and asks him to get a "quote" and sell his stock. That order too is wired to the floor. Stan's broker also hurries to the post. As soon as he enters the AT&T "crowd," he hears Wild's broker yelling, "How's Telephone?" Someone— frequently the specialist—answers, "50 to a quarter."

Wild's broker could without further negotiations buy the 100 shares offered at 50¼, and Stan's broker could sell his 100 at 50. In that event, if their customers had been looking on, they probably would have demanded, "Why were you not able to get a better price for us?" They would have been right; that is precisely what the broker has to try to do. When a broker enters the "crowd" of a stock on the floor, he applies his skill and knowledge to get the best possible price he can for his customer.

Here is how Wild's and Stan's brokers might argue as each seeks the best price for his customer. Wild's broker: "I can't buy my 100 at 50. Someone has already bid 50 and no one will sell at that price. I think I am going to have to bid up the price to 50⅛." Stan's broker hears Wild's broker bid 50⅛ and instantly shouts, "Sold 100 at 50⅛." These brokers have agreed on a price and a transaction has taken place.

You can see how basically similar are the operations of the Floating Market of Bangkok and the New York Stock Exchange. Here is the auction market in operation. Thousands of times every day the same kind of bidding is repeated on the floor of the exchange.

The two brokers complete their verbal agreement by noting each other's firm name and reporting the transaction to their phone clerks so that their customers can be notified. In the meantime, an employee of the stock exchange at Post 15 marks a special card to indicate the stock symbol, the number of shares and the price, and places it in an "optical card reader." The card reader scans the pencil marks with its photoelectric eye and transmits the information to the Market Data System computer.

As soon as the brokers get the information on the exchange of these shares, they inform their respective clients. The clients then may request the transfers of shares and money or, alternatively, have the brokers hold the shares and money on their behalf.

In this short drama concerning the buying and selling of AT&T shares, I have considered the following five steps:

1. When you sell, you sell to another person.
2. When you buy, you buy from another person.
3. The stock exchange itself neither buys, sells, nor sets prices.
4. The exchange provides the marketplace for the exchange of stocks.
5. The stock market offers an avenue of escape for individual investors. That is, a person who has purchased stocks can recover his funds by selling them at a later date on the exchange. Knowledge that a ready market exists reduces the hesitancy on the part of investors to invest in stocks. If there

were no assurance that a market would continue to exist, few would buy stocks no matter how attractive they appeared.

The "Odd" Investors

In the preceding illustration, I assumed that you wanted to purchase 100 shares of AT&T. You may wonder if the exchange's rules would have permitted you to buy 1, 5, 15, or 99 shares of that stock. Yes, you could have bought any amount of shares you wished. However, if you purchased less than 100 shares, your order would have been handled slightly differently. Also, your order would have been called an *odd-lot* order. Let me elaborate.

Assume you called your broker, Kay, and asked him to buy five shares of AT&T at the market. Kay would direct his clerk to send the order to an odd-lot dealer in Telephone. The dealer would fill the order at a price based on the next round lot (of 100 shares) transaction in AT&T. If the next round-lot price of AT&T happened to be 45⅛, the odd-lot dealer would purchase five shares at 45½. The additional one-eighth point, or 12½ cents per share, included in the odd-lot price is known as differential. For stocks selling at more than $55, it is one-quarter point, or 25 cents a share. The same procedure would be followed if you ordered 1, 9, or 97 shares.

What's for the Broker?

As the current wave of mergers, liquidations, or bankruptcies of brokerage firms attests, all brokers do not strike it rich every trading day. Stock exchange brokers charge on the average between 1 percent and 2 percent of the dollar value of each transaction. In general, for each 100 shares traded, the charges are as follows: On a purchase or sale between $100 and $399, 2 percent plus $3; from $400 to $2,399, 1 percent plus $7; from $2,400 to $4,999, one-half of 1 percent plus $19; and above $5,000, one-tenth of 1 percent plus $39. In addition, there is a 50 percent surcharge imposed on the total dollar value of every exchange, subject to a maximum of $15 per trade.

Other Exchanges: More of the Same?

I am sure you know that the NYSE is not the only stock exchange in the United States. However, you may not realize that besides the NYSE there are 17 other stock exchanges, excluding the over-the-counter market, about which I will speak later. Thirteen of these are registered stock exchanges; the rest are exempt stock exchanges. Of the 17 exchanges, the American Stock Exchange (AMEX) is the largest, handling over 7 percent of dollar volume of all stock transactions. Since the AMEX is the fascinating hub of a lucrative business, I will discuss the vital role it plays in the financial and industrial organization of the nation.

Founded in the 1850's, the AMEX was known as the New York Curb Exchange until it acquired its present designation in 1953. There was no such occasion as the opening of doors, however, for at the start the AMEX had no doors at all. It operated under the open sky in one of the narrow streets of lower New York. Today the AMEX is located in Trinity Place, New York City. On the trading floor sometimes more than 10 million shares change hands in some 50,000 individual transactions. The total value of a day's trading may reach as high as $350 million, and sometimes higher.

The functioning of the AMEX resembles that of the NYSE; the trade is made in a similar way in both exchanges. However, there is one very important difference. The listing requirements for the AMEX are less stringent than for the NYSE. Generally, the companies listed on the AMEX are less well established, and it serves as a proving ground for fairly new small and medium-sized companies which meet certain basic standards and expect to grow rapidly. The industrial giants like GM, U.S. Steel, and AT&T are traded on the NYSE.

The AMEX is not a corporation but a membership organization owned by the 650 regular members of brokerage firms. It is governed by a Board of Governors. The annual budget of the AMEX is in excess of $20 million, which is indicative of its importance in the financial world.

The various regional exchanges (such as the Midwest Stock Exchange, the Pacific Coast Stock Exchange, and the Detroit Stock Exchange) were originally for the purpose of effecting transactions in stocks of local interest, but this is no longer the case. At present over 90 percent of the trading on regional stock exchanges is in securities also traded on the New York Stock Exchange, and less than 10 percent of their business is in securities traded solely on regional exchanges.

The Wonder That Is OTC

The over-the-counter (OTC) market, which is actually a way of trading stocks rather than a central marketplace, is probably the least-known segment of the securities industry. All transactions not occurring on a regular exchange are included in over-the-counter transactions. About 10,000 common stocks are actively traded over-the-counter, more than three times the number of issues listed on the 18 stock exchanges in the United States and Canada. According to another estimate, there are over 550,000 corporations in the United States, of which about 10 percent, or 55,000, have stocks in public hands. In a year's time, the National Quotation Bureau representing the OTC market quotes prices on approximately 40,000 securities: 26,000 stocks and 14,000 bonds. By contrast, there are only about 1,300 stocks and 1,500 bonds listed on the New York Stock Exchange. In 1970 there were approximately 28 million shareholders in the United States and over 45 percent of these shareholders owned OTC securities. Yet the OTC market is comparatively unregulated, and it is only recently that there has been talk of computerized methods to facilitate OTC transactions.

The OTC market is unique. Though some OTC stocks are blue chips and could qualify for trading on major exchanges, many are speculative penny stocks of small, often relatively unknown, companies. This market grows as more and more companies go to the public for funds with which to develop new products and new markets. At the present time, thousands of utility and industrial stocks, most bank and insurance company stocks, U.S. government securities, municipal bonds, all railroad equipment trust certificates, and many Canadian and foreign securities are traded on the OTC market.

Any market as diversified as OTC can expect to attract people with a variety of objectives and interests. Institutions and other conservative investors use the OTC market in purchasing high-quality issues of government securities, corporate bonds, preferred stocks, and certain good-quality common stocks. People with high incomes find it advantageous to buy tax-exempt municipal bonds. Technically oriented seasoned investors go to the OTC market to buy stocks of new, small companies which have the potential for spectacular growth. In short, the OTC provides "a little something for everyone."

It might be interesting to recount here the experience of a typical OTC broker, Mr. Brown, on a typical day. Brown arrives at his office at 9:30 A.M. and soon begins to compare his own feel for the market with the views of the firm's other traders and with those of competitors who make markets in the same issues at other houses.

Brown is linked by 120 direct, private phone lines and 10 leased teletype wires to other brokerage firms, banks, and fund managers throughout the country. A number of switches on the desk in front of each trader enables him to talk on any line at the flick of a switch.

Before the market opens, Brown has compared notes with a score of traders and brokers. A clerk has mapped Brown's opening bid and asked for quotes—the prices at which he is willing to buy or sell the stocks he trades—along with those of the other traders on the big trading board. Any trader in the firm can buy or sell any security the firm trades at the price marked on the board.

At 10 A.M. trading begins. For the next 25 minutes Brown keeps talking in an attempt to make market for several stocks. For every trade he makes, he gives out 5 to 10 price quotes to potential customers shopping for the best price or to competitors checking his markets.

Later, a competitor catches Brown with a low asking price on a stock that is going up. "I want to buy 1,000" says the trader. "Why don't you buy 100?" answers Brown, who must sell at least that amount to anyone who takes his price. "Okay." Brown shouts to the clerk on the trading board to raise his quote half a point after the sale, then scribbles a sell order in his notebook.

And so the day rolls on. A Texan wants to buy a stock Brown is quoting at 50¼. A New Yorker is anxious to unload his stocks to Brown, but the asking price is too high. A young trader at another brokerage firm wants to sell 50,000 shares, but there is no ready market, so Brown is approached again.

Trading stops precisely at 3:30 P.M. Weary after a day's hard work, Brown flips through his pile of buy and sell orders, checks his "position"— the inventory of stocks he holds or is short in—and jots down his closing quotes. He has traded a total of 46,199 shares in 141 individual trades ranging from 3 shares to a block of 6,000. Brown gets out of the office into his car, and puts on the air conditioner. He deserves this comfort. After all, he has made money for the firms and for himself.

Summing Up

This chapter has dealt with the subject of stock exchanges as a market-place for stocks and bonds. I am now ready to discuss the sources of relevant market information so you may become a well informed investor.

Economists . . . [don't say] anything. . . . Very often, what they explain in 50,000 or so well-chosen technical words and phrases is that the economy will accelerate, decelerate or maintain the status quo if, perhaps, when and but.

—ANONYMOUS

4

Where Is All the Dope?

THE FUTURE IN A CRYSTAL BALL

In the investment world one bets on the future. Consequently, the more clearly one forecasts the future, the more success he is likely to achieve.

Assume you are planning to drive to the New York Stock Exchange tomorrow. It would be helpful to know what the weather will be like. You may take for granted that it will be like today's weather, or you may prefer to wait and see. You can ask a few of your friends how they predict tomorrow's weather, consult your newspaper or turn on a TV weather program, or you may make your own prediction on the basis of the barometer in your window. If none of these seems satisfactory, you may call the weather bureau and obtain the meteorologist's prediction. No matter which alternative you choose, you must not lose sight of the fact that you could not know *for sure* what kind of day tomorrow will be.

The situation in forecasting economic conditions is similar. Since you must make a guess about tomorrow's economic condition and act accordingly, you may base your decision on guesswork, on personal inquiry, on other people's views, or on the *scientific* forecasts of economists. Whether or not one of these methods of predicting the future will be accurate depends upon political and social factors, natural calamities, and the aggregate result of decisions made by millions of investors.

Data, Data, Who's Got Data?

There are four principal ways to acquire forecasting information. First, there are numerous sources of published general information about the market, individual companies and their shares, and the general state of the economy. This information comes to you in daily newspapers, weekly and monthly business reviews, reference guides and manuals, and other economic and business publications prepared by both private and public organizations.

Second, you may seek advice from a large variety of advisory services which cater to the needs of investors. These services may recommend undervalued stocks or alert investors to dispose of stocks that are no longer worth holding. Some advisory services specialize on certain types of securities, while others deal with special analytical techniques.

Third, you may obtain information from individual companies which supply their annual reports, prospectuses, and special statements to stockholders. Often these are the best sources of information for investment purposes, even though companies frequently forecast on the basis of their own business interests.

Fourth, you may obtain valuable information and advice from your broker. He stands ready to give you his information and his advice. But he cannot perform miracles. There always exists the possibility that he may transmit biases and prejudices which could be detrimental to your interests, and you should be aware of this.

Looking through the Publications Glass

Let me first explore some of the more important and easily accessible sources of information. One is The Wall Street Journal (WSJ), well known for its excellent coverage of a wide range of important information. Among the most sought-after pages in this journal are those containing market quotations. Here you will find lists of stocks traded on the NYSE, AMEX, OTC, and regional and foreign exchanges; the opening, highest, lowest, and closing prices of each stock; the highest and lowest price of each stock during the year; net change, if any, from each stock's closing price on the preceding day; volume; and so on. A typical excerpt might look like this:

| This Year | | | | Sales in | | | | | Change |
High	Low	Stocks	Div.	100's	Open	High	Low	Last	+ or −
$78\frac{1}{2}$	$68\frac{3}{4}$	Kirk Co.	3.50	76	$75\frac{5}{8}$	$76\frac{7}{8}$	$75\frac{1}{2}$	$76\frac{3}{4}$	$+1\frac{3}{8}$
(A)	(B)	(C)	(D)	(E)	(F)	(G)	(H)	(I)	(J)

Let me interpret the table: On a given day, 7,600 (E) shares of Kirk Company (C) were traded. The first trade for the day was at 75⅝ (F). During the day the price dropped to 75½ (H) and reached a high of 76⅞ (G). The last transaction took place at 76¾ (I) per share, which was 1⅜ (J) higher than the previous closing price. During the year this stock traded between 68¾ (B) and 78½ (A) a share, and the company paid dividends at an annual rate of $3.50 per share (D).

The *WSJ* publishes similar data on all stocks listed on the NYSE, the AMEX (also abbreviated as ASE), and selected stocks traded on the OTC and regional exchanges. Those who do not have time to read the complete list of quotations can scan the section which gives the opening, high, low, closing, and changes in prices, as well as volume, of the most active issues each day. On another page it frequently gives the Dow Jones averages, other financial indices, the total number of issues in which trading occurred, the number of stocks that advanced, the number that declined, the number of new highs, the number of new lows, and odd-lot statistics. Full lists of sales and prices on the ASE are also quoted, but only leading stocks are given in the quotations for regional exchanges, such as the Toronto, Philadelphia-Baltimore-Washington, Midwest, Salt Lake City, Detroit, Pittsburgh, Boston, Cincinnati, Pacific Coast, and Honolulu exchanges.

The *WSJ* also covers stocks traded on the OTC, although the information given is not so extensive as that for stocks listed on the NYSE and the ASE. Typically for each stock, bid and asked prices, bid change from the previous day, and dividend information are furnished.

For the sophisticated investors, the *WSJ* publishes a wealth of information. For example, bonds traded on the NYSE are quoted "plus accrued interest," implying that the purchaser paid the price quoted for the bonds plus the accrued interest from the last interest date to the date of purchase. The *WSJ* also publishes data on dividends and annual earnings of various companies. In addition, readers are informed of all new issues being floated on the market. Another type of information of considerable interest to some investors is known as "changes in insider stockholdings." The Securities and Exchange Commission requires that anyone who owns more than 10 percent of any stock listed on a national exchange or who is a director of the company issuing a stock must report changes in his holdings. By publishing these actions of insiders, the *WSJ* indirectly divulges confidential information to the public. Finally, the *WSJ* publishes information on various types of money rates and prices on commodity markets.

Broadly speaking, variations in stock prices reflect fluctuations in general business and economic trends. Consequently, you would want to keep abreast of current business news. I mention here only the sources of such news; the method of analyzing this information will be discussed in the next chapter.

Financial pages of the *WSJ* are an important source of information on broad economic and business trends. Typical news items which reflect overall business conditions include information on changes in production, wholesale and retail price indexes, department store sales, housing starts, liquid position of banks, and bankruptcies. Information is also provided on auto, steel, and oil production, electrical power output, and business inventories. Typical major news items of financial significance include international developments, imposition or relaxation of federal regulations, special legislation, mergers, strikes, wage agreements, and, above all, actions of the Federal Reserve System to ease or tighten credit conditions. I should mention too that from time to time the *WSJ* carries news items on gross national product, level of unemployment, the level of disposable personal income and savings, and magnitude of installment credit.

Many brokerage houses regularly publish research papers on individual companies, while their research departments frequently issue bulletins suggesting sample portfolios, reviewing the state of the economy and making investment suggestions. Here is a concrete example. A recent bulletin issued by the Investment Research Department of E. F. Hutton & Co., Inc., recommended the purchase of Eaton Yale & Towne in the following words:

Sales this year are estimated at over $1 billion . . . compared to $889 million last year. Earnings have been projected by management at $3.50 a share. Assuming a slowdown in the economy during the first half of 1970 has some impact on Eaton Yale & Towne, we estimate 1970 sales at $1.15 billion and earnings at $3.75 a share. With prospects of a better than average auto year in 1971, the air bag, and the benefits from the improvements made in the materials handling division, the company appears capable of reaching the $6.00 a share 1972 earnings goal set last year. The investment grade shares represent good value at 11.2 times estimated 1970 earnings. Purchase for long-term capital gains is recommended.[4]

In addition to periodic bulletins, many brokerage firms put out important monthly publications. For instance, every month Paine, Webber, Jackson & Curtis publishes the *Security Buyer's Guide*. This guide classifies selected stocks into the following categories: (1) investment grade, (2) capital gains and good quality, (3) businessman's risk, and (4) special situations. Periodically, for the benefit of the general public, brokerage houses also publish special booklets, such as *What Is Margin? How Over-the-Counter Securities Are Traded, Convertible Bonds,* and so on.

There is no lack of pertinent data if you are statistically oriented. For instance, you may follow the coverage of economic developments in specialized newspapers and journals such as the *WSJ, Barron's National Business and Financial Weekly,* and the *Journal of Commerce.* The Sunday edition of *The New York Times* provides weekly and monthly statistical comparisons boxed under the title, "Economic Indicators." The

Times also publishes an "Index of Business Activity," derived from data on carloadings, output of electricity, steel, paperboard, and lumber. *Business Week*, a McGraw-Hill publication, features an "Index of Business Activity." A variety of statistics usually appears in the Thursday edition of the *Commercial and Financial Chronicle.* The *Magazine of Wall Street, Financial Analysts Journal, Dun's Review, Fortune, Forbes Magazine of Business and Finance,* and many others contain articles which discuss current business trends.

While I am on this topic, I would also like to mention some of the standard statistical publications which provide a vast amount of information. The *Statistical Abstract of the United States* includes a variety of statistics in its one thousand pages relating to the industrial, political, social, and economic fields. Then there is the *Survey of Current Business,* an unusually detailed and broadly ranging source of data covering every aspect of domestic and foreign business. The *Wall Street Transcript* also contains a wealth of information.

A useful periodical that briefly summarizes current statistics on the overall economy is the monthly, *Economic Indicators.* In the area of money and banking, of course, the best source is the *Federal Reserve Bulletin,* a monthly publication of the Federal Reserve System.

I should also mention the *Business Conditions Digest,* published by the U.S. Department of Commerce. This digest provides the analyst with the kinds of data he needs to make an informed judgment on current and prospective business conditions. One of the facilities the *Digest* has developed for studying the indicators of business activity is a punched-card file of its statistical series. This has now been made available to the public so that anyone can analyze his own special business problems in relation to national data. Another feature included in the *Digest* is the grouping of cyclical indicators into time categories described as "Leading, Lagging, and Roughly Coincident," a concept originated by the National Bureau of Economic Research.

Bank Letters

Research reports of leading banks which usually emphasize current economic rather than stock market conditions should be of interest. The three leading reports are published by the three leading New York City banks: First National City Bank's *Monthly Economic Letter;* the Chase Manhattan Bank's *Business in Brief;* and Morgan Guaranty's monthly *Survey.* Other banks across the nation offer their own economic letters as well.

The Advisory Services

All of this readily available information will be of little value unless you can interpret it properly and translate it into positive action. In this respect, the advisory services can be of great assistance. Most services interpret economic developments, analyze past trends, explain the current situation, and forecast future prospects. They also present background information to help you understand financial developments. Ideally, an advisory service performs two functions: informational and directional. These are related but separate functions, and to take full advantage of the services you should understand the distinction between them.

The informational function of an advisory service consists of making available as much pertinent information as possible in the most comprehensible form. Thus, information is given to you in the form of discussions of market highlights, statistical tables, charts, and graphs. In a recent article,[5] Robert Burgess of the State University of New York at Albany recommended four specialized services, all of which perform an informational function. The first service, America's Fastest Growing Companies, selects approximately 150 companies on the basis of exceptional past earnings records and follows them as long as earnings continue to increase. The second service, I.Q. Trends, places 250 selected blue chips into overvalued and undervalued categories based on comparisons of historic yield data with current yield levels. The third service, R.H.M. Warrant and Stock Survey, employs a sophisticated approach to speculation, using warrants and volatile low-priced stocks. The fourth service, The Contrary Investor, has a skeptical, psychological approach to investment decisions. These advisory services are supplemented by excellent chart services (for example, Mansfield Stock Chart Service, Trendline Daily Basis Stock Charts, Paflibe, Andrews Technical Services, and Wyckoff Charting Service) which assist an investor in making sophisticated investment decisions.

In addition to the above, I should mention the three major services which are widely used by investors: Moody's Investor Service, Inc., Standard & Poor's Corporation, and the Value Line Investment Survey. Every year Moody's Service publishes five volumes of Manuals, each covering one of the following fields—industrials, public utilities, transportation, governments, and fianance. These Manuals are kept up to date by a semiweekly report. In addition to the Manuals, Moody's publishes (1) a weekly Stock Survey, (2) a set of compendiums on individual companies called Moody's Handbook of Widely Held Common Stocks, and (3) a weekly bond guide called Bond Survey.

Standard & Poor's publishes Corporation Records, listing corporations alphabetically, regardless of field. The Records are supplemented by a daily bulletin. This service also publishes: (1) a weekly magazine, The Outlook, (2) a pocket-sized handbook called Stock Guide, (3) a compendium, Stock Market Encyclopedia, (4) and a bond guide known as Bond Outlook.

The third service, Value Line Investment Survey, covers 1,100 stocks in

60 industries. The coverage of this service is excellent. Each stock covered by the service is reviewed in detail every three months. Weekly supplements are issued to report new developments that might be of interest to the subscribers. In addition, each week the Survey analyzes several industries on a rotating basis.

The directional function is really the major objective of all advisory services. Most people who have any background in economics and business can follow the myriad details made available by these services. But when it comes to interpreting and translating information into positive action, few people feel at ease. Consequently, the advisory services' recommendations provide direction to their subscribers. The recommendations range from an appeal for inaction to a go-ahead for positive action. These services want you to utilize investment opportunities, but they do not want you to take hasty, dangerous, or irresponsible steps. However, in this connection a word of caution is in order. When consulting an advisory service, you should remember that advice is given to suit mass tastes and may not be consistent with your own investment philosophy. Hence you should use caution and judgment before accepting the recommendations of these services.

About Themselves

All companies supply pertinent information about themselves through annual reports and prospectuses. A typical annual report of a company contains a statement about achievements of the past financial period, a table showing current financial highlights, and predictions for the future. Financial highlights include information relating to net sales, net income, earnings, dividends per share, number of shares outstanding at year-end, working capital, and common shareholders' equity per share of common stock. In the statement of financial condition or balance sheet are shown details of assets (current and fixed) and liabilities (current, long-term, and stockholders' equity). A statement of income and retained earnings may also be provided.

In its prospectus, a company usually spells out its objectives, its capitalization plans, names and qualifications of its board of directors, and its main business. The prospectus offers a brief history of the company, possibly a 10-year summary of earnings if it has been in business for a long time, and a listing and description of any property it owns. The annual report and the prospectus, together with special statements to stockholders by a corporation are among the best sources of information on any corporation.

Before leaving this topic I should mention a publication by the Leasco Information Products entitled *Now You Can Get the Corporate Reports*

You Use Regularly—without a Hassle. The preface to this publication reads:

If you are involved in any activity which requires a familiarity with the finances and/or administration of publicly-owned companies, you're always looking for more complete, efficient, and faster ways of handling large amounts of data. Leasco's new Disclosure service makes this possible by offering complete SEC filings.[6]

In convenient subscription packages, Leasco now offers on microfilm valuable information on individual companies.

THE FRIENDLY BROKER

We now come to the cheapest and the most convenient source of information: your broker. Realistically speaking, a broker has many facets to his personality. He has a moral obligation to report faithfully all the relevant information to help you develop a *sound* investment program. While it is not his prerogative to decide whether or not to buy one stock or another for you, a broker should always emphasize the need for careful and intelligent use of funds.

The broker assumes the role of a "stockwatcher" as well. He has instant access to the ticker tape and quotron, and he should possess the skill to catch instantly any unusual fluctuations in the prices of the stocks you own. Within limits, you may expect him to contact you if he has detected any developments which require your immediate attention.

A broker is also an informer. He has access to tons of valuable material, not all of which is of interest to you. According to what he can surmise about your educational background, market interests, and temperamental makeup, he keeps the relevant information flowing. It pays for you to know that he is the best and the cheapest source of information. You may obtain from him, at no cost, research and informational bulletins, stock guides, Standard and Poor's sheets, special write-ups on individual stocks and, above all, a technical analysis of the day-to-day fluctuations in the market.

You would be unwise not to recognize that a broker is also a businessman seeking to maximize his own income. And since he earns a commission both when you buy and when you sell, he has a vested interest in your *trading* in stocks, even when trading is not in your best interest. Do not become too critical of your broker for sometimes furthering his self-interest; considering his struggle to survive in this competitive business world, he cannot be blamed if he sometimes puts his own interests first. However, you have a right to expect that his self-interest will be of the enlightened variety and that, hopefully, it will not often conflict with his obligations to you. If it does, you should seek another broker.

While your broker is the best market friend you have, do not expect him to be a substitute for the homework which you alone must do. Your broker does not have a crystal ball. Besides the possibility of his misguiding you to serve his own self-interest, there is also the chance that he may not fully understand or correctly read your needs. Therefore, use your broker not as a crutch but as a friend whose advice and help you value immensely.

Microscopic View of Information Explosion

Sometimes you must wonder where in the world all this valuable information is stored and how to find it quickly when you need it. The information explosion does offer a serious problem, although a near-term solution seems to have emerged. During the last two years or so, there has been quite a revolution in the availability of corporate financial information. This has come about mainly through the application of microfiche— microfilm in card form—to the information reproduction and distribution processes.

There is nothing new about microfiche; it is simply a photographic reduction process used to copy material onto a 4" × 6" acetate or polyester film. This standard-size card provides space for 60 8½" × 11" pages arranged in five rows with 12 pages to the row. There is a top strip which is used for identification (company name, document number, type of report, etc.) and which can be read without optical devices. You can see that the advantages of microfiche over paper are space saving, lower acquisition cost, longevity of file, and easier accessibility.

Let me tell you what types of information are available in this form. In 1967, Merrill Lynch and the National Cash Register Company undertook the major task of reducing Merrill Lynch's corporation files to microfiche. Their files, the most complete in the financial community, contained data on some 15,000 companies. The job was completed in 1969; today about 4 million pages are reproduced on 100,000 microfiches. The price of this basic file, currently available only from the NCR Corporation, is approximately $45,000 (45 cents per fiche). If you are not interested in all 15,000 companies, the following subsets are available individually: NYSE— approximately 1,300 corporations; ASE—1,050; OTC—11,000; OTC, listed in the *WSJ*—1,200; and *Fortune*—500. The price of the NYSE subset is $12,000; prices of other subsets are approximately half of the NYSE price.

The technique used by the NCR Corporation to handle mergers, requisitions, and name changes is particularly interesting, since each of these eliminates corporate identities. The identification strip across the top of the fiche refers to acquisitions. Corporations with many acquisitions have a leading card devoid of microimages but carrying names of all acquired companies. Corporations which no longer exist have a title-only card referring to the new corporation.

In addition to the Merrill Lynch–NCR Corporation information system, information is available from other sources as well. In cooperation with the NYSE, University Microfilms, a subsidiary of Xerox Corporation, supplies microfiche documents (annual and interim earnings, reports, prospectuses, etc.) filed with the NYSE by individual corporations. University Microfilms also serves the financial community with microfiches and microfilm of the *Commercial and Financial Chronicle* and the *Bank and Quotation Record*.

Another reputable concern, Bell and Howell, provides microfilming coverage of several Dow Jones publications. *WSJ* and *Barron's* may be purchased on roll film. There is also a printed monthly *WSJ Index* which is particularly useful for reference articles.

I should mention here that the stock exchange transaction microfiche is also available. This is a weekly service which provides the daily NYSE, ASE, OTC market listings, bond listings, commodity listings, and city market listings. Since it arrives a week or two after Friday's transactions, it can function as a handy price source.

Because of the high cost of obtaining the data films and cards, only large corporations and brokerage firms can afford to purchase them regularly. But this should not dampen your interest in them. It will pay you to know whether or not your broker has access to this information so that you may obtain the requisite data from him.

What's Next?

In this chapter I have described the four major sources of investment information. As you can see, there is plenty of material available to anyone who cares to collect it. However, that is not an end in itself. What you really need is to evaluate systematically all this information in order to decide which stocks to buy or sell. This involves forecasting economic and market trends. Economic forecasting is the subject of the next chapter.

The average professional . . . economic forecaster is a bit like the average weather forecaster; he
gives you a 40% chance of precipitation and a 40%
chance there will be no rain. The extra 20% is your
problem and the forecaster is right either way.

—JOHN W. DAY

5

Oops,
the Economy Is Changing

THE OBJECTIVE

You need no longer be a casual bystander. You have learned a great deal
about the stock market, about its instruments, about the participants, and
about the numerous sources of information available. What you need now
is the ability to evaluate this information and apply it in your investment
planning. Especially important are the decisions you will make about the
future of your stocks based on how you assess future trends in the market
and the economy.

In this chapter my objective is to discuss the methods for forecasting the
economy. In Chapters 6, 7, and 8 I will talk about the market and
about the ways in which you can select stocks at the right time with
confidence.

THE KEY INDICATORS

Let me take up the matter of identification of the key indicators. As a
general rule, every conscientious investment analyst studies the movements
in important economic indicators in order to determine the long-term
economic health of the nation. Of course, the term economic *indicator*
means different things to different people. It may refer to any measure of

economic activity—from broad measures like gross national product (GNP) to very limited ones like paperboard production. One cannot hope to keep up with all indicators because data are available to any investor so cheaply and so plentifully that one is likely to be deluged. It is therefore more advisable for you to be basically interested in a limited range of indicators. For example: How fast is the real GNP rising? How much are people receiving after taxes? How many people are employed? How fast are the production of industrial goods and houses expanding? How fast are prices rising? What are the government's fiscal plans? How much gold is the nation losing as a result of deficits in its balance of payments? Finally, how is the money situation changing? It is true that these indicators would give you only a *limited* insight into the economic health of the economy; nevertheless, if you are an investor with limited resources and limited need for assimilating and interpreting available data, a narrower view of the economy would appear justifiable.

The most important indicator is the real rate of growth in GNP—the total new output of goods and services produced on an annual basis. Since the degree of affluence of an economy is primarily dependent upon its capacity to supply more and better goods, a high rate of increase in GNP with a reasonable degree of price stability indicates a healthy economy, whereas a slow or negligible rate of growth of GNP is indicative of slackness in the economy.

The second major indicator is disposable personal income, which in layman's language is known as the "take-home" pay. Most of this money is spent for consumer goods and services. The more take-home pay people have, the more they will buy; the more goods and services are sold, the more businesses will produce, thereby creating more jobs and disbursing more income.

Another indicator of major interest is the rate of employment, which is the ratio of working people to the total labor force. Since some people are always unemployed by choice (travel between jobs, vacationing, etc.), an employment rate equal to 96 percent is considered to be consistent with full employment. As a general rule, a high rate of employment (close to 96 percent) indicates a healthy economy, since it reflects an interest on the part of businesses to hire people in order to meet a high-level demand for their goods and services. Conversely, a low level of employment is associated with a sagging economy. But let me caution you against trying to read too much into this variable alone, because employment data are obtained by interviews of a sample of all households in the United States, and the results are not always accurate.

Two very popular indicators are the production of industrial goods (such as steel and automobiles) and construction starts. Indexes of industrial production (an abstract measure of the increase in the production of industrial goods in relation to a base period) indicate the trend in the production of industrial goods. The healthier the economy, the more prosperous people feel and the more they buy. As the demand for goods rises, businesses accelerate their supply lines, and more durable goods (machinery, lumber products, and transportation equipment), nondurable goods (foods, paper, and rubber products), consumer goods (automotive products, home furnishings, apparel, equipment, and materials) are produced. Another related indicator is new housing starts. Americans naturally desire to own residential property, and in times of prosperity they buy more homes, which results in a rise in the rate of new construction. The reverse is true when the economy experiences a recession.

No discussion of major indicators is complete without mentioning prices, which represent an important focal point of economic activity. In a general (and somewhat loose) way, you may think of the forces of demand and supply coming together in markets and forming prices. Of course, there are many different kinds of prices ruling in the market; however, our interest here is primarily in the general level of prices. Changes in the general level of prices may affect the volume of economic activity, the amount of employment, and the distribution of real income.

Unfortunately, monthly data on the general level of prices are not available, but two important measures of particular aspects of the price level can be obtained with relative ease. These are the *Consumer Price Index* and the *Wholesale Price Index*. The former is a measure of price changes in typical goods and services purchased by urban wage earners, salaried clerical worker families, and single individuals. The primary purpose of this index is to serve as an indicator of the purchasing power of wage income. The Wholesale Price Index, on the other hand, is a measure of price movements in commodities (ranging from raw materials to fabricated products) at the time of the first commercial transactions in them.

Interpreting the price (consumer or wholesale) index remains a tricky business. The relative strengths of demand for, and supply of, a commodity determine its price. An excess of demand over supply generally pushes up the price, whereas the price goes down if the reverse is true. Against this background let us recall that an excess of demand over supply is a reflection of a healthy economy, since this indicates people's willingness to buy, and a condition which encourages businesses to expand production. While this is true, a price level that rises faster than production of goods, that is, an inflationary rise, erodes the value of the dollar, which no consumer in his right mind would appreciate.

Government's fiscal (debt management) plans constitute another indicator of interest. The government's major avenues of expenditure are defense, social insurance, services, and education. Whenever the government needs money to meet its expanded expenditures, it borrows from the public (by selling them bonds and Treasury bills) or absorbs a portion of individual and corporate incomes by increasing taxes. Furthermore, government projects provide jobs and disburse new incomes which would not otherwise be generated. It is difficult to judge what the combined effect of these transactions is likely to be; however, as a general rule, higher rates of public expenditure are indications of higher levels of economic activity.

I should like to mention balance of payments as another important indicator. A nation does not operate in isolation, and its trade relations with the rest of the world are reflected in an international balance sheet known as balance-of-payments accounts. A deficit in the foreign trade account is indicative that the nation's purchases of foreign goods is greater than the foreign market for domestically produced goods, whereas a surplus in that account indicates the reverse. A chronic trade deficit is unhealthy, since ultimately the nation may have to finance this deficit with gold and hence progressively may lose the power to buy essential commodities from abroad.

Finally, the indicator of money should be mentioned. This is a tricky indicator to tackle, since there is no positive and direct relationship between money and the economic health of a nation. Most people think that the more money they have the better off they are and the better off the whole society is. This is just not true. A society is most affluent when it has neither more nor less money but just the right quantity of money. Let us see what this really means.

It is universally agreed that the mark of national affluence is the capacity to produce goods and services. However, simply producing goods will not be of much help unless people are willing and able to buy these goods. Clearly, money provides purchasing power. While money is essential for exchange, too much money without a simultaneous increase in the supply of goods and services merely pushes up prices without benefiting anyone. Hence, an excess money supply beyond what is considered the "right quantity" must not be permitted; controls must be effectively imposed to check unwarranted increases in money supply. I should add that, while anyone can easily find out the total money supply at any given time, most people are not qualified to determine the "right" quantity of money.

The money indicator that one watches has many facets. In addition to the rate of increase in money supply, one must note changes in free reserves of banks (the amount of money banks can safely lend), money rates (which are controlled by the Federal Reserve as a means of regulating the quantity of money), and loans and investments by banks. I will have more to say on money in Chapter 9.

FORECASTING: WHEN FACTS ARE STRANGER THAN FICTION

We live in a dynamic world in which the state of the economy is ever changing, and considerable uncertainty beclouds the horizon. Forecasting the future in such an uncertain environment is therefore a formidable task.

In a delightful article, John Day[7] quotes a friend who has underscored the plight of those who try to follow professional forecasts:

In the first place, the jargon of economics was invented to impress the people who were paying the economists to give them advice. This game eventually got to the point where the economists had invented a whole new language, understood only by themselves. This made it necessary to employ semi-economists—people who were not so far gone they had ceased to be able to communicate with the laity but who, at the same time, had a vague idea of what it was the full-blown economists were saying.

In many cases, it turns out that the economists aren't saying anything. . . . Very often, what they explain in 50,000 or so well-chosen technical words and phrases is that the economy will accelerate, decelerate or maintain the status quo if, perhaps, when and but.

The difficulties in forecasting are not all based upon the incomprehensible language of the economist. Oftentimes the problem is to digest the data. As Day[8] points out:

The Treasury will give you figures on money supply. If the supply is shrinking, this is bearish. Figures also are available on industrial production (to tell you what everybody else is doing), retail sales (to help you form an opinion about the mood of the consumer), new construction (to tell you what everybody else expects will happen), employment (if it's high, more people will have more money to spend), hours and earnings (to tell you about demand and buying power), personal income (to tell more about buying potential).

These figures, with complete breakdowns—construction, for instance, is given in private, residential, nonfarm, commercial and industrial, and public categories—are available from the Board of Governors of the Federal Reserve System, the Department of Commerce, the Department of Labor, the Bureau of the Budget and from banks . . . if all these indicators signal a downtrend, a downtrend will surely occur. Unfortunately, some are often up while others are down. . . .

This simultaneous up-and-down fluctuation in indicators creates a thorny problem. When all major economic indicators are marching uniformly in one direction, it is easy to believe in them and to accept the conclusions drawn from them. But when the indicators are mixed, then the question is: Which ones should you trust? And that is by no means an easy question to answer.

Here is an illustration based on recent experience. During the third quarter of 1969, important statistics published by official and private sources were baffling. Most of the indicators that lead the business cycle (boom and recession) were headed downward, and most coincident indicators were at least static. Yet GNP grew faster in that third quarter of

1969 than in either the first or the second quarter. In addition, personal incomes continued to set new highs.

But that's not the end of the figure-watcher's troubles. The Federal Reserve continued to revise some of its published data, occasionally reversing their trend. For instance, originally the index of industrial production for March, 1969 was published at 170.5; but later it was raised to 171.0, 171.3, and 171.4 in successive monthly revisions. The figures for May, June, and July, meanwhile, were revised downward. Similar problems arose with money supply data. During 1969, the Federal Reserve twice released new data on money in circulation that changed the figures for the money supply's size and growth rate. To complicate matters, giant computers used for forecasting the future of the economy spewed out information directly contradictory to the actual economic conditions. And yet, in his 1968 *Economic Report* the President of the United States stated: "The United States has the most accurate, comprehensive, and detailed economic statistics in the world, based on information that has consistently improved in accuracy, speed, and coverage."

If you conclude from the above statements that forecasting is going to become completely scientific and reliable, you will be mistaken. Judging from the conflicting views of different agencies on what the future will be, it would appear that there will always be an element of uncertainty in forecasting. Let me illustrate this point. During their annual convention in September, 1970, members of the National Association of Business Economists (NABE) painted a *bullish* picture for most economic indicators in 1971. The forecast, representing the median opinion of the 194 private, academic, and government economists responding, called for an overall gain of 6.4 percent (to $1.04 trillion) in the GNP for 1971. It predicted that corporate profits before taxes would rise by 6 percent in 1971, while private housing starts would jump by 19 percent during the same period. Industrial production would show a gain, though not a very impressive one.

There was a *bearish* side as well to these forecasts. The forecast indicated that gain in real GNP (actual production of goods and services) would be only 2.8 percent, while the rest of the gain in GNP (3.6 percent) would come from inflation. Spending for plant and equipment was expected to show little increase in 1971, while the rate of unemployment would continue to be high. Finally, during 1971, inflation would continue to plague the economy, with the consumer price index rising 4.3 percent.

What I have said above constitutes only one set of forecasts. Many other reputable groups have attempted to forecast the U.S. economy in 1971, and no consensus appears to have emerged on this issue. This does not mean, however, that it is impossible to know the direction in which the economy is heading. If you are confused by conflicting reports, you may depend upon the advisory service of your choice.

Your major objective is not just to gather data, for, as I indicated earlier, there are sources galore to give you all the data you want. The objective is to evaluate *all the important economic indicators at once*. In attempting to achieve this objective, you are likely to meet at least three complications. First, not all indicators move up or down by the same percentage. Second, not all of them move up or down simultaneously; some may rise, others may decline, while still others may remain unchanged. Third, not all indicators are of equal importance in evaluating the long-term economic health of a country, and it is difficult to assign appropriate weights to these indicators.

There are many agencies which attempt to forecast the future on the basis of indicators moving in all possible directions. One of these agencies, which I will call the prophetic leader, has achieved excellence in this field. The National Bureau of Economic Research (NBER) regularly engages in forecasting activities by tracing the relationships among various business statistics (called "indicators") and publishing the results in its journal, *Business Conditions Digest*.

Jesse Levin[9] explained the ways in which the NBER uses a group of indicators in explaining what the economy is doing at a given time and what it is likely to do in the foreseeable future. The NBER constructs a composite index of 12 leading indicators (for example, new orders of durable goods industries, prices of 500 stocks, change in consumer installment debt, and so on) which it calls *Leading Indicators of Business*. The index of these indicators usually reaches its peak and then heads downward months before the trend of general business starts downward. Similarly, during recessions, this index turns upward while the economy is still following a downward course.

The NBER classifies another group of indicators (for example, total unemployment rate, industrial production, personal income, and so on) as *Coincident Indicators of Business*, on the grounds that they move with the general economy. Similarly, for obvious reasons, another group of five economic indicators is classified as *Lagging Indicators of Business*.

This is not the place to write a treatise on how to tell what the economy is doing. Suffice it to say that the NBER's "leading," "coincident," or "lagging" classification of indicators should prove to be the most valuable tool. And there are other ways (not discussed here) to approach the problem, should you find the necessary resources and the time to do so. If, however, you do not wish to get involved in forecasting the economy yourself, you may depend upon the forecasts of your favorite advisory service or upon those of the NBER.

[Learn] how to make money in bear markets, bull markets, and chicken markets.

—CONRAD W. THOMAS

The Market Indicators

THE MARKET SIGNALS

In Chapter 5 I discussed the ways in which you could determine what the economy will do in the months ahead. A more practical investment question is: "How do you know what the market will do?" As a general rule, today's market reflects developments in the economy that are expected to occur six months to a year from the present. This complicates the task of market evaluation, since today's market developments may have no direct relevance to what the key indicators indicate.

The stock market is complex. There are countless factors to consider in determining what the market will do. However, for practical purposes I have developed a set of 12 indicators, called APPROPRIATES, which should provide you with a comprehensive background for judging the market.

Before explaining the 12 indicators, let me list them, to make it easier for you to follow:

A: Averages of the market's performance
P: Performance of top management
P: Popular groups of stock
R: Relationship of quality to quantity of stocks
O: Odd-lotters
P: Profit picture
R: Range of highs and lows

I: Impact of fund activities
A: Advances and declines
T: Trading volume
E: Effective yield
S: Short interest

LET'S DIG IN

The first and most important indicator is the market averages. There are at least three market averages which are widely quoted and used by investors: the Dow Jones Industrial Average (DJIA), the New York Stock Exchange (NYSE) Index, and the Standard & Poor's Index. I will discuss the relative advantages and disadvantages of each of the three averages in Chapter 8. At this point, it is sufficient to note that you should follow at least one of these averages. Furthermore, you should learn to look not only for the level of the average but for the percentage change in it. For instance, the proper way to interpret a 20-point drop (from 1,000 to 980) in the DJIA is to recognize that it is merely a 2 percent drop.

The trading of stocks by top managements of large corporations is the second important indicator. Each month the Securities & Exchange Commission publishes a list of purchases and sales of listed stocks by officers, directors, and large stockholders. When directors of a large number of corporations begin to unload substantial amounts of their holdings, such actions are generally to be taken as a bearish sign for the market as a whole.

The third indicator of the market's condition is the diverse groups to which popular stocks belong. The market has a way of recognizing certain industries (electronics, airlines, and so on) as the most attractive groups, and the active stocks easily identify these groups. Of course there are exceptions to this rule. For instance, a stock may become active, say, purely on the rumor that the company will be taken over by a well-known firm and not on the basis of its belonging to a favorite group.

The fourth indicator is the relationship between quality and quantity of stocks traded on the market. In common stocks, as in all other business assets, quality as well as quantity is important. As a general rule, the market exhibits strength when the stocks which top the active lists are of relatively high quality. Interest shown by investors in high-quality stocks is a clear indication of their confidence in a strong, rising market. Speculative buying of low-quality, poor stocks, on the other hand, is a sign of nervousness and a quick profiteering spirit and is therefore indicative of an unfavorable market trend. An exception to this rule is at the end of a major bull or bear market, when low- and medium-quality stocks are actively traded. The reason is that a long and sustained bull market induces investors to try their luck on cheaper-quality stocks.

Odd-lot purchases and sales constitute the fifth indicator. Odd-lot traders are those millions of small investors who naïvely enter and leave the market without ever acquiring the technical knowledge and skills required to make them astute investors. What is pathetic about these investors is that they buy when prices are high and sell when prices are low. But more importantly, these traders usually become increasingly wrong near the end of a major bull or a bear market.

The *sixth* indicator is the profit picture. As a general rule, corporate profits tend to decline in a falling market and rise when the market is scaling new heights. For instance, during 1969 and 1970 when the market suffered a major setback, profits of most corporations belonging to industries ranging from electrical equipment to food registered sharp declines. In the fourth quarter of 1970, for instance, earnings of 422 concerns lagged 17.6 percent below the year-earlier total. However, as the market began to rally toward the end of 1970, the corporate profit picture, so gloomy for so long, began to brighten. During the first quarter of 1971, most corporations falling in the major industrial categories (such as auto, rubber products, steel, building, airlines, and so on) were predicting sharp rises in the earnings. Corporate profits should, therefore, be treated as an important market indicator.

The *seventh* indicator of the market's health is known as "new highs and new lows." Each day the WSJ publishes a list of individual stocks which have made new highs and those which have made new lows, for the current year, on that day. Ostensibly, a large number of stocks reach new highs when the market is high and rising, and reach new lows when the market is low and falling. The failure of as many stocks to make new highs or new lows as would normally be expected is a clear signal for a reversal of the existing market trend. As a matter of practicality, during a given year, until the end of March the high and low figures for the previous year are also included; after April 1, the previous year's figures are dropped.

The *eighth* indicator might be called the impact of fund activities on the market. A development of more recent vintage is the increasing participation of mutual and pension funds in market activities. These funds command huge financial resources and are generally managed by highly qualified, thoroughly trained professionals who have a complete grasp of the market. They have the power not only to sway the market in either direction but also to provide footprints which could be advantageously followed. I will have more to say on mutual funds in Chapter 16.

The *ninth* indicator is the number of advances and declines in stock prices on a typical day. Each day the WSJ publishes figures showing the number of issues advanced, the number declined, and those which remained unchanged. The rule of thumb is that the cumulative total of advances and declines often starts to fall in advance of the DJIA at important major turning points.

The *tenth* market indicator is the number of shares traded on a particular day, technically known as "volume of trading." The number of shares which changes owners on a given day or given week is a clear indication of the degree of interest of investors in the market. Here again, a change in the volume of trading is more significant than an absolute volume. For instance, if 8 million shares change hands on the NYSE on the average, an increase in volume to 12, 15, or 22 million stocks should be taken as a positive indication of some major change in the market trend.

At this point let me introduce an interesting idea. An increase in volume by itself does not signify a rising or falling market, since every exchange must take place between a buyer and a seller, and either one might be the more anxious to transact business. If buyers are more eager to buy stock than sellers are anxious to sell, the exchange can take place only if the price rises. Technically, this is called "buying pressure," and the exchange of shares takes place on an "uptick." The reverse is true when sellers exceed buyers and exchange takes place on a "downtick." An increase in volume of trading must therefore be examined vis-à-vis buying or selling pressure in order to determine whether the market is rising (a bull market) or falling (a bear market).

While the market volume is an important indicator, it must be interpreted in light of the fact that you do not buy the market; rather, your stake is only in a small number of selected stocks which fits into your investment plan. Unfortunately, the market volume and the volume of individual stocks do not necessarily move hand in hand. It is not unusual for the total market volume of one day to be 50 percent higher than the volume of the previous day, while the turnover of your stock shows no change at all. Conversely, on a typical market volume day, the volume of your stock may amount to 4, 6, or even 10 times its volume of the previous day. Consequently, you do need a general rule of thumb to evaluate volume changes in individual stocks by comparing them with changes in market volume. Here are four generally recognized rules:

1. If the present bull market has lasted for a relatively short time in comparison with past bull markets, the chances of your stocks going up are bright.
2. If volume of your stock increases on advances and shrinks on declines, this is another plus factor in favor of your stock.
3. If the general market has just suffered a major setback, while your stock has refused to fall below a certain level, that is, if it has formed a solid base, the chances are that this stock is ready for a major upward move.
4. If your stock penetrates its previous top price level by high volume, it is usually set for a major advance.

The *eleventh* indicator is the "effective yield" or the spread between the yields on stocks and bonds. As a general rule, yields (returns) on stocks are higher than those on bonds, since there is more risk in holding the former than the latter. The difference between the two yields, which is generally positive, is known as *spread between the yields*. If the spread is negative, that is, if the yield on bonds is higher than that on stocks, this would indicate a weak market and a loss of investor confidence in it.

Finally, there is the *twelfth* indicator, the "short interest" ratio. A short interest arises when a person sells shares that he has borrowed on the expectation that the price of the stock will be lower at a future date. The short interest ratio is the ratio of total short interest outstanding for any month to the average number of shares traded during that month. If the ratio is above 1.5, it indicates that the market will turn bullish within three to six months. If, however, the ratio is below 1.0, it is considered bearish, also with a lead time of three to six months. *Barron's* data on short interest ratio published once a month are widely followed by investors.

I have discussed in detail the importance of a group of market signals and how they might help you to judge the market. I have omitted some other market signals for the simple reason that they are neither understood easily nor are they followed widely. My next task is to analyze stocks of special interest to you.

A Stock isn't everything—
That's truth I can't dispute;
But it'll do, until they make
A better substitute
—DICK EMMONS

7

That Stock
Is a Sure Buy—Maybe

A Stock Is a Company Is People

The main purpose of studying the economy or the stock market is to develop a basis for selecting the *right stocks at the right time*. You have already learned something about how to evaluate the strength of the economy and to judge the character of the market. Now it is time for you to study the technique of stock selection.

As Lawrence Rader wrote, "A stock is a company is people." The attractiveness of a stock is partly related to the performance of the company (earnings, dividends, and so on), and partly to the confidence (or lack of confidence) in it expressed by investors. Thus, whether or not a stock is an attractive investment opportunity depends upon a combination of *objective* and *subjective* factors. In this chapter I propose to discuss the two types of factors separately and in conjunction with each other so as to develop a practical theory of stock selection.

The Company: What It Is or Isn't

The first major step toward selecting stocks is to learn more about the companies in which you are interested. Company prospectuses, their latest balance sheets, and the Standard and Poor's sheets are readily available just

52

for the asking. All the companies with securities listed on the NYSE and the other major exchanges publish extensive annual financial statements. What's more, almost all listed companies supplement these annual reports with quarterly reports.

It might interest you to know that corporation annual reports haven't always been so informative. Shortly after the Civil War a railroad company, whose stock was listed on the stock exchange, was brief and to the point when it was invited to contribute its report. The company replied that it "makes no reports and publishes no statements—and has done nothing of the sort for the last five years." Luckily, the times have changed. Over the years, corporations have expanded, their capital needs have increased, and the number of shareowners has grown far beyond the boundaries of a particular region. Hence, the need for exhaustive annual and quarterly reports has become obvious.

Once you have the relevant material on a number of companies, the next step is to undertake an in-depth study of their operations. Start with the earnings, or more precisely, the earnings per share of a company. If Dandy Company has 1 million shares outstanding and it earned $2 million in 1970, then the earnings per share in 1970 would work out to $2. If this company issues quarterly earnings per share, and you intend to use its data, be sure to take into account the fact that quarterly financial data have certain limitations. Different companies use different rules for allocating fixed costs to the quarters, allocating windfall gains or miscellaneous revenues to the quarters, and accounting for needed adjustments which are discovered only at year-end. In addition, the seasonal nature of some firms' activities limits the usefulness of quarterly statements issued by these firms. Finally, as company auditors audit only annual and not quarterly statements, there is opportunity for every firm to rearrange the quarterly data to look well to the public eye. For these reasons, you should use quarterly earnings data with caution.

Growth in earnings per share is an index of the prosperity of a company. Shareholders directly share in this prosperity whenever these earnings are distributed. The distributed portion of corporate earnings, known as dividend, may be paid in cash or it may be in the form of issuance and distribution of additional shares of stock. When a company's board of directors decides to pay a dividend, it announces the amount of the dividend on a per-share basis. Each shareholder thus receives an amount equal to the per-share dividend multiplied by the number of shares he holds. The dividend is sent to the person whose name appears on the records as the owner of the shares on the date of record. The importance of dividend lies in the fact that it is a return on investment of a kind very different from the appreciation of the value of stocks held by an investor. Dividends are in a way comparable to the interest paid by a bank on a quarterly basis on its savings or time deposits, with two major differences. First, unlike bank interest payments, dividends are never guaranteed. Second, all bank interest is taxable, whereas no tax is paid on tax-free dividends declared by special companies, such as regulated investment companies.

While dividends per share constitute an important statistic, a more meaningful and widely used indicator is known as *dividend yield*. To figure the divident yield on common and preferred stocks, divide the cash dividend per share paid in a given year by the market price of the stock. This gives the annual percentage rate of return, or current yield, on the amount it costs to buy a stock. For instance, if a stock pays an annual dividend of $5, and is selling at $50, then the dividend yield is 10 percent ($5 \div 50 = 0.10$, or 10 percent). Of course, it is worth remembering that no company ever promises to declare dividends on a regular basis (some companies declare no dividends at all), so it is unwise to expect a *fixed* rate of return on this form of investment.

You should also look at net sales of the corporations in which you are interested. If sales are slowing down while earnings keep on rising, this implies that the company is either cutting costs or juggling figures to show gains in earnings. It may also imply that the company has closed down, phased out, or sold its unprofitable operations.

An important measure of the worth of a company is the net book value of a share of common stock. This value is equivalent to the amount of money which, in the event of liquidation, each common stockholder would receive from the sale proceeds of the company's assets *after* the creditors, the preferred stockholders, and all others holding claims have been paid in full. Here is a simple illustration of how the net book value of a company can be calculated:

Sale proceeds (expected) of assets	$10,000,000
Amount required to pay all claimholders	$ 8,000,000
Amount available for distribution to common stockholders	$ 2,000,000
Total Common Stocks Outstanding	1,000,000
Net Book Value per Share	$ 2

WHAT, IF ANYTHING, DOES THE P/E RATIO SAY?

Now that you have learned something about the relative attractiveness of the companies in which you are interested, the next order of business should be to decide upon the right price for the related stocks. The *right* price, of course, is an elusive term. In order to arrive at the right price of a stock, you need to relate the most recent price of that stock to its latest earnings. The resultant figure, known as the price-earnings (P/E) ratio, deserves closer examination.

The P/E ratio is one of the best indexes, though not the only one, of the attractiveness of a stock. Since current earnings provide one of the best possible indexes of the true investment value of the corporation, one should calculate from the latest income statement of that corporation the amount of earnings per share. For instance, if the total earnings of the company in 1970 are $10,000 and 2,000 shares are outstanding, then in that year the company's earnings per share are $5. If the current price of that stock is $50, then the *P/E ratio* is 10. You now have a basis for comparing the attractiveness of this company with another company producing the same or a similar product. If the P/E ratio of another company within this group is 8, other things being equal, you should not hesitate to buy the stock of the latter company in preference to that of the former, because the lower the P/E ratio, the more value you receive for your money.

In the above example, the P/E ratio was calculated by relating the price of the stock of a corporation to its *past* earnings. Such a method of calculation has a serious shortcoming in that it does not take into account the future *expected* earnings of the company. After all, when you buy the stock of a company, you buy its future and not its past.

While in theory it is easy to conclude that *future earnings* should be used in calculating P/E ratios, in practice it is very difficult to make such a calculation. No one can ever be sure how far into the future investors should look or on what forecasts they should rely. Nevertheless, if your objective is to use the P/E ratio for discovering whether prices are at bargain levels or whether the averages (or specific stock prices) can be expected to sink still farther, you have little choice but to use some type of future expected earnings in calculating such a ratio.

In this connection I should point out that the published data on P/E ratios are generally based upon *past* earnings and can be of little use to you. Most studies, including Dow Jones reports, use earnings for the 12-month period *prior* to the date of the price index. What is worse, no one is quite sure just *how significant* the P/E ratios of the DJIA or the S&P's 500 Stock Index are. They are seldom the measure of what these ratios should be.

While the P/E ratio has some serious shortcomings, it can be used as a policy indicator. In a recent article Charles Rolo[10] points out that in the 94-year period, 1871–1965, the average annual P/E ratio for Standard & Poor's 500 Stock Index was 13.9. Contrary to a prevalent impression, P/E ratios in the peak years of bull markets and the low years of bear markets were not very different. One policy conclusion to be drawn from the above findings is that barring exceptional circumstances, one should not dream of making a killing in the market by banking on runaway P/E ratios (such as in 1932 when the P/E ratio jumped to 139).

In his article, Rolo notes some historical variations in P/E ratio and indicates the way that information can be used for formulating an investment policy. According to Rolo, the *average annual P/E ratio* for the Standard & Poor's 500 stocks has not fallen below 14 since 1957. For the decade of the 1960's, the average annual ratio works out at around 17. In the latter part of 1970, the P/E ratio reached 14.5. On the basis of these statistics, Rolo concludes:

What inferences can be drawn from these data? Clearly, P/E ratios . . . are roughly in line with the historical average and conspicuously below the average for the past decade. Thus there is room for them to widen . . . in the face of a decline in corporate profits. Moreover the historical record encourages the assumption that any abatement of inflationary pressures would give a lift to P/E ratios. Translating this reasoning into numbers . . . these P/E ratios suggest a possible price range of 700 to 900 [on the Dow for the foreseeable future].[11]

I might add that, assuming Rolo's prediction to be correct, you should have sufficient reasons for believing that some of the depressed segments of the stock market during the first part of 1971 offered attractive opportunities.

It is appropriate to point out here that it is unwise for anyone to make his investment decisions on the basis of the P/E ratio alone, for under certain circumstances it can give a very distorted view of the stock or the market. There are several reasons for this. Joel Stern[12] has shown that the P/E ratio is a satisfactory indicator as long as the company's capital structure remains unchanged and acquisitions by this company of other companies are not contemplated. If either of these changes occurs, the P/E ratio will no longer serve as a valid indicator for stock selection. Another reason is that the P/E ratio does not adequately register differences in the *quality of earnings* between two companies. Also, not all earnings reported by individual companies can be taken at face value. Some companies deliberately juggle their figures to meet certain objectives, while others employ tricky manipulations in order to make their earnings appear larger. I should also mention here that growth stocks, in which immediate earnings are consistently less important to the growth companies than capital growth, should not be judged on a pure P/E ratio basis. The final reason for not using P/E ratios as the sole stock selection indicator is that oftentimes this ratio changes for no other reason than a change in *investor psychology*. Before I elaborate on this last point let me say that, despite several limitations, when used cautiously and judiciously P/E ratio can be a very important investment tool in judging the relative attractiveness of a comparable group of stocks.

When Investors Call the Shots

One of the most intriguing aspects of the stock market involves the decision of whether or not to buy or sell shares at a particular price. If you hold shares of a corporation, and on a certain day you decide to sell them, it follows that in your judgment the price of those shares quoted in the market is high enough so that you would rather exchange the shares for cash than keep them. But if you want to sell your shares, you must first find a buyer who considers the same shares at the same price an attractive buy.

How could it be that the same price is highest for one person and lowest for another? After all, there is no pressure either on the seller or on the buyer to trade in these shares. It stands to reason, therefore, that each of the two parties must be satisfied with his decision. Perhaps the explanation is that the price of a particular stock at a particular time is contingent upon the *psychological evaluation* of the situation by the buyer and the seller. You have to have an understanding of the price mechanism before you can understand this phenomenon.

When a person wants to buy a particular stock, he places an order with his broker to buy a specified quantity of that stock. The broker, in turn, seeks the help of a specialist operating in one of the several stock exchanges. I will explain the important role a specialist plays in the stock market in Chapter 12. Let me just mention here that the specialist places an order to buy a certain quantity of that stock at or below the current market price. At any given moment, there are a certain number of sellers and a certain number of buyers for that stock. In case the number of people anxious to buy the stock at a certain price exceeds those eager to sell at that price, there cannot be any meeting ground between them. The only thing that equalizes the number of buyers and sellers is the market price. Consequently, if buyers exceed sellers, the sellers bid up their prices so as to discourage those potential buyers who would consider the price too high to interest them. This price mechanism, which continuously shifts in either direction, is a rationing mechanism, permitting sellers to find the exact number of buyers for their stocks. Thus, the relative forces of demand for and supply of any given stock determine a unique market price, through the bargaining process, which is the most appropriate price for equalizing the number of buyers and sellers of that stock.

So far I have assumed that you know what price you are willing to pay for the stock you wish to buy. There is no such thing as the "right" price for a stock. Your decision to buy or not to buy a stock at a certain price rests upon your evaluation of "true investment value" vis-à-vis the "going market price."

There is nothing complicated about the "going market price" of a stock. It is the price you would have to pay if you bought the stock and that you would receive if you sold it. This price is not necessarily related to the true investment value, which may be higher or lower than the market price.

A stock is, as you already know, an earning asset. If you put your money into it, you hope to participate in the future expected earnings of that company. Notice that I used the words "future *expected* earnings." Future earnings are never guaranteed; they are estimates based upon a number of relevant factors, such as the demand for the product, growth of the economy, possibilities of product improvement, and so on. The use of the word *expected* is thus appropriate, since it carries with it the connotation of uncertainty as a result of wide differences in individual estimates of future earnings.

But the problem is still not solved. The old adage that a bird in the hand is worth two in the bush may well explain the fact that today the value of $105 which you are *likely* to receive a year from now is *not* $105, since you have to wait for a year to receive the money. What, then, is the *present* value of the *future* earnings of $105?

If you put $100 in a savings account earning 5 percent interest, you will receive $105 a year from now. It is easy to see that, given the 5 percent rate of interest, the present (discounted) value of $105 which you expect to receive a year from now is $100.

Applying this savings-account logic to buying stock, the true investment value of a stock today is the present (discounted) value of the future expected earnings. Since the true value of a stock is based upon future expected earnings, which in turn vary widely because of differences in individual estimates, no unique "true investment value" for a stock exists in the market. As a matter of fact, there exist as many opinions about the present worth or the true investment value of a particular stock as there are persons expressing such opinions. Thus, what is so interesting about the price of a stock is that opinions of the present value of that stock depend upon future expected earnings which vary considerably.

Ostensibly, the price of a stock prevailing in the market at a particular time can vary, sometimes a great deal, from the true investment value of that stock. The reason is that the market price reflects a number of divergent opinions concerning the present worth of a particular stock. The prospective investor first decides independently the present (discounted) value of the future expected earnings of a corporation. Having decided upon the true value, he then presumably compares this value with the current market price of that stock. If the market price happens to be lower than what he has determined as the true value, the investor either buys the stock or decides to hold it if he already has some of that stock. If, on the other hand, the price on the market is higher than his estimate of the true investment value, the investor may decide to dispose of his stock immediately.

To recapitulate, the exchange of a stock between the buyer and the seller is not just a matter of determining accurately what the price of that stock ought to be. Rather, it is a matter of making the best possible estimate of what the present investment value of that stock is on the basis of the expected future earnings of that corporation. Since the decision has to be made on the basis of *expected future* earnings, which are necessarily uncertain, the decision to buy or sell a stock has to be contingent upon the psychological state of each of the two parties involved. This phenomenon is the most intriguing characteristic of the stock market.

Why Can't Stock Prices Stay Put?

In the previous section I described how two different investors might simultaneously arrive at two different "right" prices for the same stock. But I did not explain why stock prices *change* and *how* the change takes place.

If you regularly follow the market quotation pages of the *WSJ*, you will notice that rarely does an active issue fail to change in price during the day. You will recall from our earlier discussion that a share of stock represents part ownership in a company. A fall in the share price of a corporation's stock thus represents a decline in the total valuation of the company, while the reverse is true when the price of the stock goes up. Viewed this way, stock prices should not fluctuate on a day-to-day or even on a week-to-week basis.

Why not?

Well, here is the reason. Take, for instance, two giant corporations, General Motors and AT&T. It is highly unlikely that either of these two corporations becomes any more or less valuable from one day to the next. But the shares in them do change in value almost every day. The explanation lies, as I explained before, in the frequent changes in the relative forces of demand for, and supply of, these stocks.

As you already know, the price you pay for a particular stock depends upon a host of factors, such as strength of the economy, general market conditions, earnings and dividends of the company, and its future prospects. It stands to reason that these factors will affect buyers and sellers of stocks differently, since the hopes and fears, caution and daring, courage and hesitation of individuals vary considerably. Thus, individual decisions, based on people's price opinions and personal requirements, are translated into buy and sell orders.

But why should a buy or a sell order for a particular stock be priced differently from the previous exchange price? Because when more people want to buy a stock than are willing to sell it, the price for that stock will rise. You can look at this exchange from the seller's point of view as well. He is likely to ask a price that reflects the present status of the company. In addition, he will ask for an extra premium if you agree with him that the company will grow in the future. Hence, the exchange will take place at a higher price, or, what is technically known, at an *uptick*. Similarly, when buyers and sellers both agree that the future of a stock appears gloomy, the number of sellers will exceed buyers, and the price will decline. So, the exchange price of a stock is influenced by (1) the mutual feeling of buyers and sellers about the prospects of the company, and (2) the relative number of buyers and sellers bidding for the stock at a given time.

ODDS AND ENDS

The *timing* of buying a good stock can sometimes be just as important a factor as the price at which it is bought. In order to decide whether or not it is the right time to buy a stock, find out how high and how low the price has gone, what *kind* of a move the stock has had in the recent past, and whether or not the volume (number of stocks traded) has picked up as the price has advanced. If the stock is near its previous low or high, it might be a good time to buy if the future looks good. However, if the price has advanced substantially in the immediate past, it might fall back before making another major advance. Also, a price advance with high volume indicates substantial investor interest in that stock and is bullish. These factors, together with the others discussed in previous sections, should provide you with the background for selecting the right stocks at the right time.

THE SUM AND THE SUBSTANCE

I have pointed out that a prerequisite to a wise selection of a stock is the collection and analysis of relevant information. Important data relating to a corporation comprise net sales, current assets and liabilities, earnings, and dividend record. The P/E ratio and dividend yield, both of which are easily calculated, are the two most important financial indicators which help you determine the quality of a stock.

I should like to emphasize the need for seeking *dependable* information. Information is only as dependable as its source. It is therefore imperative that you select only those sources possessing a reputation for accuracy, access to facts, the ability to substantiate the information supplied, relatively unprejudiced reporting, and an established policy of making recommendations based on sensible judgment gained from experience. In the final analysis, the responsibility for evaluating information in the light of your specific investment objectives is entirely your own. It will help you minimize your risks if you are a shade more pessimistic than optimistic when reviewing and analyzing corporate financial reports. You should also be flexible in your decisions, since they are necessarily based upon today's information, which is subject to radical changes tomorrow.

What is the worth of a market average . . .
which works except when it doesn't work?

—DAVID L. HOFFLAND

8

The Market's Ripples,
Waves, and Tides

MR. DOW AND HIS MAGIC FORMULA

One of the most popular and widely held market beliefs is that there exists one unique, magic formula, or average, by which everyone can judge the state of the market. The fact is, there is no such thing as a single formula or average which can be described as *the market average*. Several averages are used, of which the Dow Jones Industrial Average (DJIA) is the most popular. Let me give you the history of this average and then explain the importance of some of the others relative to the DJIA.

In the latter part of the 19th century, Charles H. Dow of New York City evolved a stock market theory that was ahead of his time and is, owing to his farsightedness, still with us. He realized that astute investors operated not on the fluctuations of individual stocks but on the basic trend of the market as a whole. This was possible because most stocks tended to move up and down together. There were exceptions, of course, but most well-known stocks showed some advance on a strong market and decline in a weak market. If this is basically true, argued Mr. Dow, then it should be possible to judge the market trend by computing an average for a carefully selected sample of stocks. This marked the beginning of what are popularly known as the Dow Jones (Industrial, Transportation, and Utility) Averages. The first Dow Jones Industrial Index, introduced on May 26, 1896, was an average of the prices of 12 major stocks of that period. In 1916, a need was felt to make the index more representative. Accordingly, the list of stocks was broadened to 20 in that year, and in 1928 the number was increased to 30.

Charles Dow, also notable as the founder-editor of the celebrated *Wall Street Journal*, died near the beginning of the 20th century. William P. Hamilton, who succeeded Dow as editor of the paper and who was a staunch supporter of the Dow theory, went further than Dow in analyzing the relationships between stock market movements and general business. It was Hamilton who associated the Dow theory with the technical approach and pointed out the distinction between that approach and the fundamental approach.

Basically, these are the two approaches to practicing the investment art. The fundamental approach associates purchases and sales of stocks with changes in national economic trends, in corporate earnings, and in general business conditions. By contrast, the technical approach is based upon the hypothesis that since astute investors and traders buy and sell stocks on the basis of advance information and deep insights into future stock prices, their pattern of trading can be detected early by watching price and other formations on charts. The latter fact, which in a nutshell is the basis for the Dow theory, is clearly explained by Dana Thomas in the following words:

According to Dow and Hamilton, stock prices represented the sum total of what everybody felt, knew, dreamed and feared, distilled into the "bloodless verdict" of the marketplace. And a careful study of the averages as a barometer enabled a student to anticipate how the public appraised American business even before it was consciously aware of its own analysis.[13]

Dow and Hamilton argued that at any given moment the stock market reflects three movements: a major trend (like the ocean's tide) either upward or downward; an intermediate trend (the wave); and the day-to-day fluctuations (ripple). If this is true, they argued, then one must have a satisfactory way of identifying the major (tides), intermediate (waves), and minor (ripples) trends. After all, a price fluctuation lasting a few hours, in which the price of a stock goes from 90 to 90½, falls back to 90¼, and then rises to 90¾, is of little consequence; whereas an increase in the Dow Jones Industrial Average from 631 to 775 over a period of six months must be recognized as a major uptrend. So Dow and Hamilton explained their formula for identifying the three trends as follows. The market is always to be considered as having three movements, or trends, all going on at the same time. The first is the narrow movement, from day to day, which might be called a minor trend. The second is the short swing, running from two weeks to a month or more, which is more likely a secondary trend; the third is the main movement covering at least four years in its duration, or what might be conveniently called a major trend.

The original theory, as developed by Charles Dow, was made more sophisticated by Hamilton in at least two ways. Hamilton maintained that a major uptrend in the market is confirmed when either the industrial or the rail (now transportation) average advances beyond the previous high followed by similar advances in the other. Similarly, when both the averages dip below a previous important low, this should be regarded as a signal for the decline in the market.

Another dimension that Hamilton added to the Dow theory can be called the *equilibrium concept*. When stock prices move within a narrow range for several weeks, that is, when the market moves sideways, it indicates a period of *accumulation* and *distribution*. During this period, buyers and sellers reach a state of equilibrium, and the upper and the lower levels are established. When the two averages rise above the upper level, the market can be said to be ready for a major upward move. Conversely, when the averages fall below the lower level, this should create a strong bearish sentiment in the market.

Surprisingly, the above approach, formulated several decades ago, still reigns as all-important in the minds of devotees of the Dow theory. However, an important modification deserving special mention has been incorporated into this approach. For the major trend, the four-year minimum has now been modified; on the basis of recent studies it is now believed that a major movement can last from less than one year to as many as half a dozen.

What Do Dow Averages Tell?

Since Dow Jones averages are so popular among market watchers, it might be pertinent to ask: "What do Dow averages tell?" Unfortunately, there can be no straightforward answer, since there are three distinct Dow averages, and you should first try to understand what they represent.

The most important of the three is the Industrial Average. This consists of 30 industrial common stocks (for example, AT&T, Chrysler, General Electric, Woolworth). The second, the Transportation Average, comprises 20 railroad common stocks (for example, Canadian Pacific, Great Northern, Penn Central, Western Pacific). The third, the Public Utility Average, consists of 15 utility common stocks (for example, American Electric Power, Detroit Edison, Pacific Gas & Electric, Panhandle E.P.L.).

Let us examine a recent change in the Industrial Average. On January 4, 1970, the Dow Jones Industrial Average closed at 800, down 15 points from the previous closing. Two questions can be asked concerning this change. First, since the average price of 30 stocks was 800, were all of these stocks priced as high as $800 a share? If so, why were only the high-priced stocks included in the computation? Second, since the average dropped 15 points in one day, is it correct to say that the market fell out of bed?

The first question cannot be properly answered unless you learn the computational technique. Here is a simple example. Assume that the average is made up of only three companies: Haden Company, selling at 50 a share; Standard Company, selling at 40; and Daton Company, selling at 30. The average price for these three companies can be computed as follows:

Haden Company	50
Standard Company	40
Daton Company	30
Total	120
Divided by 3 = ...	40

The average in this case, then, is 40.

Now the next week Haden Company splits its stock 2 for 1. The stockholder who owned one $50 share now has shares worth only $25 per share, but he has two shares, so his total holding is still worth $50.

Let us recompute the average after the split:

Haden Company	25
Standard Company	40
Daton Company	30
Total	95
Divided by 3 = ...	31.67

Thus, the new average is 31.67, down 20 percent from the previous average, without any change in the market condition. Since this appears odd, an appropriate measure must be devised to "adjust" for the stock split. The common practice is to change the divisor so as to leave the average unchanged. In this case, if the average is to be left unchanged at 40, the divisor must be changed from 3 to 2.375 (as though the number of companies is reduced from 3 to 2.375), so we get $95 \div 2.375 = 40$. Thus:

Haden Company	25
Standard Company	40
Daton Company	30
Total	95
Divided by 2.375 = ...	40

You can see that if this method is consistently followed, each stock split will drive down the divisor. Today, when the DJIA is computed, the total of 30 stock prices is not divided by 30. By prewar 1939, the divisor had already shrunk to 15.1, and by 1950 to 8.92; currently, it is 1.826.

Let me now answer your first question. The DJIA of 800 (on January 4, 1970) does *not* imply that the average price of the stocks included in the average was $800, or anywhere near it. As a matter of fact, if you add up the per-share price of the 30 stocks used in the DJIA on January 4, 1970, the total would be $1,796. Dividing this number by 30, you would get a simple, current average price of $59.87. But if you divided $1,796 by 2.245, which was the divisor on that date, you would get a closing average of 800. I hope you can see that the DJIA *is not an average* but rather a *market index*. The index has deviated farther and farther away from the *true* average share price of 30 stocks because of numerous stock splits over a period of seven decades.

Any theory, however simplified, which has survived for more than 70 years normally will be well established and accepted. Unfortunately, this is not true in the case of the Dow theory. To some it is merely a definition which says in effect that a price movement is upward until clearly it is downward. Others criticize the theory on the grounds that when the change from bull to bear market—or vice versa—takes a long time, or when there is a series of reversals, this theory appears anachronistic. A statistical study conducted by Alfred Cowles many years ago showed that over a 26-year period, buy or sell signals beamed by the Dow theory have been right 45 times and wrong 45 times. Despite these criticisms, however, the theory has many devout followers, and many investors still claim that movements in the Dow averages provide a basis for selecting investment opportunities in which risks are much less than average.

NYSE INDEX: A BETTER ALTERNATIVE?

For years the Board of Governors of the NYSE has been dissatisfied with the DJIA. However, it was not until July 14, 1966, that it began to publish new indexes of the prices of common stocks listed on the exchange. These include a composite index covering all of the more than 1,250 common stocks listed on the Big Board and four separate indexes representing broad industry components of the whole list. The composite index is sent over an international network of some 4,000 tickers every half hour, while the component indexes are flashed once every hour.

The technique of construction of the NYSE Index is very simple. The price of each of the 1,250 stocks included in the index is weighted by the number of shares listed on the stock exchange; that is, the bigger the company, the greater the weight given to it. When the index was first computed, the starting figure worked out close to the $50 average price of all shares on the exchange. To be sure that the exchange would never be embarrassed by its own index, it was simultaneously announced that the index would be split 2 for 1 if it ever reached 100. In addition to the composite index, the exchange also initiated four group indexes—for industrials, transportation, utilities, and finance.

The NYSE Index has had only a short history, and it is too early to tell whether or not it will stand the test of time. However, many people believe that it is the most comprehensive, consistent, logical, bias-free, and accurate measure of market conditions. Besides, the possibilities of using this index are virtually unlimited. Only a beginning has so far been made, and in the years to come analysts will surely discover new uses for it.

OTHER INDEXES: MORE OF THE SAME?

The two averages I have so far described give the point variations (for example, the DJIA increasing 15 points to 800) but not the percentage changes. The former could be misleading, since a rise of 15 points when the average is 800 is a very different matter from the same point rise when the average is only 500. Another problem with the calculation of the DJIA is stock splits, which, as I explained, makes it necessary to lower the divisor and raise the average. Standard & Poor's (S&P's) Index is calculated so as to solve these problems. Let me elaborate.

Using the method of S&P's 500 Stock Index, first multiply the price of each share by the number of shares in that issue. For instance, if Whitney Corporation is selling at $10 a share and 1 million shares of this corporation are outstanding, its value will be $10 million. Likewise, the value of each of the 500 stocks is calculated by following the same procedure. Then all the 500 values will be added, thus arriving at the aggregate value of the issues covered. Notice that this procedure automatically takes care of stock splits, and no adjustments need be made to correct the situation. If Whitney stock were to split 2 for 1, the result will be 2 million shares at $5 a share, and the total value of these shares will remain unchanged at $10 million.

I mentioned earlier that S&P's index is expressed as a percentage so that more meaning can be attached to the fluctuations in stock prices. The composite values of all stock prices are expressed as a percentage of the average market value during the years 1941–43. However, in order to make the index more in line with the average prices of the stocks it represents, the percentage figure is finally divided by 10. The resultant index, although strictly speaking not a percentage, does provide its users with a close approximation of percentage variations.

Besides the 500 Stock Index, Standard & Poor's prepares an index based on 425 industrial stocks. It also has a 25-stock railroad index and a 50-stock utility index. Because of their many important features, these indexes have now become very popular, and many investors study them rather closely.

So far, I have been discussing various averages for the stocks on the

NYSE. In 1966, the American Stock Exchange introduced its own stock price index (AMEX), which is computed by adding all of the positive net changes and negative net changes above or below previous closing prices. The total is divided by the number of issues listed on the ASE, and the result is added to (or subtracted from) the previous average to arrive at the current AMEX average.

An example will clarify the computational technique. Suppose the changes in the total of prices of ASE stocks were $200. If there were 1,000 stocks listed on the ASE on that day, the ratio would be $200 \div 1,000 = 0.20$. If the previous AMEX average was 9.80, then the current average would be $9.80 + 0.20 = 10.00$.

I should mention that there are some averages which represent specific industries only. For instance, *Computerworld* publishes the Computer Stocks Trading Index (CSTI). If you are a computer fan, you will want to subscribe to this journal. Besides CSTI, it publishes indexes on computer systems, peripherals and subsystems, software and EDP services, and leasing companies.

Averages or Witchcraft?

So far I have only reviewed the various types of market averages which are available just for the asking. However, I have neither discussed their limitations as market predictors nor examined them to discover what they *really* show. It is time to address myself to these tasks.

In an important article, "The 'Averages': What Do They Tell Investors?"[14] Robert Puff has demonstrated that the popular market indexes are designed to answer the question, "What has an *average of stocks* done?" rather than "What has *the average stock* done?" The difference between the two is of utmost importance, since for most investors the second question is more meaningful.

Here is a gist of the way Puff demonstrates the difference. It is convenient to begin with the Dow-Jones Industrial Average because it is the most popular and the most frequently quoted average. The DJIA is compiled by adding up the prices of the 30 selected stocks and dividing the total by a divisor (currently 1.826). Obviously, this method gives disproportionate weight to the higher-priced component shares. For instance, a 10 percent price change in Du Pont affects the DJIA by about 6.50, whereas an equal percentage fluctuation in Allied Chemical causes little more than a 1.00 change. In the short run the DJIA shows what an average of higher-priced stocks has done and not how the average stock has behaved. Similarly, Standard and Poor's 500 Stock Index is biased in favor of large corporations such as AT&T, General Motors, and Jersey Standard because this index is weighted according to the number of shares each corporation has outstanding. The NYSE and the AMEX indexes are also "size-weighted" and hence suffer from a deficiency similar to that of S&P's index.

No index has been devised which can be called an ideal average. However, two new averages compiled by the Indicator Digest Organization come closer to perfection than any of the others. These two are the New York Stock Exchange Average (IDA) and the American Stock Exchange Average (AIDA). Both of these represent simple averages of the percentage price changes of all stocks traded on a given exchange in a given day and are more representative of the average stock than other market averages.

Table 8–1 shows the relative performance of six stock averages since the market reached (1) its all-time high in late 1968; (2) its seven-year low in May, 1970; and (3) its "recovery high" in September, 1970.

TABLE 8–1

RELATIVE PERFORMANCE OF SIX STOCK AVERAGES

	Closing Prices			% Decline	% Increase
	12.3.68	5.26.70	9.8.70	12.3.68 to 5.26.70	5.26.70 to 9.8.70
DJIA	985	631	773	−36	+22
S & P's Index	108	69	83	−36	+20
NYSE Index	61	38	45	−38	+18
IDA–for NYSE ..	84	39	45	−54	+12
ASE Index	33	19	21	−41	+11
AIDA–for ASE ..	61	19	21	−69	+11

Source: Robert Puff, "The 'Averages': What Do They Tell Investors?" p. 2.

Note that the conventional averages did not fully reflect either the drastic decline or the limited recovery of the "average stock" during 1969–70. However, during the same period, IDA showed a decline of 54 percent (as against the DJIA of only 36 percent) and a rise of 12 percent (as opposed to a rise of 22 percent in the DJIA).

SWITCHCRAFT FROM WITCHCRAFT

A far more effective method of studying the averages, as suggested by Puff, is to study the DJIA in conjunction with historical data relating to earnings, dividends, P/E ratios, and yields. These data are brought together in Table 8–2.

Notice that the fluctuations in prices, dividends, earnings, and P/E ratios have been wide and erratic. Since the past is the best guide we have for the future, it is almost certain that we will continue to have similar fluctuations. With that in mind, you may argue that, since the high-grade stocks were selling in the fall of 1970 near their lowest P/E multiples in 15 years,

TABLE 8–2

HISTORICAL DATA RELATING TO DJIA

	Dow-Jones Industrial Averages			Mean	
	Mean Price	Earn-ings	Divi-dends*	P/E Ratio	Yield
1922–26 Avg.	116	$11.62	$ 4.42	10	3.8%
1927–29 "	238	16.16	8.07	15	3.3
1930–35 "	122	4.49	5.96	27	5.0
1936–39 "	147	9.17	6.73	16	4.6
1940–46 "	142	10.83	6.87	13	5.0
1947–50 "	188	24.03	12.28	8	6.5
1951	266	26.59	16.00	10	6.3
1952	275	24.76	15.13	11	5.8
1953	275	27.23	15.51	10	5.7
1954	342	28.40	16.83	12	5.1
1955	438	35.78	17.82	12	4.1
1956	492	33.34	20.22	15	4.2
1957	470	36.08	20.20	13	4.4
1958	510	27.95	18.95	18	3.8
1959	627	34.31	19.38	18	3.1
1960	626	32.21	20.46	20	3.3
1961	673	31.91	21.28	21	3.2
1962	630	36.43	22.09	17	3.6
1963	708	41.21	23.20	17	3.3
1964	829	46.43	25.38	18	3.1
1965	905	53.67	28.17	17	3.1
1966	870	57.67	30.11	15	3.5
1967	865	53.87	29.84	16	3.5
1968	905	57.89	31.34	16	3.5
1969	870	57.02	33.90	15	3.9
9/23/70	754	50.00E	31.85†	15	4.2
1922–69 Avg.	332	22.58	13.16	15	4.5

* Prior to 1948 includes value of stock dividends.
† Current annual rate.
E   Estimate
Source: Robert Puff, "The 'Averages': What Do They Tell Investors?" p. 3.

it was possible to pick up many bargains in the market in making up an investment portfolio.

CONFIDENCE IN A CONFIDENCE INDEX

Although strictly speaking it is not a market average, and therefore perhaps does not belong here, I should like to explain Barron's Confidence Index (CI). Many adherents claim that a study of the CI helps one to discover the major trends in advance. As a matter of fact, some people have actually demonstrated that in the past many of the tops and bottoms of the CI have coincided with the tops and bottoms of the DJIA of a future date. Others have also shown that movements of the CI are correlated with the movements of the stock market. This implies that if the CI continues to predict the future correctly, by studying it you could "beat the market."

Barron's Confidence Index is constructed in three steps. First, an average yield on Barron's 10 highest-grade corporate bonds is calculated. (You will recall that the yield on a bond is the rate of return from that bond.) Similar average yield is calculated for Dow Jones's 40 medium-grade bonds. Finally, a ratio of the Barron's yield to the Dow yield is taken, and this ratio is called the CI. When the ratio is high, it is claimed, confidence of investors is likewise high, and the demand for lower grade securities is either high or will be high. The reverse is true when the CI is low or declining.

I can feel your excitement over the discovery of the prizewinner. At last all your market worries are over! But alas, a recent analytical study by Jack Gaumnitz and Carlos Salabar[15] concluded that there is not much support for the theory that the CI reflects the decision of smart investors, who act ahead of the average investors and thus signal in advance the future path of stock market prices. I am afraid this means that we have still not found a substitute for homework.

WHERE DO AVERAGES LEAVE YOU?

Now that you are conversant with several averages, you should do fairly well in conversing with other investors. So if someone asks you how the market did today, you will not answer by just saying: "Up 10 points." For, as you well know, there are the DJIA, the NYSE Index, S&P's 500 Stock Index, the IDA, and the AIDA. And besides these averages there are others: New York Times Industrials, Associated Price Industrials, Barron's Averages, and . . . . Well, have fun with the averages.

I feel I should end this chapter by recommending frequent use of only a few of the many averages we have discussed. I suggest that you use the NYSE Index for evaluating the performance of the NYSE stocks and the AMEX Index for analyzing the ASE stocks. I would also advise you to keep track of fluctuations in the DJIA, if only because this index is quoted most widely by business and investment publications.

CRAFT, NOT WITCHCRAFT

We must have a good definition of Money,
For if we do not, then what have we got,
But a Quantity Theory of no-one knows what,
And this would be almost too true to be funny.
So your definition's no better than mine.
Still, with credit-card-clever computers, it's clear
That money as such will disappear;
Then, what isn't there we won't have to define.
—KENNETH BOULDING

9

Dough Makes a Difference

MONEY: MASTER OR SERVANT?

Not so long ago a cynic conceived the role of money in our society in these words:

> Money is the Nothing
> That you get for Something
> Before you can get Anything

Actually there is more to money than just that. Money is something one handles every day, and it seems a simple fact of life; yet few understand all its effects and complications. Money cannot buy the finer things in life, but without money it is impossible to maintain a sufficiently high level of living to permit one to devote sufficient time or energy to the pursuit of these finer things.

In order to understand why money, which in itself cannot be consumed or enjoyed, commands such high value, you must recognize that when you buy or sell a good or a service you always exchange it for money. Therefore, the market in general, and the stock market in particular, where the amounts involved are usually large, is extremely sensitive to developments in the monetary area. In fact, many people assert that the primary impulse behind broad movements of stock prices is usually of monetary origin. This may or may not be absolutely true. But no one has ever denied that there is some relationship between monetary changes and changes in stock prices.

73

It follows, therefore, that if you wish to take advantage of fluctuations in stock prices you must first understand something about money; namely, what it is, what it does, who controls it, and how it affects stock prices.

What Money Is

Money is, in a sense, any object that is generally accepted in payment for goods and services. It could be, and at various times has been, such varied objects as large round stones on the island of Yap, cattle and sheep, cowrie shells, wampum, and beads. Gold and other metals were long the main form of money.

It would be misleading to limit the concept of money to printed bills (that is, currency) and coins. Actually, most transactions in the United States and other developed countries are made by means of bank accounts, checks, charge accounts, and IOU's of various kinds, which act as pseudo money. Although you can go to your bank and draw out your balance in currency, not many people could do that at the same time because the amount of currency in existence in the country is much less than the amounts people have in the banks as deposits. Hence, as a practical matter, money, or money supply as it is commonly called, is defined to include currency, coins, and demand deposits (checking accounts).

It is clear that money is used to buy things, that is, it acts as a *medium of exchange*. Unless it is generally accepted by those who have something to sell or some service to perform, it will not be money.

Money functions as a *measure of value* and often as a determinant of quality. And even if you argue that the value of money almost always changes, you will roughly know what it means to buy a $30,000 home or a $3,000 car.

Money also acts as a *standard* of deferred contracts. Experience has shown that it serves better than any other known medium as the basis for contracts which take a long time to fulfill. Finally, money is a *store* of value or, you might say, a conduit to future purchasing power. The major functions are neatly stated in this little rhyme:

> Money is a matter of functions four:
> A Medium, a Measure, a Standard, a Store.

An important fact about the power of money is that, with the advancement in monetary theory, money has in recent years become an effective regulator of the economy. This implies that changes in the volume of money have brought about predictable effects upon the level of economic activity. If this is true, then as an investor you might draw valid conclusions regarding future price developments in the security market by examining the changes in the volume of the money supply. But more of that later.

Money in a Fist

One of early man's most notable discoveries was the use of fire, which became a valuable tool for preparing food, providing warmth, manufacturing tools and equipment, and so on. The later history of industrial progress is largely one of developing more and more energy from the use of fire—in the kitchen stove, in the steam engine, and in the automobile—by burning wood or coal or petroleum. Throughout the ages man has sought to keep fire under strict control. There is a similarity between the story of fire and the story of money. Because money is such an all-pervasive and powerful influence in our life, plans and policies to control it must be devised and applied, mainly by the federal government. Man has always used money in some form, repeatedly attempting to find new ways of making it more powerful and always ensuring that it is effectively controlled. Today there is as much reason to control money as there is to control fire.

In order to understand the ways in which money can be controlled, you have to identify first the institutions which are primarily responsible for the creation and destruction of money. Bills and coins are, of course, issued by the government; but by far the greater proportion of the money supply—75 to 80 percent—comes from private sources through checking accounts in commercial banks. Checks are money because they are readily accepted in payment for goods and services. The money in a checking account is called a "demand" deposit because the owner can withdraw it without giving any advance notice.

There is one important aspect of the creation of checking accounts. Contrary to what most people believe, not all checking accounts are opened when customers bring cash to their banks for deposit. Quite frequently commercial banks open checking accounts against loans granted by them. Thus, in addition to receiving ordinary demand deposits, banks can build up deposits by granting fresh loans, so long as they keep adequate currency on hand to meet depositors' needs. Because demand deposits are money, commercial banks are said to possess the power to create money.

Since commercial banks possess the very important power of money creation, it is reasonable to assume that some powerful agency should be charged with the responsibility of controlling commercial banks. The controlling agency in the United States is a superbank known as the Federal Reserve System (FRS), which is responsible for determining and maintaining the "right" quantity of money. There are 12 Federal Reserve Banks in the United States, each dealing almost exclusively with the commercial banks in its district. Notice that the term "right quantity" is an elusive concept: what is right for one set of economic conditions may not be right for another; what is right at one time may not be right at another. Despite these limitations the FRS maintains the right quantity of money in much the same way that a mechanic lubricates a machine with the right quantity of oil.

The FRS attempts to maintain the right quantity of money through the use of three major policy instruments: open-market operations, discount rate, and reserve requirements. *Open-market operations* generally consist of purchases and sales by the FRS of readily marketable federal government securities in the open market. When the FRS desires to increase the money supply, it buys securities from the banks and the public. Conversely, when the FRS desires to reduce the money supply, securities are sold.

The second instrument by which the Federal Reserve influences the availability of money is *reserve requirements*. The use of this tool is straightforward. All member banks of the Federal Reserve are required by law to set aside with the Federal Reserve a certain percentage (say, 20 percent) of their demand deposits (and a lower percentage of their time deposits). This implies that the more money each bank has to set aside, the less it has for lending, and the less money is likely to be created by it. Thus, when the Federal Reserve wishes the money supply to contract, it increases the reserve requirements, and vice versa.

The third instrument, the *discount rate*, is the rate that the Federal Reserve charges member banks against loans granted to them. Since most banks that borrow from the Federal Reserve use the funds for making loans to their customers, a higher discount rate generally implies a higher interest on bank loans. And as you well know, the more interest one has to pay on the funds he borrows, the less money he is likely to borrow and spend. Since you need money to buy stocks, an increase in the discount rate usually means that less money will be borrowed for buying stocks.

The FRS from time to time uses the instrument of *margin requirements* to regulate directly the amount of money which can be borrowed for buying stocks. Under Regulation T the FRS controls the percentage of the cost of stocks purchased that the broker can lend to you for this purpose. Under Regulation U, it limits the amount that can be loaned by banks for buying and carrying stocks registered on the exchanges.

The percentage of margin which the purchaser of registered stocks has been required to pay has varied, historically, from 40 percent to 100 percent of the purchase price. On January 1, 1971, it was 65 percent. This 65 percent applies, of course, to *initial* margin. There is also a *maintenance* margin set by the NYSE.

What Difference Does the Supply of Money Make?

In previous discussions, I have assumed that money does make a difference. Let me now ask: What difference does money make? First, there is no mechanism by which any institution can exercise complete control over the money supply. Second, no matter how sophisticated your method may be, you will never be able to predict fluctuations in stock prices with complete certainty. Finally, since variations in stock prices are the result of many factors, an examination of variations based only on the money supply can never give a complete explanation of variations in stock prices. Keeping these limitations in mind, let me state our goal clearly and then discuss the possibilities of reaching that goal.

For most investors the only objective in engaging in stock market activities is to make money. This implies that investors want to buy stocks when prices are down and sell when prices are up. In a nutshell, this is the name of the game. But the question is: How do you achieve this? After all, every investor has the same objective, which in all probability will make things difficult for you. If everyone tried to buy a stock at its lowest price, this would create so much demand for that stock that the price would not remain low very long. Similarly, if everyone tried to sell a stock at the highest price, the consequent selling pressure would force the price down. What, then, is the answer?

The answer simply is that you must "beat the market." You must correctly anticipate changes in the prices of your favorite stocks and act before others have a chance to act. Your chief goal is to develop a system by which you can anticipate major movements in common stock prices. Mind you, movements in general stock prices do not necessarily coincide with movements in prices of an individual stock. Therefore, the system that you develop may sometimes be inappropriate for determining movements in individual stock prices.

Furthermore, while the search for a system for predicting future stock prices has been carried on for a long time, success has been as elusive as the search for flying saucers. There is no close and simple relationship between stock price trends and general patterns of business and prices. Besides, economic activity and stock prices go hand in hand only two thirds of the time, and it is difficult to identify the remaining third.

There are other problems too. Stock price changes generally move well ahead of subsequent business changes, so that economic activity and stock prices are moving in opposite directions at the turning points (shifts from lower to higher or vice versa) of the stock averages. Worse, it is impossible to judge the state of the economy on a day-to-day or even a week-to-week basis, since data pertaining to the state of the economy become available only after a substantial delay. Also, on many occasions stock prices forge a unique pattern, apparently unrelated to developments in the economy; thus, it is futile to look into the economy for exact market predictions. All this points to the fact that anticipating stock price movements is hazardous; yet, if caution is exercised, attempts to develop a predictive system for stock price movements can still be a profitable venture.

I mentioned that stock prices and economic activity move in the same direction about two thirds of the time. *Economic activity* is an all-inclusive term which must be broken down into segments if any meaning is to be attached to it. Unfortunately, so many important things make up the total picture of the economy that it is virtually impossible to separate the relevant from the irrelevant. There is one ray of hope, however, in an old and celebrated theory popularly known as the Quantity Theory of Money. According to this theory, fluctuations in the money supply will influence the willingness of individuals to spend money. Changes in total spending will in turn exert important influences on the economy. Although the theory does not establish this, it is frequently argued that a weak economy (recession) leads to lower stock prices whereas a strong economy (boom) pushes up stock prices. In short, changes in the money supply cause (and therefore precede) changes in the level of stock prices.

An attempt to establish a firm relationship between changes in the money supply and fluctuations in stock prices was recently made by Michael Palmer.[16] Palmer studied the relationship of movements in the nation's money supply to fluctuations in common stock prices over a period of 10 years (1959–69). Palmer assumed that changes in the money supply were the major causal factor producing fluctuations in (among other things) stock prices. His study supported the belief that there is a distinct relationship between changes in the nation's money supply and movements of common stock prices (see graph in Figure 9–1).

FIGURE 9–1

Money Supply and Stock Prices, 1959–69

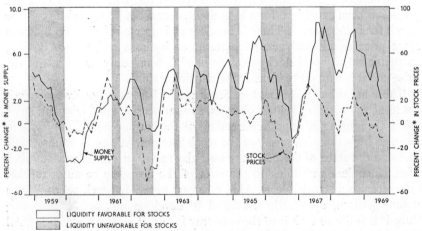

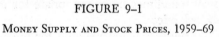

☐ LIQUIDITY FAVORABLE FOR STOCKS
▨ LIQUIDITY UNFAVORABLE FOR STOCKS

° Annual rate of monthly change, six-month moving average.
    Source: *Federal Reserve Bulletin* and Standard & Poor's Security Price Index. Taken from Michael Palmer, "Money Supply, Portfolio Adjustments and Stock Prices," *Financial Analysts Journal*, July–August, 1970, p. 21.

Many studies, such as Palmer's, have tried to determine the causal relationship between the money supply and stock prices. The findings of these studies suggest that a declining money supply usually precedes both declining stock prices and sagging business activity. The average time span between a decline in the money supply and a fall in stock prices has turned out to be about 15 months, whereas contraction in the money supply has preceded a business contraction by 20 months on the average. Therefore stock prices have usually declined on an average of about five months prior to a weaker business trend. In the last 50 years, there have been only three significant exceptions to this rule, all of which have occurred under abnormal conditions.

Statistics also indicate that increases in the money supply precede increases in stock prices and an expansion in economic activity. However, the lead time in this case (a bull market) is less than the lead time expected in a market with falling stock prices (a bear market). An expanding money supply typically precedes a rise in stock prices by about two months, whereas it precedes an expanding business by about eight months. What is more phenomenal is that during the last 50 years there has been no significant exception to this rule.

I think you can see what these observations indicate. They suggest that during the last 50 years, if you had blindly followed the money indicator system for buying and selling stocks, you would have participated in all bull markets and would have avoided all but three bear markets. Of course, you would have run the danger of being overcredulous had you accepted this system as the universal law of movements of the stock market. This system only suggests that if you properly measure and interpret changing money trends you will have sufficient lead time to develop adequate safeguards against the normal hazards of forecasting.

How Money Affects Stock Prices

These safeguards cannot be developed unless you have a grasp of how monetary policy affects stock prices. As will become clear, money affects the level of economic activity, which in turn affects stock prices. Keep this interrelationship in mind as we discuss the role of money in influencing stock prices.

The capacity of our economy to produce goods and services is dependent upon the size and quality of the labor force, the level of technology, the availability of raw materials, and the efficiency with which these resources are combined. Whether or not this capacity is fully utilized rests upon the willingness of people to buy what is being produced; their willingness is in turn dependent upon personal incomes and upon the cost of borrowing money (that is, interest rates), both of which can be affected by varying the supply of money. Generally, the larger the quantity of money in the hands of the people, the more the demand for goods and services and the greater the possibility of increased production and higher economic activity.

Although stock prices sometimes move erratically, most of the time they do reflect the potential strengths and weaknesses of our economy. Consequently, strong economies are generally associated with bull markets, whereas bear markets accompany sagging economies. There is a direct and positive relationship between money and economic activity and an indirect but positive relationship between money and stock prices.

INTERESTING ASPECT OF INTEREST RATES

I have just explained how money affects stock prices. Now I would like to speak about the relationship between interest rates and the supply of money. Lower interest rates imply a greater supply of money, which in turn generally leads to higher stock prices. The reverse is true when the interest rate rises.

The intricacies of the effect of interest rates on stock prices are as mystifying as the Mock Turtle's description in *Alice in Wonderland* of "the different branches of arithmetic—Ambition, Distraction, Uglification and Derision." One simple explanation of the interest rate is that it is a price which the borrower of money has to pay to the lender. This implies that the higher the price of money, the less is the demand for it. When people have less money with which to buy stocks, demand for stocks declines and, concomitantly, stock prices go down.

This seems clear enough, but you may ask: What has all this got to do with the *lowering* of interest rates and an *increase* in stock prices? The answer lies in the maneuvering of interest rates by the Federal Reserve.

As I said before, the FRS has the power to increase or decrease the prevailing interest rate by appropriately changing the interest rate charged to banks. When there is inflation in the economy, the FRS raises the discount rate in order to check the increase in the money supply and in this way attempt to control inflation. The reverse action is taken by the FRS when recession threatens the economy.

During all of 1969 and the first part of 1970, the U.S. economy suffered from sustained inflationary pressures, and the interest rates were pushed by the FRS to incredibly high levels. The prime rate (interest rate on bank loans to the best customers) climbed to 8 percent. Yields on a number of good utility bonds rose to between 8 and 9 percent. House mortgage rates shot up to 8 percent. These high interest rates pointed to one simple fact: money had become tight and very little was available for buying stocks.

Against the background of such a tight money situation, momentous words seeming to promise lower interest rates were spoken by Secretary of the Treasury Kennedy. Before long, the stock market moved sharply upward in anticipation of larger amounts of stock purchases to be made by the Federal Reserve.

What lessons can be learned from the above? As a general rule, an increase in the interest rate means lower stock prices, while a lowering of the interest rate implies higher stock prices. There are exceptions to this rule, of course; however, experience suggests that the "interest rate–stock prices" rule applies most of the time, and it is useful in making meaningful investment decisions.

FED UP WITH THE FED

Here is an account of how the Federal Reserve in 1969 wiped out the chances of millions of investors to make lots of money in the stock market. To buy stock you need money. According to the established stock market theory, a bull (rising) market—and particularly a speculative one—needs big injections of (new) money to keep it going. For instance, the 1967–68 bull market was supported by a rapid expansion in the nation's money supply and by an even more rapid growth in loans to stock buyers by banks and brokers, a situation that has not been very different from that prevailing in other bull markets. The result was that many potential stock buyers were able to lay hands on the money to buy as many shares as they liked.

Money makes its pressure felt in a down market as well. For instance, how far a full-fledged money squeeze can push stock prices down—quite independently of whatever happens to the national economy—was demonstrated in 1966. In 1966, between February and October, as measured by the Dow Jones Industrial Average, stock prices fell 25 percent when the Federal Reserve clamped down hard on credit availability throughout the economy and for a time actually shrank the total money supply. The slump, which made the 1966 bear market one of the most severe in recent years, was all the more striking because business activity and profits kept rising throughout most of 1966.

That "money makes a real difference" was again observed in 1969. The Federal Reserve embarked upon a severely tight money program and the "money panic" became rampant. Using every monetary tool at its disposal, the Federal Reserve clamped down on borrowers early in 1969 and did not relax its policy during the year. This action is to be viewed against the background that today's market has become particularly dependent on generous credit and is thus peculiarly vulnerable to a drop or even a leveling off in the volume of stock-buying loans.

Let us look at the situation more closely. In 1968, the Federal Reserve increased the money supply at the annual rate of 10 percent, twice the rate that the economy could absorb without inflation. What was the effect on the market of such an increase in money? As a general rule, money pumped into the economy tends to produce excess liquid funds that find their way into the market, supplying buying power that pushes up prices. And that is exactly what happened. The DJIA rocketed from the low of 817 during the early part of 1968 to the high of 985 in December of the same year, or a gain of 20 percent during the year.

In 1969, the Federal Reserve switched to its present restrictive monetary policies. Money supply increased at the annual rate of only 2 percent, while the nation's output of goods and services grew at an annual rate of 6 percent. Thus, with money supply growing less rapidly than business activity, overall additions to the money supply were not large enough to overflow into the market. Indeed, there was clear evidence that money was leaving the stock market because investors needed funds to finance their business operations.

In less technical terms, the point is simply that when money and credit are plentiful, investors can carry on their normal activities and have cash left over to buy stock too. An investor who is buying a house, for instance, may be able to borrow 80 percent of its price on a mortgage loan, make the 20 percent down payment in cash, and buy some stocks as well.

But when money and credit are tight the investor may be able to borrow only 60 percent of the price of a new home, and he may have to use for the higher down payment the cash he otherwise would have used to buy stocks. If there is a real squeeze and he can borrow only 50 percent of the price of a new house, he may have to sell stock he already owns to raise the cash to meet the down-payment requirement.

There is another very good reason why money supply and stock prices should move hand in hand. When the money supply is expanding rapidly, direct loans to finance stock purchases are easy to obtain. In fact, they may become so easy to get that stock market credit grows at an explosive pace. For instance, during the last quarter of 1968, "net debit balances"—money owed to brokers by customers who had borrowed to buy stock—hit about $9.8 billion. Bank loans to stock buyers also rose swiftly; the total dollar volume of stock-buying loans doubled over that at the peak of the 1961 bull market, one which brokers viewed as highly speculative. When the rate of increase in the money supply slowed down in 1969, however, loans for stock buying tended to dry up, thereby dampening the demand for stock.

In view of what has been said, it was easy to predict the market trend in 1969, and stock prices behaved very much as predicted. The DJIA nose-dived from the post-1966 high of 985 reached in December, 1968 to the low of 631 in June, 1970.

Where Are the Turning Points?

I have pointed out that as a general rule stock prices tend to decline when the FRS pursues a tight money policy and that stock prices move upward when an easy monetary policy is being pursued. In order to make use of this insight, you must be able to discern at once any shift in monetary policy from ease to tightness or from tightness to ease. In other words, you must be able clearly to recognize the *turning points*.

In a recent article[17] Stephen Barnett pointed out that a large part of the problem of recognizing the turning points is choosing the indicators that accurately reflect shifts in monetary policy. Barnett examined a set of important monetary indicators (such as the money supply, three-month treasury bill rate, net free reserves of commercial banks, and so on), in order to determine whether any of these indicators pinpointed shifts in the direction of monetary policy between May, 1960 and January, 1970. He concluded that it is the federal funds rate (the rate one bank charges another for short-term borrowing) and the three-month Treasury bill rate, rather than the money supply, which react most quickly and reliably to changes in monetary policy. This information should prove to be interesting, since throughout this discussion I have used money supply as the most important monetary indicator.

Money Talks

Let me summarize my money comments:

First, to buy stock you need money.

Second, the more money people can get their hands on, the more stock they will buy.

Third, the Federal Reserve attempts to regulate the money supply available in the economy.

Fourth, the more money there is in the economy the easier it is for people to borrow.

Fifth, given the supply of stocks, the more stocks people want to buy the more they push up stock prices.

Sixth, besides money supply there are other monetary indicators which help one in pinpointing the turning points.

In conclusion, I must warn you against the pitfalls in relying solely upon the monetary indicator system. It is true that there is an observable and, to a large extent, predictable relation between changes in the money supply and changes in the prices of stocks. Although it is possible to apply this relation to your investment policy, many uncertainties which should never be lost sight of cloud the investment horizon. If you don't take this warning seriously, you may follow the path of the man who drowned while attempting to cross a river that averaged only 3 feet deep.

Highly skilled manipulators are born, not made. Anybody can buy or sell a security. But only the most highly talented operator can unload a stock while conveying the impression that he is buying it and that the price of the security is bound to climb higher.

—DANA THOMAS

10

The Great Society
of Master Craftsmen

In this chapter I plan to talk about the behavior of the sophisticated, elite investors popularly known as fundamentalists or technocrats. Actually, they are a small minority, since very few investors systematically take into account all fundamental and technical factors before arriving at investment decisions. It should be interesting to learn what constitutes fundamental and technical factors and how these factors might assist one in making the right investment decisions.

FUNDAMENTALISTS' MAGIC CARPET

The fundamentalists are those astute investors who operate on the basis of fundamental factors. These factors include, among other things, the prevailing economic situation in the country, the economic status of the industries within which the companies issuing stocks fall, and the relative strength of these companies. The strength of any given company, in turn, is a function of its earnings and dividend records, its historical growth rate, and its future prospects. These considerations depend upon whether or not a company is soundly managed, is making reasonable profit, has a bright future, and is liberal in terms of disbursement of earnings. It should be recognized, of course, that since we are dealing with a dynamic situation,

84

these fundamental factors are not fixed but change over a given time span.

Here is how information about these factors can be utilized by the seasoned investor. First, on the basis of an evaluation of the fundamental factors the fundamentalist estimates a stock's fundamental price, or "true investment value." He then obtains from his broker the current market quotation of that stock. If the market price is lower than the fundamental price, he buys the stock; otherwise, he passes it up.

Let me explain the importance of the key fundamental factors. Fundamentalists examine the current state of the economy as the basis for their stock selection. Although there is no direct causal relationship between the state of the economy in general and the behavior of the stocks chosen, most stocks generally advance when the economy is booming and decline when the economy is in the grip of a recession. Thus, there is a positive, albeit indirect, relationship between fluctuations (boom or recession) in the economy and the behavior of stock prices.

It is also important for a fundamental-factor watcher to judge the state of the industry which the stock represents. The reasons are: (1) growth in individual industries does not necessarily move hand in hand with the growth in the economy, and (2) at any given moment some industries are popular with investors while others are jinxed. Clearly, then, stocks belonging to a popular industry group have a much brighter future than those falling in the unpopular group.

The major objective of every fundamentalist is to evaluate carefully the strengths and weaknesses of a selected set of companies before he makes his investment decisions. The price of a stock is positively related to the earnings and dividend policy of the company; in most instances, higher earnings and dividends imply higher stock prices. The future growth prospects are also of great importance because the demand for (and therefore the price of) a stock reflects the expectations of future growth of the company.

As I said, a fundamentalist evaluates a stock on the basis of a set of fundamental factors. If, on the average, the factors are favorable, a stock is said to be in a fundamentally strong position. On the other hand, if the weak factors outweigh the strong ones, then the stock is naturally fundamentally weak.

This notion of a single stock being fundamentally sound or weak can be expanded to reflect the position prevailing in the stock market. When, on the average, true investment values of average stocks in the market are higher, the market is said to be "fundamentally strong." When the reverse is true, the market is said to be "fundamentally weak."

One of the interesting but erroneous conclusions you may draw from the above is that all "good" stocks are fundamentally strong and all "bad" ones fundamentally weak. In general, there are no inherently good or bad stocks, if one omits the obviously bad ones of a few unsound and unviable corporations. There are instead "popular" and "unpopular" stocks, the former attracting the attention of traders and investors for a variety of reasons, and the latter awaiting their chance to be the darlings of the market.

The Technocrats and Their Tricks

The technocrats deal with more complicated and involved factors and are therefore more difficult to understand. In a recent book, a group of authors characterize technocrats as members of a cult wearing many faces and possessing widely diversified interests. According to them:

The market is made up of investors (shareholders interested in price *trends*) and traders (shareholders interested in near-term price *changes*); of bulls (those hoping for *rises*) and bears (those hoping for *declines*); of longs (those who *own* the shares they hold) and shorts (those who have sold shares they *borrowed*); of the floating supply (shares that can be purchased at prices *slightly* higher than current quotations) and investment holdings (shares that can be purchased only at prices *much* higher than current quotations). All these conditions taken together make up the technical position of the market at any one time.[18]

Let me explain various aspects of this quotation by putting you in the technocrat's seat and giving you a grand conducted tour of the technical territory.

As a technocrat, you are concerned with examining the past history of prices and volume of trade of a selected number of securities in order to determine the relative strengths and weaknesses of these securities, or of the market as a whole. Mind you, you do not care *why* the prices change. All you are interested in is determining whether or not there exists any *pattern* in the price changes, so that you may use the past price change patterns to predict future price changes. That is why you are called a technocrat. If, for instance, on the basis of past study you predict that the price of a stock would increase, that stock is said to be "technically strong," and this provides you with a buy signal. On the other hand, future price declines expected on technical grounds make a stock "technically weak," and you become a net seller in that stock. Similarly, the market can be technically weak or strong, depending upon the general weaknesses or strengths of average stocks trading in it.

Getting Technically Involved

My next task is to discuss the ways in which you might determine the technical strength of the market. The basic ingredients with which you must work are a stock index of your choice, data relating to volume, and important variables, such as highs and lows, odd-lot statistics, and so on.

There is no better way to begin a discussion of the forces which underscore the technical strength of the market than to examine the Dow Jones Industrial Average (DJIA). As you already know, the DJIA may be used to determine whether or not there is a clearly discernible major trend in the market. Experience suggests that this theory works when a long, wide, upward or downward movement is registered in the market. Conversely, the theory is unsuitable as a market predictor when the market trend frequently reverses itself in the short or intermediate run. Whatever the limitations, the greatest contribution of this theory is that it has made us aware that the law of inertia applies to the securities market and that, once a trend is established, the market trend appears to remain stable.

We have just noted that one limitation of the Dow theory as a technical indicator is that it becomes virtually ineffective in a sideways market when the trend changes direction in quick succession. Another major drawback of this theory is that it does not attempt to explain a consistent pattern of the stock price movements. One theory which attempts to do just that—to develop a consistent pattern in the stock price movements—is the *Elliott Wave Principle*, worked out in the 1930's by R. N. Elliott and later popularized by Hamilton Bolton. The Elliott principle states that major moves take place in five successive steps resembling tidal waves. In a major bull market, the first wave is upward, the second downward, the third upward, the fourth downward, and the fifth and final phase upward. The waves have a reverse flow in a bear market. This theory—when it works— provides the user with a highly valuable tool for market prediction. The Elliott Wave Principle is demonstrated in Figures 10–1, 10–2, and 10–3.

A somewhat different view of the technical performance of the market is that arrived at by use of the *advances-declines indicator;* that is, by taking into account the number of issues traded on the stock exchange on a given day, the number of issues that advanced, the number that declined, the number that were unchanged from the previous day, and the movements in the stock price index. The traditional belief is that, given the behavior of the DJIA and the number of stocks which rise and fall, it is possible to predict the short-term market trend. The nature of these predictions is summarized in Table 10–1.

The logic for the above predictions is simple. The Dow Jones Industrial Average is constructed on the basis of only a few stocks, whereas *the*

TABLE 10–1

PREDICTION WITH FLUCTUATIONS IN DJIA

DJIA	Stock Advanced less Stocks Declined	Future Market Trend
Rise	Positive number	Up
Fall	Positive number	Up
Rise	Negative number	Down
Fall	Negative number	Down

FIGURE 10–1
GRAPH SHOWING A MAJOR MOVE IN FIVE SUCCESSIVE STEPS

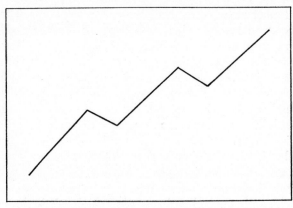

Source: Edmund W. Tabell and Anthony W. Tabell, "The Case for Technical Analysis," *Financial Analysts Journal*, March–April, 1964, p. 68.

FIGURE 10–2
A CLOSE-UP OF THE FIVE-STEP MARKET MOVES

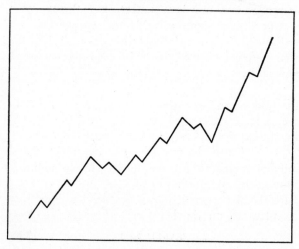

Source: Tabell and Tabell, "The Case for Technical Analysis," p. 68.

market embraces all stocks traded in it. Consequently, it is believed, for a few days the DJIA may move counter to the all-inclusive market trend; but eventually the DJIA must move in the same direction in which the majority of stock prices are moving. The advances-declines indicator is graphically illustrated in Figure 10–4.

FIGURE 10-3
WAVES, SUBWAVES, AND THE DJIA

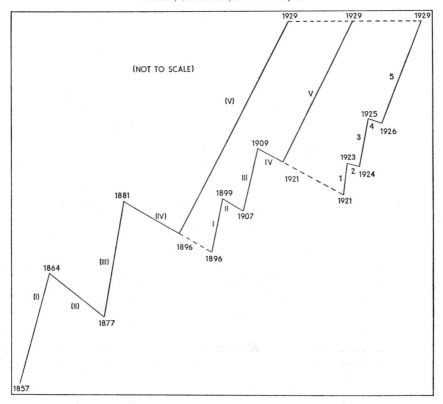

Note: Each of waves (I) (III) (V) breaks down into five subwaves, as do waves I, III, V, and waves 1, 2, 5. Corrective waves (II) (IV), II, IV, and 2, 4 break down into three subwaves.
Source: Tabell and Tabell, "The Case for Technical Analysis," p. 69.

An important variant of the advances-declines indicator is popularly known as the *breadth index.* This index is computed by taking the difference between the number of advances and the number of declines every week and dividing the result by the number of stocks that remained unchanged during the same week. Thus, if during a certain week 1,000 stocks advanced, 500 declined, and 500 remained unchanged, the breadth index would work out to be (1,000 − 500) ÷ 500 = 1. Each week, the index figure for that week is added to the prevous week's figure (or subtracted from the previous week's figure if declines exceeded advances). These data are then plotted on a graph, and the trend in the market is determined from the direction of the movement in the breadth factor. The breadth index is shown in Figure 10-5.

An excellent indicator of the technical strength of the market is the

FIGURE 10–4
THE ADVANCES-DECLINES INDICATOR

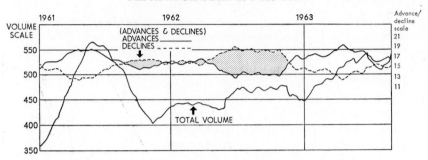

Source: Tabell and Tabell, "The Case for Technical Analysis," p. 71.

high-low index. Every trading day the *WSJ* publishes the number of stocks which reached their new highs and the number of stocks which fell to their new lows during the day. The presumption underlying the validity of this index is that if more stocks rise to their highs than decline to their lows, then the market could be said to be technically strong. The historical high-low index is given in Table 10–2.

FIGURE 10–5
THE BREADTH INDEX

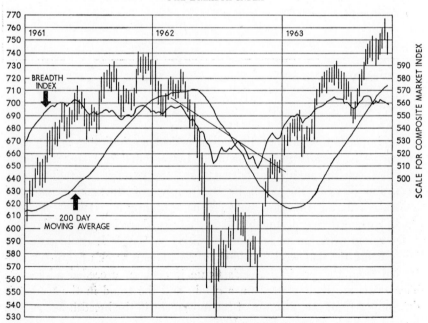

Source: Tabell and Tabell, "The Case for Technical Analysis," p. 71.

Another indicator, which is related to the one just mentioned, is *large block transactions*. Frequently, the *WSJ* and other journals such as *Barron's National Business and Financial Weekly* publish data on large transactions (say, 10,000 shares and over) in specified stocks and the prices at which these transactions were made (see Table 10–3). If most large blocks of shares are traded on downticks (that is, at prices lower than the previously quoted prices), then that would indicate a weak market. Conversely, large transactions on upticks would represent a strong bull market.

Your next consideration is to examine the size of the *short interest*, which is a measure of short sales. You are said to be selling short when, without first owning a stock, you sell it at a certain price in the hope that soon you will be able to buy it at a lower price and realize a profit. A short sale constitutes a built-in demand for stocks, and it is also indicative of a bearish outlook prevailing in the market.

The process by which a short sale is transacted is rather interesting. Assume that you expect the market to go down in the near future. You instruct your broker to sell short 100 shares of Control Data at 60. Your broker borrows the stock so that he can deliver the 100 shares to the buyer. The money value of the borrowed shares is deposited by your broker with the lender. Sooner or later you must cover your short sale by buying the

TABLE 10–2
YEARLY HIGHS AND LOWS OF DOW JONES INDUSTRIAL AVERAGES

	Industrials		Transport Cos		Utilities	
	High	Low	High	Low	High	Low
1970*	811.31	631.16	183.31	116.69	118.71	95.86
1969	968.85	769.93	279.88	169.03	139.95	106.31
1968	985.21	825.13	279.48	214.58	141.30	119.79
1967	943.08	786.41	274.49	205.16	140.43	120.97
1966	995.15	744.32	271.72	184.34	152.39	118.96
1965	969.26	840.59	249.55	187.29	163.32	149.84
1964	891.71	766.08	224.91	178.81	155.71	137.30
1963	767.21	646.79	179.46	142.03	144.37	129.19
1962	726.01	535.76	149.83	114.86	130.85	103.11
1961	734.91	610.25	152.92	131.06	135.90	99.75
1960	685.47	566.05	160.43	123.37	100.07	85.02
1959	679.36	574.46	173.56	146.65	94.70	85.05
1958	583.65	436.89	157.91	99.89	91.00	68.94
1957	520.77	419.79	157.67	95.67	74.61	62.10
1956	521.05	462.35	181.23	150.44	71.17	63.03
1955	488.40	388.20	167.83	137.84	66.68	61.39
1954	404.39	279.87	146.23	94.84	62.47	52.22
1953	293.79	255.49	112.21	90.56	53.88	47.87
1952	292.00	256.35	112.53	82.03	52.64	47.53
1951	276.37	238.99	90.08	72.39	47.22	41.47
1950	235.47	196.81	77.89	51.24	44.26	37.40
1949	200.52	161.60	54.29	41.03	41.31	33.36

* Estimated.
Source: *Barron's*, October 5, 1970, p. 26.

TABLE 10–3
Large Block Transactions, New York Exchange
(20,000 shares and over)

	Price	Volume	Previous Sale
SEPTEMBER 28			
Upjohn-c	47	111,100	47½
Amer.Hosp.Sup.-c	33½	287,300	34
Mfrs. Hanover-c	66¾	42,600	67
Std. Pkg.	9	28,000	8⅞
Safeway Stores	31	20,500	30¾
Ky. Fried Chicken	17⅝	25,100	18
Rollins-c	22¼	52,300	23
CrownZellerbach-c	31½	37,800	31⅞
Telex	19¼	25,000	19¼
Grand Union-c	25	50,000	25
Plessey	3⅛	180,000	3½
Pub. Serv. E&G	22⅛	50,000	22⅛
Gulf Oil	27¼	93,900	27½
Gulf&West part-c	16½	54,000	16⅝
West'ghouse part-c	63	44,900	63¼
Ginos-c	28	79,400	28¼
Chrysler-c	27⅛	20,000	27⅜
PanAmWldAir-c	12¼	103,000	12¼
U.S. Fid.&Guar.	35⅞	27,000	36
McDonald	41¾	24,700	41⅝
S.S. Kresge	48½	73,400	48¾
Phillips Petr.-c	29⅛	28,200	29¼
Pennzoil (pfd.)	39¼	28,700	39¾
RCA part-c	26	21,000	26⅜
Telex-c	19¼	25,000	19⅜
Plessey	3½	37,400	3⅝
Plessey	3⅜	25,300	3½
SEPTEMBER 29			
FMC	22	29,200	21⅞
Carrier	33½	34,300	34
Heublein-c	40	47,500	40
Plessey	3½	45,000	3⅝
Occid. Petrol.	19½	57,400	20½
Eaton, Yale	30¾	49,000	31
Kinney Natl.	28¼	25,000	28½
Telex	17⅞	90,000	19
Skyline	29	28,000	28⅞
Pittston Co.	33	23,000	33
Pittston Co.-c	33	27,000	33
SC E&G-c	26¾	59,600	27⅛
Walter E. Heller	19	24,000	19¼
Faberge	17¼	20,900	17½
Pitney Bowes-c	26½	149,000	26⅞
PanAmWldAir-c	13⅝	50,000	13¾
Lone Star Gas	24	23,600	24
Baxter Labs	23¾	23,600	23⅝
CorningGlass part-c	170	72,000	174
Fed. Dept. St.-c	36¾	30,000	36¾
Chrysler-c	27	49,700	27
U.S. Ind.	16	33,300	16½
East. Gas & Fuel-c	30½	55,600	30½
Am.Airlines part-c	20¾	20,000	21
DeltaAir part-c	29½	31,200	29¾
Pitney Bowes-c	27	20,300	27
Chadbourn	8¾	20,000	9¼
Amer. Air	21	20,000	21¼
GreenShoeMfg.-c	28¼	20,000	28¼
Cunningham Drug	8¾	25,600	8⅞
KinneyNat'lServ.-c	28	50,000	28½
Pfizer	33½	57,500	33⅞
Sunbeam-c	21¼	173,000	21¾
Northwest Air	19¼	25,000	19¼
Carrier	33½	21,900	33⅞
Purex	14	41,500	14⅜
SEPTEMBER 30			
Gulf Oil	28	75,000	28
Ky Fried-c	20	40,500	20
PanAmWldAir	14	21,300	13⅞
Ex-CellO	19⅛	48,900	19⅛
Motorola part-c	46½	33,400	47
Baxter Labs-c	24	41,100	23⅞
Nalco Chem.-c	38¾	45,800	39⅝
Bell & Howell	37½	36,000	37¾
Control Data-c	46½	26,900	47
Seatrain Lines-c	23	29,000	23⅜
Walter E. Heller	19¼	30,000	19⅜
Sony part-c	17	49,900	17¼
Dexter Corp.-c	16	61,600	17½
Kaiser Cement-c	20	22,500	20
S. S. Kresge	50	31,000	50
ITT (pfd N)-c	55½	29,900	55⅝
Campbell Soup-c	27½	60,000	27½
Amer.Hosp.Sply.-c	33¾	24,700	34
Std. Oil Ohio	70	24,900	70¼
Genstar Ltd.-c	7⅝	44,900	7⅝
Plessey	3⅜	20,000	3½
Plessey	3½	20,000	3⅝
NorthwstAir part-c	20¼	52,900	20⅜
Colgate Palmolive	39¾	49,100	40
StudeWor(pfd A)-c	43	20,000	40¼
Std. Pressed Steel	6¼	24,400	6½
Publ. Serv. E&G-c	22⅞	24,400	22⅞
CBS	31½	24,900	31¼
Cleveland Elec.-c	34	22,400	34⅛
Sony part-c	15⅞	46,100	15¾
Plessey	3⅜	24,300	3⅜
OCTOBER 1			
Shulton-c	25½	41,900	25¾
Hanna Mining	47	25,700	46½
PanAmWldAir	14	27,600	13⅞
Phillips Inds.-c	15¾	30,000	15⅞
Masonite	44¼	69,400	44⅝
Ralston Purina	23¾	20,200	24⅛
Goodyear Tire	27⅛	22,000	27
Minn. Mining-c	87	94,900	88
Amer. Cyanamid-c	30	57,400	30
McGraw-Hill part-c	15	49,500	15⅛
Amer. Cyanamid-c	30	63,600	30
Nat'l Lead	21	50,000	20⅞
Genesco-c	24	21,800	24
Long Is. Lgt.-c	23¼	49,400	23¼
Amtel	6⅜	35,500	7
Pitney-Bowes-c	27¼	24,900	27⅜
Pitney-Bowes-c	27¼	23,800	27½
Great A&P-c	26¾	72,000	26¾
Control Data-c	45½	28,200	45¾
Beneficial Fin.-c	46	23,000	46¼
Skil part-c	17	31,000	18½
VCA Corp.-c	20½	20,700	21½
OCTOBER 2			
Sony	17⅜	43,400	17½
Household Fin.	37	24,000	37¼
Occid. Petr.	22	20,000	22
Avery Prod.-c	28¼	50,000	28
Brit. Petr. (fn)-c	8¾	80,000	9
Baxter Labs-c	24	28,700	24½
Publ. Serv. E&G	22⅞	20,000	23¼
Albertson's-c	11⅛	21,400	11⅛
R. R. Donnelley-c	16	26,900	16¼
Continental Can-c	40⅝	41,800	40⅝
Int'l Min.&Chem.	12⅞	26,300	12⅞
Sony	16¼	110,000	17⅞
Sony	17¼	20,000	17⅜
Tenneco-c	20	20,000	20
Gen'l Cable-c	19¼	30,300	19½
Brit. Petr.-c	9	962,000	8⅞
Hshld Fin.-part c	37	29,900	37¼
Delta Air	30	20,200	30¼
Newmont Mining	25¾	23,200	25¾
Sedco-c	22⅛	71,500	22½
Heublein-c	39	50,000	39½
Sony	17¼	20,500	17¼
Xerox	88¼	25,000	88½
Bethlehem Steel-c	21¼	60,000	21⅜
Eastern Air-c	17¼	45,500	17⅛
Denny's Rest.-c	9¼	49,000	9⅜
Brit. Petr.	9½	25,000	9¾
S.W. Publ Serv.	12	29,900	11¾
Plessey	3⅜	27,300	3½
R.T.E. Corp.	15¼	34,700	16
Faberge	17	74,900	17¼
PanAm Wld Air-c	14¼	58,000	14¼
Martin-Marietta	15½	61,500	15½
Std. Pkg.	9½	25,000	9½
Weyerhaeuser	55½	20,200	55½
Black & Decker-c	50	20,200	50

c-Cross sale.

The total number of large block transactions (trades of 10,000 shares and more) for the week ended October was 405.

Source: Barron's, October 5, 1970, p. 26.

same amount of stock as you borrowed. If you are lucky enough to buy Control Data at less than 60, your profit is the difference between the two prices, less commission and taxes. But if you are forced to buy the stock at a higher price, you will incur a loss. A short interest is thus an index of the amount of stock borrowed in expectation of price declines.

The size of the short interest outstanding in the NYSE, as reported by the exchange every month, is subject to two contradictory interpretations. A trader who has a short interest in the market is naturally bearish and expects prices to go down in the near future. Judged from this aspect, a large short interest indicates widespread expectation of a price decline and is thus bearish. On the other hand, a trader who is short must purchase stocks in the near future to cover his obligations. From this point of view, a large short interest indicates a strong potential demand for stocks and justifies bullish sentiments.

In this connection, a word of caution is in order. Not everyone can or should indulge in short sales, for they go against the normal human instincts. Most people who operate in the market assume that the market is upward-bound, and it takes a highly skilled investor to enter the market believing that the immediate trend is a downward one. As Daniel Drew, an astute investor in Wall Street's early years, once cautioned: "He who sells what isn't h'sn, must buy it back or go to prison." The short-interest indicator, therefore, reflects more the activities of seasoned investors than of small investors.

Another fact you will need to consider is popularly known as odd-lot trading. An odd lot is an amount of stock less than the established 100-share unit or 10-share unit of trading: from 1 to 99 shares for the great majority of issues; from 1 to 9 shares for the so-called inactive stocks. Trades of less than 100 shares are dealt in by odd-lot dealers. An odd-lot dealer is a member firm of the exchange which buys and sells in odd lots. These dealers accept the responsibility for buying and selling stocks (numbering 1 to 99) for their own accounts, the prices of which are geared to the auction market.

The broker's fees for odd-lot transactions are a little higher than round-lot fees. More specifically, if the price of a stock is $55 or more, the odd-lot differential is one-quarter point (25 cents) above. For stocks of less than $55 the differential is only one eighth of a point (12½ cents).

Suppose for a moment that you wish to buy at the market 20 shares of International Stretch. Your order is transmitted by your broker to the representative of an odd-lot dealer at the post where International Stretch is traded. A few minutes later there may occur a 100-share (or round-lot) transaction in International Stretch at $10 a share. The odd-lot price at which your order is immediately filled by the odd-lot dealer is $10.125. If you had sold 20 shares of International Stretch, you would have received $9.875 a share.

Odd-lot statistics derive their importance as a technical indicator from a theory, popularized by Garfield Drew, according to which changes in odd-lot transactions portend significant market trends. A basic assumption of the theory is that small investors, who typically buy and sell less than 100 shares, are ill informed and can be counted upon for making wrong moves at critical moments. This implies that if odd-lotters are net buyers (that is, if they are buying more than selling), then small investors are entering the market and are "providing the opportunity" for smart money to get out. In general, therefore, a small investor can be expected to sell when the market is about to resume its upward trend and buy when a downswing is in the offing. This rule undoubtedly has some exceptions and is valid principally in the short run. Despite these limitations, however, you may gain valuable insights into the market by carefully scrutinizing the odd-lot trading figures.

The stock market is an exciting place, and its barometer of excitement on any given day is the volume of trading; that is, the number of issues changing hands. Ostensibly, a high trading volume shows greater interest on the part of investors, either in the form of buying or selling interest, whereas a low volume suggests lack of interest in the market. A study of the total volume of trading figures is significant because the number of issues changing hands on a given day or a given week is indicative of the future market trend. Let me explain to you some of the accepted volume theories.

It is generally believed that a rise or decline in stock prices on high volume signals a continuation of the existing price trend; whereas a rise or decline of prices on low volume usually points to a reversal of the price trend. It is also an accepted belief that volume tends to be high after a long advance and low after a long decline. This is so because most investors feel rich enough to buy stocks after a long bull market but hesitate to take losses at the end of a bear market. In addition, bull markets are associated with spectacular stories about fortunes made overnight. Such stories inevitably attract small investors into a rising market. Once they enter the market, many of these investors continue to operate there, even during a long declining market.

Another interesting interpretation of fluctuations in market volume is that volume increases on successive days of advance in a bull market and decreases on successive downswings in a bear market. When volume and prices move hand in hand, they are said to be "in gear," since they reinforce each other. However, if the volume and the price average do not move in unison, a reversal of the existing market trend is said to be in the air.

In passing, I should mention that in recent years some technocrats have raised serious doubts as to the usefulness of market volume as an important indicator. For instance, Godfrey, Granger, and Morgenstern[19] found no connection between stock prices and the corresponding volume of transactions. They concluded that "the application of conventional demand and supply theory would prove useful in the study of stock market behavior." However, the matter did not end there. Robert Crouch[20] took issue with the finding of Godfrey and his colleagues. On the basis of an econometric study, Crouch concluded that, if properly used, volume can act as a useful predictor of the market.

In an article in *Barron's* Edson Gould[21] explained that since early 1966 in the market, there has been a rotation of interest in individual securities and groups of securities. In the periods of advance, some stocks and groups of stocks have advanced significantly; but in the periods of decline, some have registered precipitous declines while others have held against the trend. In markets such as this, said Gould, it is most helpful to attempt to ascertain the "intermediate-term points of reversal." In recent years the investor who has adopted an overall cautious policy with due regard to reserves but who has taken action at intermediate-term turning points, increasing risks at low points and decreasing them at high points, has attained a fair measure of success.

In order to identify these intermediate-term points of reversal, *Barron's* has developed the *Daily Trading Barometer* (DTB), which is a weighted composite and three separate oscillators. One is based on the last seven days of advances and declines on the NYSE. The second is the algebraic sum of the last 20 days of plus and minus volume on the NYSE. The third oscillator is simply the ratio of the DJIA close to an average of the last 28 days' closes.

As mentioned, the DTB is an oscillator. It moves up and down within well-defined limits. Many investors claim that the DTB is the most reliable indicator of overbought and oversold market junctures. They claim that by using this index they can predict intermediate-term moves fairly successfully. The DTB is graphically represented in Figure 10–6.

A technical factor of major import is the nature of the stocks which are *popular* among investors and traders. Every day the *WSJ* publishes lists of the most active stocks and their average prices on the New York and American Stock Exchanges. Since the stocks included in these lists vary greatly in quality, the average daily closing prices of these stocks also vary considerably. Variations in these averages occur with changes in the *quality* of market leadership. The rule of thumb is that high-quality stocks command relatively higher prices than low-quality issues. Thus, on any given day, the majority of the most active stocks may represent the blue chips or high-quality stocks, in which case the average price will be relatively high; on another day, the active list may consist of highly speculative, low-quality, low-priced stocks, so that the average price will be lower than that of the blue-chip average. The market is generally more vulnerable when low-quality stocks become the darling of the market because of the degree of risk involved in owning them.

A loosely defined technical indicator of the market is the *directional*

FIGURE 10–6
DAILY TRADING BAROMETER

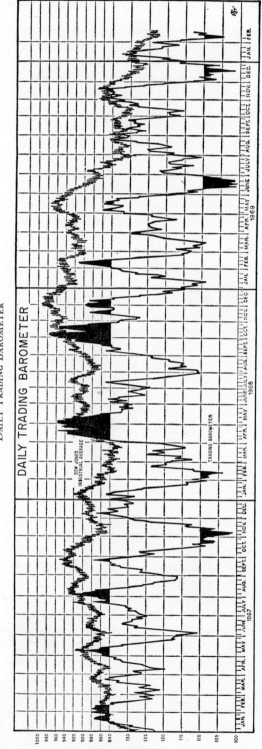

Source: Edson Gould, "Daily Trading Barometer: It Signals a Market Rally," *Barron's*, February 16, 1970, p. 26.

move of the averages. On any typical day, these averages move independently of one another. For instance, on any given day, the industrial average may go up 10 points, while the other two averages may decline by a smaller amount. On another day, all three averages may go down, or may go up or down in any combination. Such divergent movements are not unusual, but what gives this market its characteristic predictive power is the belief that this divergence in averages is not likely to persist for long. Consequently, it is frequently assumed that if these averages move in different directions the future of the market can be predicted with a relatively high degree of accuracy. In general, it is believed that movements in the weaker segment of the market precede the movements in their stronger counterparts. Since in terms of quality railroad companies are considered a poorer investment than industrial companies, during a strong market transportation averages are assumed to reach their peak and turn downward before industrial averages, and the performance of these averages in a bear market is assumed to be the reverse. In this way, watching the relative performance of the two series at critical moments may reveal significant information regarding the current status and future performance of the market.

An indicator with a venerable history is *Barron's Confidence Index* (CI), to which I referred in a previous chapter. The CI is a ratio of high-grade to lower-grade bond yields. The specific series used are *Barron's* average yield on 10 highest-grade corporate bonds, and Dow Jones' average yield on 40 bonds of a lower average quality. As a general rule, high-quality bond yields are *lower* than low-quality bond yields, since investors have more confidence in the former. During periods of economic recession, investors attach more importance to safety. Conversely, during periods of prosperity, investors are more willing to undertake risks at the cost of safety. In a rising market the CI rises, indicating investors' preference for lower-quality, high-yielding bonds. On the other hand, when the CI slides downwards, the market is believed to be getting ready for a downturn, since people are too scared to express confidence in lower-priced stocks.

I have mentioned several times before that your interest lies not in the market trend but in the stocks you already own or are likely to own. Consequently, you need to find an indicator that will indicate the performance of your stocks relative to the market. Such an indicator might be called the *relative strength* factor. Assume that at the end of every trading day you compare the closing price of your stock with the DJIA by calculating a simple ratio between the two. As long as this ratio continues to rise, your stock is outperforming the market, and vice versa.

An example should make this clear. Suppose on a trading day the price of Latex Corporation's stock is $78 per share and the DJIA is 780. The ratio of the two, or the relative strength factor, is $78 \div 780 = 0.10$. The next day the price of Latex goes up to $90, whereas the DJIA increases to

785. The factor then becomes $90 \div 785 = 0.12$. Since 0.12 is greater than 0.10, this indicates that your stock is acting stronger relative to the Dow.

Finally, let me mention a few rules for judging the strength of the market, most of which are based upon experience and observation. For instance, it is believed that a daily advance trend extended over four or five days provides sufficient evidence for a reversal of this trend. Another superstition prevailing in the market is that if stock prices advance when the news is bad, the market is technically very strong. Or, if prices fail to rally on bullish news, a weak technical position is generally inferred.

I will add that in analyzing the technical factors to help you judge the technical strengths or weaknesses of the market or individual stocks, you can do no better than to resort to *charting*. I will go into the technique of charting in the next chapter.

Like everything else, technical position in the market may be either good or bad. A good technical position is one in which the number of trading stocks which traders hold or wish to buy at the prices prevailing in the marketplace is precisely equal to the total supply of those stocks held by the investors. In such a situation the market is said to be in "short-term equilibrium." Sometimes, however, traders find that they have accumulated more shares than they are able to distribute to investors at the prices ruling in the market, while at other times they realize they have purchased fewer shares than they wish to buy and that investors wish to sell at the prevailing price. In these cases, the market is said to be in "short-term disequilibrium," and this is considered a poor technical position. It is interesting to note that whenever the market is in a state of disequilibrium, the invisible hand of the market automatically activates the opposite forces to bring the market from disequilibrium to equilibrium. Of course, a minor disequilibrium does not always trigger an opposite reaction. However, as the market deviates more and more from the normal short-term equilibrium position, the strength of the deviation forces diminishes and that of the corrective forces grows progressively stronger, eventually bringing about a reversal of the existing demand and supply structure. If such a reversal is reflected in widespread declines in stock prices, the market is said to be "technically weak." If, on the other hand, the reversal of the existing trend calls for an upward adjustment in prices, the market is considered to be "technically strong."

The Meaning of It All

Stock prices may move upward or downward because of two major factors: fundamental and technical. An interplay of these two may result in four distinctive situations ruling in the market at any one time. First, a market can be both fundamentally and technically strong. Second, it can be both fundamentally and technically weak. Third, it can be fundamentally strong but technically weak. Fourth, it can be fundamentally weak but technically strong. The market will tend to advance for an indefinite period in the case of the first situation, while the second situation will lead to an extended decline in the market. Market predictions in the case of the third and the fourth situations are not so clear-cut, however. In either of these two cases the market may advance or decline, depending upon the relative strength of the fundamental and technical factors operating on it.

As a general rule, you should buy in a weak market and sell in a strong one. The fundamental and technical factors help you determine the state of the market, which in turn provides you with the basis for generating appropriate market actions.

Charting stocks is a never-never land. Some deprecate it as abracadabra.

—DAVID L. MARKSTEIN

Craftsmen as Chartsmen

In the preceding chapter I stated that a seasoned investor examines both the fundamental and technical factors in stock selection. While both the fundamental and technical factors are important to astute investors, one aspect of the latter deserves special mention. This aspect is known as *charting*, which is the art of using charts and graphs to forecast the future market trend. Charting is a difficult art. It requires some quantitative background, and it is a time-consuming chore. Besides, there are many different kinds of charting techniques, not all of which are easily understood or practiced. However, anyone who wishes to become a successful investor must eventually develop the background and find the time to practice this art. Fortunately, information about charting has now become so readily available that thousands of ordinary investors now use them where once they were the tool only of the professional.

Of the several techniques followed by chartists, I will explain the methodology and thinking of only the most important ones in this chapter, leaving the others for you to investigate yourself.

The Chartist Philosophy

It might seem far-fetched, but John Maynard Keynes could be thought to be describing the chartist philosophy when he wrote:

. . . newspaper competitors have to pick out the six prettiest faces from a hundred photographs . . . each competitor [chooses] . . . those which he thinks

100

likeliest to catch the fancy of the other competitors, all of whom are looking at the problem from the same point of view.[22]

Consistent with this philosophy, your objective as a chartist should be to spot the winners among the thousands of stocks traded on the various exchanges. By analyzing the results of one of several different kinds of charts, you should be able to identify those stocks which will appreciate the most in price. This is a difficult task, but certainly well worth the effort.

The belief that good stocks can be identified through charting is based upon the fundamental principles relating to the Dow theory. As I have mentioned, although some stocks move differently from the average stocks in the market, as a general rule stocks exhibit strong tendencies to move as a group. In a bull market, most stocks tend to rise; the reverse is true in a bear market. It is this "association of price movements" which chartists attempt to capture and use as a basis for future market predictions.

GETTING A LINE ON THE MARKET

The chartists, busily shifting stock statistics, are constantly putting together a jigsaw puzzle. Not all agree on what the market has done lately. As for the future, some predict a rally, some foresee a selling climax, and some anticipate other moves in between. They work with as many different-looking charts as there are charting techniques employed by them. There is, however, one practice which is commonly followed by all. In one form or another, all chartists chart the Dow Jones Industrial Average and the Dow Jones Transportation Average, if only because they are popular and are reasonably representative of all stocks traded in the market. Since almost all the information needed by chartists is published daily in the WSJ, collecting relevant data poses no serious problem.

VERTICAL LINE OR BAR CHARTING

Let me begin with vertical line charting, sometimes called bar charting. Most people interested in charting use this technique, partly because vertical charts are easy to draw but also because they have meanings familiar to a technical analyst.

The procedure for preparing a vertical line or bar chart is relatively simple. Suppose you were to draw on graph or logarithmic paper a series of vertical lines, each line representing the movements of price for a time period—a day, a week, or even a year. The vertical dimension of the line will represent price; the horizontal dimension indicates the time involved by the chart as a whole. In making a daily chart, for example, each vertical line will represent the range of each day's price activity, and the chart as a whole may extend for a month. You extend the line on the graph paper from the highest transaction of each day down to the lowest and make a cross mark to indicate the closing price.

Another feature of the vertical line chart is that volume can also be shown on it by the inclusion of a second set of vertical lines at the bottom of the chart. Each line is proportional in height to the total number of shares traded during each time period shown in the upper part of the chart. In Figure 11–1 a vertical line chart for movements in the stock of

FIGURE 11–1
Sɪᴍᴘʟᴇx Cᴏʀᴘᴏʀᴀᴛɪᴏɴ

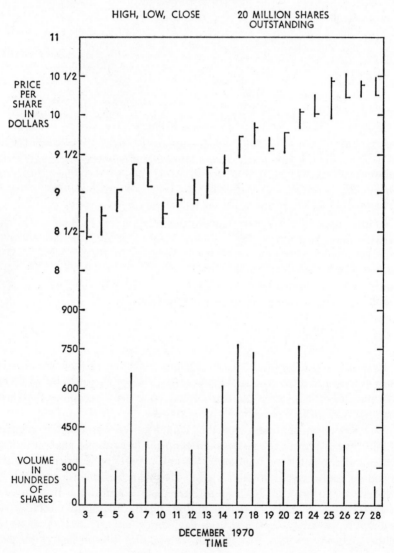

the Simplex Corporation is shown. The chart covers a month's activities and each vertical line represents one day's action.[23]

Essentially, a vertical line or bar chart is a pictorial representation of market action representing a chosen stock, and it has little predictive value. However, many of the tools of technical analysis discussed earlier can be used on a vertical line chart to forecast future changes in stock prices. For instance, if a reasonably long period is covered, a vertical line chart is likely to show *support* and *resistance* levels. A support level is a barrier to price decline, whereas a resistance level is a barrier to price advancement. A vertical line chart can also show basic trend lines in the stock price, thereby confirming the theory that most stock price movements follow a certain pattern, which may be up, down, or sideways (fluctuating within a narrow range). The basic trend lines have some predictive value, the vertical line chartists claim. Rising trends on a vertical line chart indicate higher prices; the reverse is true if the lines follow a downward pattern.

It might interest you to know that as practitioners of a highly sophisticated science, the vertical line chartists have developed a very interesting method which they use to predict future stock price trends. A typical set of their technical terms includes, besides *uptrend, sideways,* and *downtrend: throw-back effect, break-in trend line, fans, triangles* (symmetrical, reversed symmetrical, descending, and ascending), *head, shoulders, neckline, wedges, flags, rectangles, pennants, saucers, saucepans, bedpans, bowls, W-Triple tops and bottoms, gaps and islands,* and so on.

So far I have talked about charting the course of individual stocks. Bar chartists frequently chart Dow Jones averages as well, in an effort to determine where the general market is headed. In Figure 11–2, the bar chartist tries to discover the trend existing in the market, to determine whether the market is headed upward or downward. In short, a vertical line chart can be constructed to forecast individual stocks as well as general market trends.

An outstanding example of the application of vertical line chart technique for charting the course of future market action can be found in an article by Charles Collins.[24] Collins constructed several charts of Dow Jones averages in order to test the celebrated Elliott theory. You will recall from an earlier discussion that according to R. N. Elliott every market movement, regardless of size or importance, has three impulses in the primary direction, impulses numbers 1 and 3 being separated by secondary or corrective swings in the opposite direction. Elliott found that the corrective swings consisted of only three impulses, two tending to correct the previous trend, separated by a counterimpulse. Collins constructed the graph shown in Figure 11–3, analyzed it by parts, and came to the conclusion (April, 1970) that the market bottom for the correction that began in early 1966 was still to come. In retrospect, I can say that Collins was right.

FIGURE 11-2

DISCOVERY OF TRENDLINE IN THE DJIA

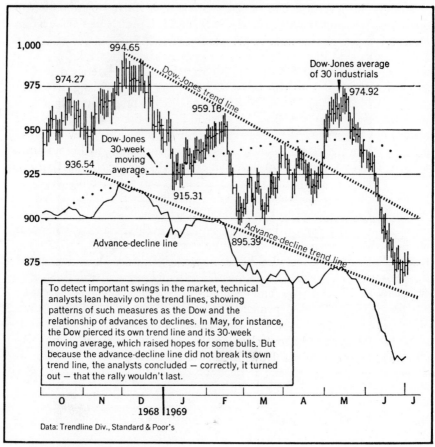

To detect important swings in the market, technical analysts lean heavily on the trend lines, showing patterns of such measures as the Dow and the relationship of advances to declines. In May, for instance, the Dow pierced its own trend line and its 30-week moving average, which raised hopes for some bulls. But because the advance-decline line did not break its own trend line, the analysts concluded — correctly, it turned out — that the rally wouldn't last.

Data: Trendline Div., Standard & Poor's

Source: Business Week, July 5, 1969, p. 66.

Let me sum up the discussion of vertical line or bar charting by quoting from an article by David Markstein:

. . . the bar chartist observes the upward zigs and downward zags which form a trend. From those, and with the help of a number of rules worked out by experience, he attempts to spot a trend.

Other readings of support and resistance levels, trendlines and trading area patterns tell him that the probabilities (never the certainties, for no serious technical analyst would claim that his methods are infallible) favor the end of a trend or, perhaps, the beginning of another trend.[25]

The bar chartist is interested in physiological elements (head and shoulders) and the woman's world (saucers and bowls), and he works only

FIGURE 11–3

THE ELLIOTT WAVE PRINCIPLE AND THE DJIA

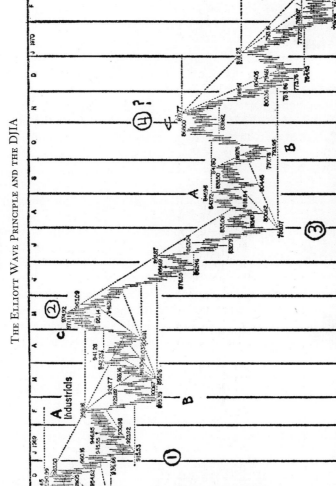

Source: Charles Collins, "Market Ebb Tide," *Barron's*, April 27, 1970, p. 20.

Courtesy of R. W. Mansfield Co.

with straight lines. A different breed of chartists makes a tic-tac-toe game out of charting. Sounds interesting? Here are the rules.

POINT-AND-FIGURE CHARTING

I have already explained that bar chartists bank upon discovering certain buying and selling forces in the market on the basis of which they predict the future price trends. These forces consist of three factors: time, volume, and price. Members of another school, popularly known as the *point-and-figure chartists*, question the usefulness of all three factors. They argue that the only way to predict future price fluctuations is to look at *price changes only*. No volume action need be recorded, and the time dimension (day, week, or month) must be pushed into oblivion.

The technique of constructing a point-and-figure chart is less complicated than you might think. If significant price changes are the only things that matter, then all you need do is to capture the significant (say, one point or more and ignoring all fractions) price changes in a stock, no matter how long it takes for the stock to register this change. The way to proceed is by putting an X in the appropriate price column of a graph. Then you enter successive price increases (of one point or more, ignoring all fractions) in an upward column as long as the uptrend continues. If the price drops by one point or more, the figures move to another column and the X's are entered in a downward progression until the downtrend is reversed. When you use such a chart over a reasonable period of time, you have a king-sized tic-tac-toe game which can then be used for prediction.

A step-by-step illustration of how a point-and-figure chart might be constructed should prove to be rewarding. In their recent book, Anthony J. Lerro and Charles B. Swayne[26] have explained this construction technique in the following manner. Take a sheet of graph paper and label the vertical axis with price of the stock selected. Unlike the bar chart, the horizontal axis does not represent time (day, week, or month). Instead, each block, rather than each line, represents each point (Figure 11–4). Notice I said, "each point." Remember that in point-and-figure charting, fractions (changes of less than one) are completely ignored. Only price changes of full points are recognized.

Whenever there is a change in price of one point, an X is placed in the appropriate box. For instance, if a stock is selling for $30, and the price advances to $31, the proper entry is made in the manner shown in Figure 11–5. If the price of the stock moves to $33, the entry will be made as shown in Figure 11–6.

Remember, too, that time is not recorded on the horizontal axis. Regardless of how long it takes for the price of a stock to go up, all price increases are recorded in one vertical column. Entries are made in different columns only when the trend is reversed. Thus, if the price of our stock

FIGURE 11-4

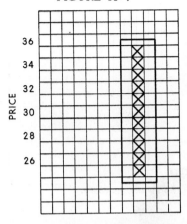

Source: Anthony J. Lerro and Charles B. Swayne, *Selection of Securities,* Braintree, Mass.: D. H. Mark Publishing Co., 1970, pp. 65–66.

FIGURE 11-5

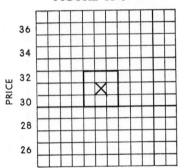

Source: Lerro and Swayne, *Selection of Securities,* pp. 65–66.

declines from $34 to $33 and then to $32, the entries representing this decline will be made in the vertical column to the right of the column in which the advance was posted, as shown in Figure 11–7.

The point-and-figure technique, which is simple to master, can be gainfully applied in developing point-and-figure charts for all the stocks in which an investor is interested. What is more significant, however, is the fact that one should continue to plot these charts for fairly long periods of time so that definite shapes can be observed on the graph paper.

FIGURE 11-6

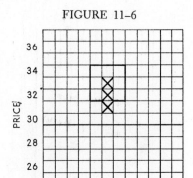

Source: Lerro and Swayne, *Selection of Securities*, pp. 65–66.

FIGURE 11-7

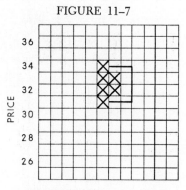

Source: Lerro and Swayne, *Selection of Securities*, pp. 65–66.

Point-and-figure chartists claim that their charts have great predictive value. They say that by concentrating on the congested area on the chart, they can estimate the next resting (upward or downward) place of the price. They do this, first, by counting the squares across a congested area and then calculating, or making an educated guess, of how far the price, which follows a breakout, will advance or decline. In Figures 11–8 and 11–9 point-and-figure charts for two companies are shown. Notice that in both instances the chartist has marked the patterns which appear on his charts so that he may tell with reasonable accuracy how stocks are likely to behave in the future.

FIGURE 11–8

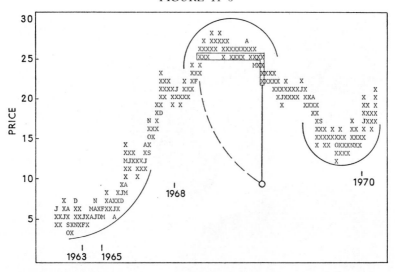

Source: Adapted from Lerro and Swayne, *Selection of Securities,* p. 10.

FIGURE 11–9

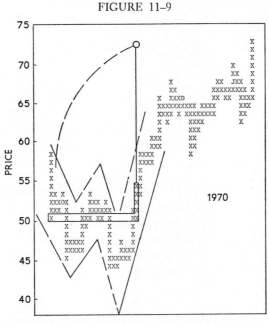

Source: Adapted from Lerro and Swayne, *Selection of Securities,* p. 10.

Volume-Price Trend

Recently David Markstein of Technical Stock Market Studies in New Orleans developed a sophisticated method of charting which he called the Volume-Price Trend (VPT) study. Markstein described his technique in the following way:

[The] Volume-Price Trend study—is to liken the market to a bucket that has a small hole in the bottom and a hose, nozzle down, which puts new water in at the top.

If an analyst assumes that the hole at the bottom of the bucket represents sell orders, some preemptory, some routine, and that the hose at the top is the inflow of new capital in the form of buy orders, he needs to know one thing: Is the hole draining away more water (capital) from the market for this stock than the hose replaces in the form of buy orders? Or are the buyers possessors of the majority of money and will the bucket, therefore, overflow and the stock in consequence go up?[27]

In short, the VPT technique expresses volume as a function of price in order to measure the flow of capital in the market. The flow of capital, in turn, forms the basis for predicting market trends.

Some Warning Signals

In quickly reviewing a few of the more important charting techniques, I have only scratched the surface. For a serious student of charting, there is no substitute for a thorough study of the various charting techniques. Nevertheless, even on the basis of my sketchy descriptions, many useful inferences can be drawn.

First of all, charting is not a science but an art. Like all arts, it must be practiced carefully and intelligently. Second, whether you prefer point-and-figure technique over vertical line or bar chart technique or whether you reject both in favor of the relative-strength technique is a matter of personal preference. You may even choose to follow more than one technique in analyzing the market condition. The main point is to discover through experience a method which proves most profitable over a period of time.

Finally, when you choose the route of technical analysis, you are not limited solely to following the charting technique. You may reinforce the effectiveness of your chart interpretations by studying other technical indicators (such as short interest, support and resistance levels, volume trading, and so on) as well as fundamental factors.

If we could bring back to life the old . . .
[specialists], because of today's conditions of sur-
veillance, they would prefer to stay dead.

—ANONYMOUS

Specialty of the Specialist

In recent years a great deal has been written about the ways in which specialists further their self-interest at the cost of the average investor. Since I do not agree with this view, and since I feel that specialists play a very important role in the market, I would like to treat this subject in a slightly different way. As a spokesman for specialists I would like to answer a series of questions and criticisms directed toward them.

Q. What are specialists for?
A. To make money.
Q. For the investors?
A. For themselves.
Q. Why don't the specialists advertise this?
A. It would not be in good taste. But it is implied. A specialist is a person who maintains, insofar as reasonably practicable, the stability and orderliness of the central market and is adequately compensated for his valuable services.
Q. Who is this remarkable person?
A. William Shepherd once characterized the specialist in the following words:

> . . . at the heart of the market for each stock stands a solitary man, cool-headed and confident while the thunder resounds about him. He is the specialist. This virtuoso, nameless to most of us, is a larger-than-life figure of extraordinary capital agility and impeccable ethics. Armed with his book of orders, the specialist quotes prices and brings together buyers and sellers.

111

Moreover, he is charged with stabilizing the market by selling when it rises and by buying when it falls.[28]

The average specialist on the exchange is probably in his forties. He is one of some 350 members engaged in the same business and associated in about 75 separate units operating on the NYSE and 35 on the ASE. The units are composed of three or more members organized in a variety of ways—joint accounts, combined books, partnerships, or corporations. On the average, each unit specializes in about 20 stocks. About 85 specialists, or a quarter of the total, have been in this profession for more than 20 years; about 175, or half, have been specialists for more than 10 years. Every specialist works at a particular location at one of the trading posts on the exchange floor. It is the only place where the stocks in which he specializes may be traded.

Q. How does a person become a specialist?

A. First he applies to the SEC and receives its formal approval. After a period of satisfactory service as an "associate" specialist, he is required to pass a rigorous examination which tests in detail his knowledge of the rules governing the specialist's function. He must also agree to conduct his business under extremely rigid, prescribed rules and policies and must observe a high standard of business ethics.

Q. Tell me, does the specialist perform any really important functions?

A. Certainly. A specialist has two big jobs. He acts as a broker for other brokers as well as a market maker. He must effectively execute orders entrusted to him by other exchange members. These orders are left with him when the current market price deviates from the prices of the orders. For instance, when a commission broker receives a limit order to buy at 55 a stock selling at 60, the specialist represents the order if and when the price declines to the level specified. Thus, he makes it possible for other members to conduct business elsewhere on the floor. In addition, a specialist has the function of maintaining, as far as practical, fair and orderly markets in the stocks which he services and for which he acts as a principal. When there is temporary disparity between supply and demand, he buys or sells for his own account to narrow the price ranges between sales and to give depth to the market. By doing this, he keeps price continuity more orderly than would otherwise be the case, thereby contributing to the liquidity of the market. He thus makes it possible for investors' orders to be executed at better prices when temporary disparity exists.

Q. How does he do that?

A. The specialist enters orders on his book under each price category in the sequence in which they are received. For each order, he indicates the number of shares and the broker from whom it was received. He represents these orders in the market, frequently competing against other members representing customers. As he is successful in executing the orders on his book, he sends reports to the members for whom he has acted according to the sequence of listings under each price category. When he makes a transaction for a broker, or when an order is canceled, he crosses it out on his book.

Q. Can you give me an illustration of the role of the specialist as a market maker?

A. Certainly. In most instances, there is a discrepancy between the price at which the buyer is willing to buy and the seller is willing to sell. Let's assume that a stock has just been sold at 55. The highest price at which anyone is willing to purchase more of this stock is 54¼ (the best bid), and the lowest price at which anyone is willing to sell is 55¼ (the best offer). If no other mechanism intervenes, there will be a stalemate. The specialist's job is to break the stalemate.

The specialist does this by purchasing the stock at a price higher than anyone else is willing to pay or by selling stock at a price lower than anyone else is willing to take. The specialist, acting as a dealer for his own account, may now decide to bid 54¾ for 100 shares, making the quotation 54¾–55¼, which narrows the spread between the bid and offer prices to half a point. Now, if the prospective seller enters the market and wishes to sell 100 shares at the price of the best bid, the specialist will be able to purchase a stock at 54¾. By doing this, the specialist will not only provide the seller with a better price, but will also maintain better price continuity, since the variation from the last sale was only ¼ of a point.

Here is an example of how the specialist may sell stock for his own account to maintain a market. Let's assume that with the last sale in a stock at 62¼, the best bid is 62, and the best offer is 63. The specialist offers 500 shares at 62½ for his own account, changing the quotation to 62–62½. The buyer enters the market and purchases the stock from the specialist. Thus, the buyer has been able to purchase the stock ½ point cheaper than would have been the case without the specialist's offer, and again better price continuity and depth have been maintained.

Q. So far you have been talking hypothetically. Can you tell me an actual incident when the specialist made the market for a specific stock?

A. Certainly. On Saturday, February 29, 1964, the President of the United States announced plans for the development of the Lockheed A-11, a revolutionary supersonic aircraft. The announcement stimulated heavy demand for Lockheed stock. Before trading opened on the New York Stock Exchange the following Monday at 10 A.M., many purchase orders had been left with the specialist in Lockheed, and the crowd of brokers around the trading post was sizable. It was obvious that Lockheed shares would open above the Friday's closing price.

With market orders to buy some 30,000 shares and market and limit orders to sell only about 17,000 shares, the specialist faced the problem of bringing supply and demand into balance. Working coolly and efficiently, he sold his previously acquired inventory of 5,600 shares to help satisfy the demands of buyers. He also decided to go short 4,000 shares —risking considerable capital—to supply additional stock to the market. Assisted by registered traders and auxiliary specialists who sold 3,200 shares (2,900 of them short), the specialist matched the buy and sell orders, and at 10:33 A.M., 30,000 shares changed hands at a price 2¾ points above Friday's close. Because of the variation from that close, Monday's opening price required and received exchange approval.

The market subsequently confirmed that the opening price was "reasonable." For the remainder of the day, there were 399 individual transactions in Lockheed, ranging from 100 to 3,000 shares. Sales totaled 111,700 shares—the third highest volume of the day. That day, the stock closed up 2⅜ from Friday's close and just ⅜ away from Monday's opening. But just as important, the price of each trade—whatever its size—did not vary from the preceding transaction by more than ¼ point. The Lockheed specialist continued to supply the market with Lockheed stock when buyers wanted it, and bought the stock when sellers appeared. He thus maintained an orderly market for Lockheed stock.

Q. Are you implying that the specialist lives dangerously both during trading hours and when the market is closed?

A. Most certainly. By the very nature of his job, the specialist is required to live dangerously all the time. He takes more risks than any other person in the financial world is ever asked to face. At times he must invest large amounts of his own money in stocks that no one else will buy at that price. At times he must sell large amounts of stock when everybody else expects the price of that stock to rise.

Let me tell you a classic story written by Dana Thomas.[29] It involves Dave Jackson, a specialist, who handled the Pantepec Oil book on the AMEX. Some years ago, during his Sunday night radio program, Walter Winchell broadcast a tip on Pantepec. When Jackson arrived at his post on Monday morning, he found orders to buy 357,500 shares. Sell orders totaled 234,500 shares, and he had only 500 in inventory. Jackson had two choices: he could stop trading in Pantepec, or he could go short the 122,500 shares necessary to meet the excess demand over supply. Even though Jackson realized that if he went short, he would lose over $100,000 for every point the stock went up, he chose to go short.

The outcome of Jackson's courageous decision was very interesting. Jackson succeeded in making the market only 2⅛ points above the close of the previous Friday. Traders crowded around Jackson's post, and a roar went up as Pantepec crossed the tape at 8⅞. By the end of the day, the demand for that stock had leveled off, and Jackson was able to cover part of his short position. Even more interesting, by the end of the week Pantepec drifted lower, and Jackson emerged with a profit of $50,000.

Q. I see. Would I be correct in assuming that the specialist tries to maneuver fluctuations in the prices of individual stocks so that no one can make as much money as he does?

A. That is simply not true. The specialist is not expected to prevent the price of a stock from declining nor is he expected to keep it from going up. He only tries to keep rises and declines in stock prices fair and orderly, insofar as is reasonably practicable under the circumstances. Of course, it stands to reason that the specialist cannot apply a single, specific formula to markets in individual stocks in order to determine whether they are fair and orderly. What is considered fair and orderly for one stock may be completely inadequate for another. It depends on such factors as market conditions, price level of the stock, normal volume of transactions, number of outstanding shares, and how closely the stock is held. Therefore, the specialist has to be flexible and subjective in carrying out his responsibility.

Q. You said that the specialist always maintains an orderly market. Do you mean to say that he is on his toes even before the opening bell rings?

A. Exactly. Most of the orders received by brokers on the floor before the opening of the market are left with the specialist. Using these orders, and also dealing for his own account in varying degrees, the specialist arranges the opening price in each stock as near to the previous close as possible. In arranging the opening, he must consider general market conditions and market circumstances in the particular stock. Of course, sometimes unusual situations demanding special treatment do arise.[30] Let us assume that on the previous day XYZ Oil Company's common stock closed at 39⅞. However, after the close of the market, an announcement was made of a new oil strike on land owned by this company. This led to a heavy influx of buy orders the following morning. A governor of the exchange was called into the "crowd" to supervise the situation. All orders to buy and sell were given to the specialist.

Let's say that after a count was made, the specialist found himself with orders to purchase 15,000 shares at the market and orders to sell 3,000 shares at the market. The specialist also had limit orders to sell (that is, sell when prices reach certain levels) at the following prices:

700 at 40	1,500 at 41
100 at 40⅛	300 at 41½
400 at 40¼	500 at 42
600 at 40½	100 at 42¾
200 at 40¾	200 at 43

Thus, an additional 4,600 shares were offered at prices ranging from 40 to 43. If it were decided to open the stock at 43, selling orders, including the market orders to sell, would supply only 7,600 shares of the 15,000 wanted—and at a price over 3 points higher than the previous close. Since this might be considered too great a variation, an attempt would be made to narrow the gap between the large demand and the small supply. To do this, the exchange authorities would have to delay the opening of XYZ Oil Company stock, and notice of the delay would have to be printed on the tape. As the business went on, floor brokers who had left orders with the specialist and others would be likely to ask, "How's XYZ?" The specialist would probably reply that there were "buyers" for the stock. The floor brokers then would relay this information to their member firm offices so that customers would know that XYZ was probably going to open at a higher price than the previous close. Similar information would also be passed along by the specialist to those firms that he knew had been interested in the security. Registered traders might also be consulted to see whether they wished to sell stock.

After the governor in charge of the operation felt that the situation appeared to have crystalized, a quotation was established, even though the spread between the bid and offer prices might be wider than usual. Let's assume that 1,000 of the 15,000 shares to buy at the market were canceled. Sellers, however, were attracted by the bid price. They put in orders to sell totaling an extra 1,500 shares.

The governor and the specialist now reappraised the situation and found that there were 14,000 shares to buy at the market and 4,500 shares to sell at the market, leaving 9,500 shares to buy on balance. The governor knew there were limited price orders in the specialist's possession to sell 3,500 shares up through 41. In other words, if the stock opened at 41, 3,500 shares could be sold on the orders limited at 41 or lower, reducing the on-balance amount to buy 6,000 shares. The governor learned that the specialist was "long" 2,200 shares, which if sold would reduce the stock demand to 3,800 shares.

At this point, the specialist and the governor decided on a quotation of 41 bid, offered at 43. This quotation was published on the ticker tape. It resulted in only one extra order—500 to sell at 41¼. The governor then discussed the situation with the specialist to see at what price he would be willing to supply the balance by going "short." As a result of this discussion 14,000 shares of XYZ Oil Company would open at 41¼, up 1⅜ points from the previous close. Four thousand shares were sold on behalf of the orders held by the specialist to sell at limits of 41¼ or lower, 4,500 shares were supplied by the market orders to sell, and 5,500 shares by the specialist (his inventory of 2,200 shares and 3,300 shares sold "short").

Q. You have said several times that a specialist performs a very challenging job. Is he rewarded for his services in many ways?

A. Yes. The specialist has three major sources of earnings. He earns a floor brokerage commission by acting as an agent in executing the orders left with him by other members. The commission ranges from $1.15 to $4.65 per 100 shares, depending on the price of the stock. It is paid to the specialist out of the commission which the commission firm receives from its customer. There is no extra charge to the investor when the specialist's services are used. Let me add here that the amount which a specialist derives from commission is determined by the particular stocks in which he specializes. Stocks in which there is usually an active public interest are known as "bread-and-butter" stocks, and in these the specialist acts principally as an agent, for which he receives commissions. Stocks in which there is less public interest are known as "dealer stocks." The specialist must own part of these stocks allotted to him.

In risking his funds, the specialist also hopes to realize a profit on the transactions which he makes for his own account. The specialist's success in making a profit, as is the case with all other dealers, is largely determined by his own judgment and astuteness as well as by general market conditions. This point requires elaboration.

Statistics show that in nearly one third of the transactions on the NYSE, the specialist is a participant; over 90 percent of these are *stabilizing transactions* (buying and selling against the market trend). Under these circumstances, one would expect the specialist to make little money. But the facts suggest the opposite.

It is generally true that the specialist is *required* to operate against his self-interest most of the time. However, he makes money by taking advantage of backing and filling. There are always temporary pullbacks from price increases and temporary declines on the way up. It is on these dips and rebounds that the specialist makes money.

The specialist also makes capital gains on his specialty stocks. Under present rules he is permitted to hold some stocks in his long-term accounts. If these stocks appreciate in value, the specialist stands to make good long-term profit on them.

Q. Now tell me, since the specialist is out to make lots of money, does he cater only to the needs of large customers?

A. Not quite. Theoretically . . .

Q. Never mind the theory. Would you just tell me the facts?

A. The specialist performs a key function by helping to execute large orders. The size of the market given in response to an investor's routine request usually is not indicative of the potential amount of stock which may be bought or sold. The specialist may be able to assist the commission broker in executing a large order by: (1) taking or supplying part or all of the stock as dealer at a mutually agreeable price within the market; (2) locating willing buyers or sellers by drawing on his knowledge of the market; (3) handling market or limited-price orders given to him by a commission broker who is executing on a piecemeal basis a large order requiring time to fill; and (4) purchasing or selling stock for his own account, with the approval of a governor of the exchange, outside the auction market to fill a block bid or offer.

Therefore, an investor who wishes to buy or sell a substantial amount of stock should let his broker know what he wishes to do so that the broker may seek to determine the depth of the market on the floor and enlist the services of the specialist if he wishes to. In such a case, the investor should not hesitate to "show his hand," since the market usually has greater depth than the nominal quote indicates.

Q. Are you saying that what specialists bank on is not having too many small orders so that they won't have to work hard?

A. I wouldn't say that.

Q. I gather that the specialist is a pretty privileged character. What special privileges does he enjoy?

A. I don't think that the specialist is a "privileged character," although he does enjoy some special privileges. For instance, in 1949 the Federal Reserve Board exempted him from margin requirements imposed on other traders. Under current exchange rules, specialists can buy stock on 25 percent margin.

Another privilege a specialist enjoys is that "he is the one player in the card game who knows everybody's hand." He represents customers with competing interests, and he has the power to deal for his own account in competition with his customers. However, in theory a specialist upholds the motto: service before self.

Q. Would I be correct in assuming that the SEC imposes many regulations on the specialist?

A. Absolutely. The exchange requires that each specialist unit be able to carry an overnight position of 2,000 shares of each 100-share-unit common stock in which specialist partners are registered. That is the bare minimum, however, and many specialists employ a great deal more capital in servicing the stocks which they handle. Some use only their own funds; others augment these funds with financing arrangements with other exchange member organizations or banks.

Besides meeting the financial requirements, the specialist has other responsibilities. The specialist is expected to keep the market a "close one." If he wishes to execute a transaction one point or more away from the last sale (in a stock priced at under 20) or two points away in a stock at 20 or over, he must obtain the approval of exchange officials. The SEC also keeps a close surveillance over specialists' activities. Computers now monitor the buying and selling patterns of stocks and alert the exchanges to any deviation from the normal. Specialists are required to submit full records, including figures on commissions, dealer profits and losses in each stock, and gains and losses made from their investment accounts.

But there is more. As Thomas puts it:

Current rules prohibit a specialist from taking orders in his stock directly from the officers of a company. He cannot effect transactions to adjust his inventory for tax purposes. He must normally avoid participating as a dealer in the opening or reopening of a stock in such a way as to upset the balance of supply and demand. There has been a tightening-up of the latitude permitted in the assignment of stocks to investment accounts.[31]

I should also mention that a specialist cannot buy for his own account at a given price until he has executed all buy orders held by him at that price.

Q. So far in all your discussions you have given me the impression that the specialist's character is beyond reproach. Perhaps you have not read Richard Ney's *The Wall Street Jungle*. In this book, Ney writes:

I will try to show that a significant cause of the market's day-to-day fluctuations is, in fact, the manipulations of the specialist. I propose to illuminate the shadows in which the specialist hides, demonstrate his effect on stock values and prices, and distinguish between the facts and the sophisticated fictions promulgated about him by the Securities and Exchange Commission and the Stock Exchanges. . . . In theory, the Exchanges are governed by a highly moral code of financial conduct; in fact, they pit the specialist's financial interests against those of his customers.[32]

Would you still like to argue that the specialist is a man of impeccable ethics?

A. Generally, yes. I have no doubt that occasionally the specialist takes undue advantage of his position and abuses his privileges. For instance, the SEC, investigating specialist behavior during the market drop of 1962, discovered that one stock opened 1¼ points below the previous close, although the specialist *sold* 500 shares, implying that demand exceeded supply for that stock. It was also discovered that another specialist who opened a stock 9 percent below the previous close had on his books 1,100 buy orders which matched with the sale orders. Other instances of abuses have been noted by the SEC. However, I maintain that these are exceptional cases. You should also remember that when a specialist outbids his customers, he may be performing his market-making function rather than shortchanging the customer to further his own interests.

Q. I don't think you can dispose of the many criticisms which have been directed against the specialist quite so lightly. Anyway, is there anything else you can tell me?

A. No, nothing. Now as an investor you can go off and safely play the market game.

Q. Just one last question. Wouldn't I do better to go off and play the market game by becoming a specialist?

A. Good. I hope you can stand the pace.

ACT **III**

PUGWASH OR HOGWASH

*All bulls dive into the market with complete
assurance that by defying the laws of gravity, for
their personal benefit, the market will go up forever.*
—ANONYMOUS

13

In a Bull Market,
Go with GOSSIP

BEGINNING OF THE "GAME"

"April," T. S. Eliot once wrote, "is the cruelest month." Anyone who
watched Wall Street come down to earth with a crash during the month of
April, 1970 would have agreed with Eliot. Rarely in the annals of finance—
with the possible exception of October, 1929; September, 1946; and May,
1962—has so much been lost by so many in such a short time. During
April the QUOTRON Market Change Index (or Qcha), which measures
the average percentage advance or decline of all stocks listed on the NYSE,
dropped 25 percent. During the same period, the AMEX average plum-
meted 25 percent, while many over-the-counter stocks lost over 33 percent
of their values. In April there existed a bear market that showed no signs of
turning around.

But this, taken by itself, would give a distorted view of the stock market.
A quick look at the performance of the market since the Great Crash of
1929 would indicate that the bull trends have dominated the scene. A
study of market trends in the United States would show that bull markets
normally last twice as long as declining bear trends. If you believe that the
bulls will play as significant a role in future markets as they have in the
past, then you owe it to yourself to develop the right perspective for
participating in the market when it moves upward.

A bull market, it is believed, is easier to deal with than a bear market because in such a market the biggest, brashest bulls flock to Wall Street and stock prices reach for the moon. While this is generally true, a word of caution is in order. Everything that smells like a rose is not necessarily a rose. Similarly, in a bull market every stock that *looks* attractive is not necessarily a good investment. In order to succeed in this type of market, therefore, you need a new framework. I call my construction of this framework the "GOSSIP" Theory. It is summarized on page 127.

Good Old Theories

The beginning of a bull market after a long and seemingly never-ending bear market can be compared with the arrival of the monsoons in India after a long hot summer. Monsoons bring great relief to those who suffer from the intense heat. But they also pose health problems for those who do not exercise caution and discrimination in enjoying rain showers. Bull markets, too, have hazards. As the market turns around, most of the badly battered stocks begin to look irresistibly good, leading to indiscriminate buying which can prove costly. Throughout the financial community during such a market, "hunches" and "tips" replace analytical thinking. New underwritings create instant millionaires by the bagful. "Onward" and "upward" become the slogans of the day, as all the bulls flock to Wall Street.

A look into the market during any major period of upswing will prove to you the validity of the above statements. For instance, from 1965 to 1969, total personnel of the Exchange community shot up from 96,300 to 165,000. Over the same time span, the price of a seat on the NYSE surged from $190,000 to a postwar high of $515,000 (on the AMEX, from $55,000 to $350,000). The number of new listings exploded, adding 529 million shares to the Big Board in 1968 and another 669 million in 1969, which were four and five times the annual number of new shares in earlier periods. The buyers of Cameo Records at $2 per share made millions, and owners of Control Data watched the price of that stock go up from $35 to over $160.

While success stories make pleasant reading, we must not fail to give adequate recognition to those who lose. In a recent book on stock market, an anonymous author tells the sad story of an investor whose resources evaporated from $62,000 in October, 1957 to $297.78 in May, 1964, during the course of a major bull market.[33] One should be able to learn from the jolted complacency and shaken confidence of this unhappy lot.

Your first objective in dealing with these rather vulnerable bull markets should be to brush up on the good old theories and follow them religiously. You will recall the time-honored market theories previously discussed, especially those based on study of fundamental and technical factors.

One theory holds that bull markets are generally associated with strong fundamental factors. These factors include the prevailing economic situation in the country, the economic status of the industry within which the company falls, and the relative strength of the company which issued the stock. The company's strength, in turn, is a function of its earnings and dividend records, its historical growth rate, and its future prospects. These considerations are dependent upon whether or not a company is soundly managed, is making reasonable profit, has a bright future, and is progressive in terms of disbursement of earnings.

In buying a stock it is necessary for you to make sure that the market is strong not only fundamentally but technically as well. The market is considered to be technically strong when one or more of the following takes place: stock prices generally rise; stocks penetrate their previous highs; the volume of short sales increases; Barron's Confidence Index rises; and line charts forecast a definite uptrend. You may rest assured that when the market is both fundamentally and technically strong, the chances of your making profitable investments are greatly enhanced.

OVERLOOK GO-GO STOCKS

One of the basic ingredients of a bull market is the spectacular performances of what are popularly known as "go-go stocks" and "go-go funds." There is ample evidence for this. In a recent bull market, Benguet Mining shot up from $2 to $22, while Burmah Mines increased 150 percent in a matter of weeks. Similar stories can be heard from mutual fund headquarters. Mates Fund, for example, had a 140 percent gain during the year 1968; during that same year, the Enterprise Fund scored a 43.6 percent gain over and above a 116.3 percent increase in the previous year.

All this sounds exciting until the latter part of the story is told; then the picture really changes. During the 1969–70 bear market, the go-go stocks and funds took their worst beating. On May 26, 1970, Burmah Mines no longer existed and Benguet sold at 5¼. The net asset value of Mates Fund fell 21.9 percent in 1969 and another 42 percent between January 1 and May 26, 1970. The value of Enterprise Fund declined over 60 percent from its earlier high. Gone are the go-go days. And even when the market turns upward, investors who have lost heavily will remain cautious and will not rally to support the go-go issues. You should therefore stay away from go-go ventures.

SEEK OUT FAVORITE CONCEPTS

In a previous chapter I mentioned that in recent years a willingness to buy "concepts" has produced some spectacular stock market gains for many investors. While the idea of concept buying is sound, following any concept blindly, in either declining or rising markets, can be disastrous.

While concepts may change at any time, the likelihood for change is much greater when a bear market gives way to a bull market. So when the market begins to rise after a recession, many of the old concepts fall out of investors' favor as new concepts emerge from behind the scene. However, to inflexible investors, the old concepts which proved good market guides in the past continue to look irresistibly good. And therein lies the danger signal, which you should take seriously. Practically speaking, if you wish to play the concept game you should seek the currently valid concepts and not stick with the old "established" concepts.

Show Conservative Enthusiasm

One of the most difficult things for an investor to do during a bull market is to apply conservative enthusiasm while buying and selling stocks—that is, be able to move with enthusiasm and confidence while retaining a conservative level-headedness and caution. It is usually true that during a bull market stock prices tend to follow an upward trend. The optimists grab whatever stocks come their way, lest the market run away from them. The pessimists worry about putting their money into high-priced stocks because they believe that what goes up must eventually come down. A successful investor should follow a middle-of-the-road policy, acting decisively while at the same time avoiding pure speculation. However, this is easier said than done. The most effective approach to this problem is to operate on a plan, or what might be called a "portfolio management concept." This means that if one seriously wishes to go about making money in a bull market, he must carefully plan and manage a portfolio with conservative enthusiasm.

Investigate before Investing

One of the common errors committed by investors in a bull market is the rather naïve assumption that the only way to make money is to buy common stocks. This is simply not true. One must thoroughly investigate all the other available alternatives before investing in common stocks. If this task of considering alternatives appears too arduous, at the very least one should study the possibilities of putting his money into preferred stocks, bonds, and warrants.

Price-Earnings Ratios

Finally, the price-earnings ratios, used as an investment tool, must not be lost sight of. Very often during a bull market, when general optimism prevails in the economy, investors are willing to pay high prices for stocks relative to the stocks' respective earnings. The opposite is true during a bear market. At the height of the bull market in 1961, the mean P/E ratio of the Dow Jones Industrial Average was 21; in contrast, the P/E ratio in 1950 was a mere 7. Let me explain how this information can be advantageously used by an investor.

During a bear market the investors' confidence is badly shaken, and the P/E ratios of some good stocks are driven to their lowest levels. Even after the market has *decidedly turned* around, many sound stocks continue to sell relatively cheaply, and their P/E ratios hover around low levels. A successful investor must single out these good, cheap stocks and, after proper investigation as to the probability of their future success, should invest in them. Experience suggests that those who are able to do this are paid off very handsomely in the long run.

THE GOSSIP THEORY

In this chapter I have explained the GOSSIP theory, which is summarized for your convenience:

G = Good old theories
O = Overlook go-go stocks
S = Seek out favorite "concepts"
S = Show conservative enthusiasm
I = Investigate before investing
P = Price-earnings ratios

I hope you will frequently indulge in GOSSIP as you play the market.

There are two types of investors in the market: one follows the UTMOST theory; the other does not. Those investors who follow the UTMOST theory will succeed.

—ANONYMOUS

14

To Succeed in a
Bear Market:
Try UTMOST

WHAT'S THE PROBLEM?

On May 4, 1970, stock prices took their steepest dive since President Kennedy's assassination on November 22, 1963, and the stock market tobogganed as the Dow Jones Industrial Average sustained its sharpest drop of over 19 points. (The market suffered another major decline of 20.81 points to 641.36 on May 25.) Bond prices also were battered, while some Treasury and corporate issues headed toward record lows.

What happened on May 4, 1970, to make the market suffer its biggest loss since it dropped 21.16 points on November 22, 1963? Underlying the general mood of investors in the market were several factors which deserve special attention.

UNCERTAINTY

Foremost among the major worries of investors was the U.S. invasion of Cambodia which, despite Presidential assurances to the contrary, was thought to be the beginning of a new war. This worry was topped by a report of an unprecedented press conference at which Russian Premier

Kosygin stated that he would take a hard line against the U.S. military campaign in Cambodia.

Movements in the DJIA on May 4 reflected the investors' apprehensive mood. The market headed down right from its opening on Monday (May 4), the average showing a loss of 14.91 points at 11:30 A.M. However, since Kosygin's remarks proved to be more diplomatic than positive, prices began to recover; by 12:30 P.M. the industrial average had trimmed its loss to 7.92 points. But shortly after noon, a statement from Communist China terming U.S. intervention in Cambodia a "provocation" to the Chinese people redepressed the market, and prices once again resumed a downward journey.

The international tension which pushed the DJIA down 19.07 points was very different from the sense of international tragedy that prevailed seven years earlier when President Kennedy was assassinated. The death of the President was a traumatic experience for everyone, and the market fell 21.16 points on that day. Is there anything in common between these two incidents other than the fact that each resulted in a stock market decline of approximately the same number of points? The answer is, yes there is another common factor. Both incidents created an atmosphere of uncertainty. In each case, nobody knew what might happen. Would World War III soon begin? Was this the prologue to a long march toward domestic turmoil and sinking corporate profits? No one could be certain.

It might be interesting to recall another major news event, no less dramatic than the two just cited, but which barely dented the market. On July 19, 1969, Neil Armstrong and Edwin Aldrin became the first human beings to step on the moon. It was a historic moment, and one would have expected a sharp upturn in the market of a magnitude at least equal to the downturns set off by the other two incidents. But the market fooled everyone; on the following day the DJIA closed at 834.02, off 1.4 points, transportation was down 1 point, and utilities were down 1.4 points.

While it appears paradoxical that the market would react as though America's great achievement in space was bearish news, there was an underlying factor which tipped off seasoned investors that the market would not rise. Apollo 11 had been so greatly publicized that everyone expected the mission to succeed; consequently, the market had already discounted the good news. So, when the historic moment arrived, the news had little consequence for investors.

TARNISHED CORPORATE IMAGE

Everyone buys stocks in the hope that their prices will quickly appreciate. Most investors also recognize that, barring temporary aberrations caused by emotional outbursts, movements in stock prices are geared to corporate earnings. An obvious corollary to this idea is that stock prices generally move up and down with the increasing or decreasing earnings of the respective companies.

If you look closely into the drop in the DJIA from the level of about 800 in January, 1970 to a little over 700 in early May, you will realize that expectations of lower earnings of most corporations in the early part of 1970 and their dismal showing of actual first-quarter earnings constituted an important reason for the market's nose dive. You need not go far to find substantially lower earnings and colossal losses of corporate giants. Thus, in April, 1970 three major steel companies reported earnings down anywhere from 11 percent to 92 percent during the first quarter of 1970. Then came the disappointing news from GM, Ford, and Chrysler, and a forecast by IBM Chairman Thomas J. Watson, Jr., that in 1970 that high-flying company would have "a difficult year." Among the industry groups, Aerospace lost 30 percent (that is, percentage change of earnings in the first quarter of 1970 versus the same period of 1969); Electrical Equipment and Electronics, 67 percent; Glass, 32.6 percent; Building Materials, 30.5 percent; and Wood Products, 20.8 percent. It is no wonder, then, that such showings have tarnished the corporate image in investors' minds, tempting many of them simply to get out or at least not get in.

MONEY

As I have explained before, money is generally expected to serve us. Occasionally, however, it becomes our master, starting monetary jitters across the stock board.

It happens this way. When the supply of money outruns the amount of goods available for purchase, an inflationary spiral begins. If inflation gets out of hand, what amounts to the most inequitable tax of all—the most regressive tax—is imposed upon the public, creating undue hardship for those with fixed incomes, loss of faith in the country's monetary system, and an all-around uncomfortable feeling among investors. Since in the long run continued inflation creates an untenable situation, the Federal Reserve almost always attempts to control it by raising interest rates and slowing down the rate of increase in the money supply. Occasionally, the Federal Reserve resorts to other measures as well, such as raising the margin requirements (that is, lowering the amount of money that can be borrowed by investors to purchase stock) and requesting member banks to exercise restraint in granting loans.

The task of the Federal Reserve might appear simple, but it is not. Attempts to control inflation by tinkering with monetary tools have economic and social costs. To begin with, when tight monetary policy is first instituted, no one can be sure just how long such a policy will continue. This creates uncertainty, and businesses and corporations hesitate to undertake long-term investment plans, which in turn act as a depressant on the economy. Also, as control over money gets tighter, plans for expanding business facilities, marketing new products, and even buying stocks are invariably curtailed. All these most assuredly lead to lower stock prices.

Just as a continuing tight credit policy aggravates the rising risk of recession, so also any hope of even a moderate easing of money buoys the market. This is a demonstrable fact; and to see how the market is affected by a relaxation in monetary policy, you need only analyze the statement of Treasury Secretary Kennedy at the beginning of 1970. On February 8, he said:

Once the inflationary psychology is broken, and the business community and the public in general begins to look forward to greater stability, interest rates will drop to a more reasonable level and other salutary effects will be felt throughout the economy. Because of the progress we are now making, that happy day may be closer to hand than most people realize.[34]

Immediately following Kennedy's statement, the DJIA spurted up 14 points. However, as soon as the investors realized that Kennedy had no advance knowledge of what the Federal Reserve *really* had in mind, and when the Federal Reserve showed no signs of letting up on monetary brakes, the DJIA faltered.

A slightly different incident occurred on May 5, 1970, when Arthur Burns, Chairman of the Board of Governors of the Federal Reserve, announced a lowering of the margin requirements from 80 percent to 65 percent, signaling a relaxation of the prevailing tight money policy. The next day the stock market opened up very strongly; within minutes the DJIA advanced 15 points. However, as investors began to realize that there had not really been any fundamental change in any of their many different kinds of worries, the market began to sag.

Let us return to the May 4, 1970 drop of over 19 points in the DJIA. It is evident that one reason for the decline was the stalemate in the administration's fight against inflation. Tight monetary and fiscal policies had produced the anticipated business slowdown; but despite the slowdown prices stubbornly resisted the pressures of tight money, thereby considerably reducing investors' expectations of an easy money policy in the foreseeable future. As a matter of fact, the continued uptrend in prices reinforced the investors' fear that the country was in for a long, arduous session with tight monetary restrictions.

It is now an established fact that money makes a great deal of difference in the way stock prices behave. Other things being equal, stock prices show signs of sluggishness under tight money conditions and tend to go up when money is relatively easy.

OTHER ALTERNATIVES

A relatively unknown factor that frequently affects the stock market adversely is the outflow of funds from the market. After the market average has suffered a long decline and the stock market still continues to tread a tenuous, downward path, the "smart money" is scared away from the market. Some turn to such offbeat investments as pistachio trees, wildcat oil wells, struggling private firms, antiques, and American paintings.

Not all investors frustrated by the performance of the DJIA turn to offbeat gambits. Many are attracted by the high interest rates prevailing in the bond market. When yields for the U.S. government, municipal, and corporate bonds climbed to record levels in 1969, for instance, individual investors pumped more than $25 billion into this market. Compare this figure with the less than $9 billion in 1968 and the previous record of $14.5 billion in 1966. But that is not all. During 1969 and 1970, at the Federal Reserve Bank of New York, droves of investors queued up to buy Treasury bills that yielded better than 2 percent more than savings banks. And at giant retail houses, such as Bache & Company, customers came in with dozens of passbooks to buy $100,000 worth of bonds at one time.

The result of this "smart money" leaking out of the market is always disastrous. Since to buy stocks you need money, when the supply of money is reduced, due partly to the pursuance of a tight money policy by the Federal Reserve and partly to the reallocation of money to other markets, stock prices generally suffer sharp setbacks.

SAGGING ECONOMY

Money is essentially a barometer of a nation's economic life; it indicates in a general way the economic conditions prevailing in the economy. However, if you are to make a sound investment judgment, in addition to looking at a barometer you must also closely examine the economy itself.

A sagging economy usually causes considerable disappointment in the minds of investors, which, in turn, adversely affects stock prices. The U.S. economy had been sagging throughout 1969, and in the first quarter of 1970 it appeared to be in limbo. The economy was drifting, following the loss of momentum in the first quarter. There was very little new strength emerging anywhere. The rate of unemployment, which stood at 3.5 percent at the end of 1969, rose to 4.2 percent in February 1970, to 4.4 percent in March, to 4.8 percent in April, and to 6 percent in July, 1970. Along with increasing unemployment, short-term interest rates drifted lower; these rates were reduced to below 6.5 percent in April, 1970 from the high of 8 percent reached in January, 1969. A look at the major economic variables (prices, housing construction, industrial production, capital spending, and so on) indicates that while trends in some of the variables were clearly unfavorable, others exhibited encouraging trends. In general, therefore, it is fair to say that when there is great indecision about which way the economy is really headed, investors are afraid to do any buying against the background of a sagging economy. A drifting economy thus contributes to a declining market.

Turmoil on the Domestic Front

The stock market frequently reacts adversely to what might be called "factors beyond economics." More specifically, investors are often discouraged by political and social turmoil. Not a day goes by that one does not hear of increasing crime rates, problems of school integration, the influence of drugs on our youngsters, acts of violence by revolutionary groups, and campus disorders. Some of these problems will naturally remain with us as our population increases and we head toward an increasingly complex society. The gap between the Establishment and the radicals, the old and the young, and the men and the women is likely to continue to widen. The apparent lack of progress in solving these problems creates depressed feelings among investors. For instance, one of the factors to which the May 4, 1970 decline in the DJIA was attributed was to the news that four students had been killed and at least 12 wounded at Kent State University. It is therefore no exaggeration to conclude that turmoil on the domestic front acts as a depressant on the stock market.

The UTMOST Theory

In this chapter I have described an UTMOST theory of investment. In developing an investment strategy, you must give serious consideration to this theory, which explicitly recognizes those factors which adversely affect the market. Here are the ingredients of the UTMOST theory:

> U = Uncertainty
> T = Tarnished corporate image
> M = Money
> O = Other alternatives
> S = Sagging economy
> T = Turmoil on the domestic front

Have fun with the UTMOST theory!

15

Buy In, Sell Out,
or Hold until Doomsday

THE ETERNAL BUY-SELL DILEMMA

One of the most difficult things that you as an investor must do at any given point in time, is to decide whether to buy in, sell out, or hold onto the stocks you own. To help you make these decisions intelligently, it would be beneficial for you to consider and study a set of guidelines. These may be based on stock market lore, investment theories, and technical approaches, tested against your own value judgments.

Before I describe a set of guidelines, it seems appropriate to mention that at any given moment you are likely to decide that some stocks should be bought and others should be sold. There is no such thing as a perfectly "good" time to buy or a perfectly "good" time to sell.

You should realize, too, that in the investment world, procrastination is a positive action. By deciding not to do anything, you in effect agree to hold the stocks you own. As a matter of fact, insofar as your performance as an investor is concerned, there is very little difference between inaction and a conscious decision to hold your stocks because of an optimistic appraisal of the future performance of the various companies involved.

Let us proceed, then, to set up some broad buy-sell-hold guidelines. Notice, I said *guidelines*. It would be unwise for me to tell you which stocks you should buy or sell or when you should take such actions. For

134

these are *personalized decisions*; they depend upon many factors which cannot be spelled out a priori. Nevertheless, the general guidelines which I am about to set up can provide you with valuable assistance in reaching your investment decisions.

At this point I must make three simplifying assumptions. First, throughout the discussion I will assume that the decision to buy and the decision to hold are identical. Second, I will assume that if a stock appears to be a good buy at a given time, you will buy it immediately if you don't own it or you will continue to hold it if you already own it. Third, I will assume that if a particular stock does not appear to be a good buy, then you will not buy it, or you will sell it at once if you own it. For purposes of this discussion, any stock which is expected to appreciate in value is to be considered a good buy.

Two Elementary Approaches

It should be interesting to begin with two elementary approaches to trading in stocks. The first one, which might be called the *quick-act approach*, goes something like this. A necessary condition for success in the investment world is to act quickly on advance information before others have a chance to act. Of course, in this day and age, where dissemination of information is fast and efficient, it is difficult to acquire valuable information pertaining to specific companies before such information becomes general knowledge. However, if you keep your ears and eyes open and do your homework regularly, you will come across news items which will tip you off to some good news about corporations, and you can use such information to make investment decisions. If your actions are correct and timely, you will be paid off very handsomely. For instance, if you had bought stocks of Syntex Corporation at the time the company announced its decision to manufacture contraceptives, you would have made substantial gains from this investment.

The second technique of buying and selling stocks might be called the *quick-dip approach*. Every so often the stock market suffers a sharp loss for any one of a number of reasons, and as a result many stocks become available at *bargain* prices. In these instances, if you are convinced that the market drop is temporary and that there is no good reason for stock prices to continue downward, then have the courage and the foresight to plunge in and buy up as many bargain stocks as you can afford. Of course, this is easier said than done, because buying stocks when things look gloomy goes against human nature. Therefore, forcing yourself to snap up stock bargains before other people overcome their qualms will entail self-discipline and self-analysis.

Let me cite one instance when the quick-dip approach could have been used with great success. On the day President Kennedy was assassinated, as the news spread and people began to fear the worst, the market dropped over 20 points, and many stocks closed at their lows. For those who had faith in America's political machinery and who concluded that adjustments would soon be made in the political structure, this was the right time to act. If you had been one of those people with the courage and resources to take advantage of this quick but temporary dip, you would have made a fortune.

UNDERVALUED-STOCK STRATEGY

One of the more sophisticated methods of buying stocks is known as Graham's undervalued-issue strategy. In 1934, Graham and Dodd published a book, *Security Analysis*, in which they developed a market strategy for operations in undervalued issues. Subsequently, other theoreticians worked on this idea and transformed it into a comprehensive, broad-based market strategy. Today the modified version of the Graham strategy has as its basis four ingredients: (1) purchase of "bargain stocks"; (2) acquisition of growth stocks; (3) buying of cyclical stocks; and (4) the acquisition of "special situations."

In following the modified Graham strategy, your foremost objective should be to buy bargain stocks. This implies, of course, that you already know how to identify these stocks. Intuitively, one might think of bargain issues as those stocks which are selling in the market at prices well below their net worth and which offer the most attractive means of obtaining above average long-term returns. On a more practical level, bargain issues might be identified in the following manner.

Stocks which are selling at a price well below their *book values* can be characterized as bargain stocks. How the market price of a stock ever reaches higher than its asset value can best be explained by an illustration.

Suppose that the ABC Company has 100,000 shares outstanding and the following information can be derived from its latest balance sheet:

Value of tangible assets to be realized, if sold $10,000,000
Amount necessary to liquidate all claims of creditors and preferred
  stock holders .... $ 5,000,000
Net proceeds for distribution to common stockholders .... $ 5,000,000
Book value of each share (5,000,000 ÷ 100,000) .... $ 50

Let us suppose, further, that the ABC stock is selling in the market for $29 a share. Why? Because in this instance investors perhaps tended to exaggerate the significance of transitory events. There is nothing surprising about this. Quite frequently, investors interpret temporary declines as major setbacks and in consequence drive stock prices down. Another reason for stock prices to decline is that quite often investors accept reported earnings uncritically and refuse to pay a fair price for the stock. Accounting practices are still open to many discretionary decisions, and sometimes the accounting reports constitute a significant understatement of both the trend and level of earnings per share. When this is so, the related stocks begin to sell at bargain prices. In our illustration, the ABC stock would continue to be a bargain stock until the market price has been driven up to $50, which is the current book value of the stock.

According to the Graham strategy, your second objective should be to acquire *growth stocks*. Here, again, the concept can only be loosely defined, since growth stocks are not necessarily the same as stocks of a growth company or a growth industry. A growth stock is one whose market value is expected to increase faster than the general market and faster than the average for the industry.

This definition brings us to the heart of the problem: What must happen to a company in order for the stock of that company to outperform other stocks? The answer is simple: Such a company must show promise of a more than average increase in sales and earnings.

Spotting growth stocks and investing in them before these stocks have made their major moves can be a very profitable venture. Texas Instruments, Fairchild Camera, Xerox, Itek Corporation, IBM, Motorola, Polaroid, SCM—all provide examples of growth stocks. However, there are some difficulties in identifying these stocks and some risks in investing in them. These difficulties should be clearly spelled out.

Eiteman, Dice, and Eiteman have pointed out that growth in sales and earnings of a company are based primarily upon an increase in the demand for the products of that company. There are two types of demand: new demand and replacement demand. The authors state:

> When a new industry first comes into being, its capacity to produce is likely to be inadequate to supply the immediate demand for its products. At such time expansion leads to lower costs, larger volume, and greater net earnings. This rapid increase in earnings during the growth period provides a basis for breath-taking advances in the market value of its shares. Then, as some of the products first marketed wear out, replacement needs further augment demand and cause profits to mount and stock prices to soar.[35]

The trick is to spot these companies *before* their earnings explosion takes place. This is easier said than done; most investors are unaware of these companies until their growth potential has become general knowledge.

Another problem associated with investing in growth companies is that they are usually quite volatile. As Cohen and Zinbarg have pointed out, when their earnings level off, their prices "collapse."[36] For instance, the earnings of Texas Instruments fell from $15 million in 1960 to $9 million in 1961; the consequent price decline was from $256 per share to $95 a share in 1961. Similarly, as a result of earnings declines, in 1966 the price of

Fairchild Camera stock fell from 216¾ to 96¾, while the stock price of Farrington Manufacturing fell from 57½ to 11 for the same reason.

In dealing with growth stocks, there is also the problem of "maturation slack." After a company has gone through a long maturation process, there usually comes a period of decadence, during which the demand for its product actually declines. When this occurs, the price of such a stock moves sideways, and during that period the investor is not likely to realize any appreciable financial gains from such an investment. Despite these problems and risks, however, in most instances investors who purchase growth stocks at the right time end up with sizable financial gains in the long run.

The Graham strategy suggests that your third objective should be to purchase cyclical stocks when they look attractive. A cyclical company is one whose earnings rise when boom conditions prevail in the economy and fall when the economy suffers a recession. Automobiles, heavy trucks, steel, copper, and railroads are some examples of cyclical companies. As you might expect, prices of cyclical stocks soar when the economy is rolling along at high speed, while the prices of these stocks plummet when the economy runs in low gear. The idea is to pick up good cyclical stocks when they are at the bottom of their cycle.

While the theory of cyclical stock buying is straightforward, there are some problems involved in its proper implementation. First of all, it is not always clear where the low point in the business cycle is. Second, it is not always easy to distinguish between cyclical and noncyclical stocks. Third, even if these stocks are identified, it is not always possible to determine accurately when they reach their cyclical lows. Fourth, at the time a particular cyclical stock looks very attractive, several other stocks are likely to appear equally or more promising, thereby further complicating the selection process.

While the problems of identification and buying of cyclical stocks at the right time do exist, they are surmountable. Advisory services and brokerage firms frequently identify cyclical stocks and advise their customers to buy the selected ones. As for the right time to purchase these stocks, I can do no better than quote L. O. Hooper, who recommended buying cyclical stocks in January, 1961 in these words:

Cyclical stocks for months have been "unwanted" stocks. The business cycle has been against them. Earnings have been declining. Most of them are not "growth" stocks, and most of them lack the glamour people have been seeking in issues representative of the electronics and advanced science industries. It is my opinion that traders and cyclical investors should take a long look at equities of the type tabulated below. I reason: (1) that the business cycle is near a probable turning point, (2) that these stocks are way down while the glamour issues are way up and (3) that investors this year will begin to look more at neglected values than at overromanced shares. The tabulation speaks for itself.

It shows that many cyclical issues, while up a little from their lows are selling at 20% to 60% under their former bull market highs.[37]

Your final objective in following the Graham strategy should be to acquire special-situation stocks when their prices suffer temporary setbacks. A special-situation stock is one whose price dips temporarily because of some adverse news affecting it or because, to paraphrase Graham and Dodd, the market made a mountain out of a molehill and exaggerated a vicissitude into a major setback. For instance, if the price of General Oil Corporation declines sharply as a result of the news that it did not find oil in a recent drilled area, but it continues to be an attractive company, then General Oil would become a special-situation stock.

While the idea of buying special-situation stocks has some merits, I must warn you against relying too heavily on it. There are several reasons for this. Special situations of any significance are encountered only rarely. Besides, the returns from purchases of special-situation stocks are usually short term in character, since they normally terminate when the particular events are consummated. Also, do not lose sight of the fact that this approach usually involves the unraveling of legal complexities. For instance, a prospective merger of two companies constitutes a promising special situation; indeed, investors might obtain substantial returns from time to time on such transactions. However, because of the legal complications which often arise in these situations, activities along these lines hardly seem advisable for a general portfolio strategy. Because of these reasons, my advice to you would be to keep your eyes open for special-situation stocks but not to commit a sizable segment of your portfolio to them.

ADVANTAGE OF TRIPLE COINCIDENCE

Buying undervalued stocks by using Graham's strategy is only one aspect of the buy-sell guidelines. Another aspect has to do with selecting among a variety of stocks, all of which appear equally attractive. For instance, how would you determine whether IBM shares are better than those of General Motors? Both are excellent companies, both pay good dividends, and both stocks are regarded as being of top quality.

A little probing into the past record of the two companies would reveal that IBM has performed far better than GM on at least three counts (see Figure 15–1). IBM's rate of growth in net income per share, as indicated by a graph showing the slope of its historical earnings path, has been considerably more rapid than that of GM. In addition, IBM's growth has been more stable in that the deviations from its trend in earnings have been much less marked than those of GM. Finally, estimates of future earnings made by these two companies indicate that IBM's per-share earnings growth will be more rapid and more stable than GM's. Any company which has these three advantages over other companies enjoys what I

FIGURE 15–1

INTERNATIONAL BUSINESS MACHINES AND GENERAL MOTORS EARNINGS PER SHARE

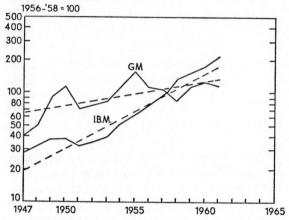

Source: Volkert S. Whitbeck and Manown Kisor, Jr., "A New Tool in Investment Decision-Making," *Financial Analysts Journal*, May–June, 1963, p. 2.

would call the advantage of triple coincidence. Investors are likely to pay a higher price for a stock with the advantage of triple coincidence than for one without it. So, in accordance with this principle, you should look for those companies which exhibit the coincident occurrence of the following performance elements: (1) high rate of growth in income per share, (2) smaller deviance from an earning trend, and (3) estimated superior future rate and stability of growth.

THEORY OF CONCEPT BUYING

Of comparatively recent development is the theory that investors should buy "concepts" rather than individual stocks. This theory involves spotting a combination of factors likely to cause a particular group of stocks to outperform the rest of the market. Many investors who bought the *right* concepts in recent times have been well rewarded, and it is worth your time to learn more about this theory than was provided in Chapter 13 and earlier in this book.

Early in 1970 two security analysts, John Greeley and John Doherty, concluded a study of a number of concept groups and, on the basis of this study, made the following observations.[38] Every "valid" concept has four common ingredients: (1) an easily grasped idea indicating that significant sustained growth is practically inevitable; (2) a favorable government or social climate to support its validity; (3) well-performing stocks within the concept group that will magnify and reinforce investor interest; and (4) substantial sales and earnings gain in the recent past. All four ingredients are essential to determining the strong performance of concept stocks.

The study points out that careful evaluation of these four factors by an investor can indicate not only which concepts to buy but when to sell them. According to Greeley and Doherty:

Changes that result in the elimination of one or two of these characteristics seem to presage a decline from investor favor. When any of the four factors we have mentioned is weakened, attacked or ceases to be valid, it breaks the chain of images conjured up by the concept. From that point, it is only a matter of time before the crowd ceases to believe in the concept [and the prices of the stocks in the group begin to decline].[39]

The two analysts applied the four key ingredients in evaluating five concept groups: specifically, the conglomerate group, the antipollution group, the cable television group, the franchising group, and the mobile home group. Of these five, the conglomerate group got the lowest score. There were several reasons for this. The idea of synergism (that is, that the total effect of a combination will be greater than the sum of the effects of its parts taken independently) was unsound. The government climate was unfavorable, and, since 1968, the earnings of conglomerates have been declining. For these reasons the two analysts felt that conglomerates comprised "a mature concept group which . . . [had] run up, [came] . . . back down and . . . [henceforth would] probably act generally in line with reported earnings."

Greeley and Doherty felt that the franchising concept had three negative characteristics and one neutral one. Arguing that proliferation of competition, a number of franchising failures, and government hearings on business practices of enfranchisers cast doubts on the growth prospects, the analysts came to the conclusion that this group should also be avoided by investors. Applying the same technique, the analysts also rejected cable television and mobile homes as favorite concept groups.

Of the five concept groups selected by them, Greeley and Doherty ranked antipollution stocks as foremost, since this group possessed three positive and only one neutral factor. Not only was the industry's potential market enormous, but both the public and the public sector were anxious to solve the pollution problem in the quickest possible time. Hence, the analysts recommended the purchase of antipollution stocks on weakness.

Just as buying concepts has proved to be rewarding for many investors, it has also been disastrous for those who did not use good judgment. It must be remembered that most concepts share an important characteristic: they generally sound irresistibly good, whether or not the reasons for their attractive appearance are valid. Consequently, before making a decision to buy a concept stock you should evaluate the concept and make sure your judgment is sound. I must also warn that concepts continually change, and you should not stay wedded to any one concept.

THE CONTRARY-OPINION THEORY

A peculiar approach to buying and selling stocks is known as the contrary-opinion theory. Actually, this theory is based upon common sense and is neither exact nor original. Formalized by Humphrey Neill, a 74-year-old native of Saxtons River, Vermont, the contrary-opinion theory attempts to anticipate market moves by reasoning which is the opposite of whatever the majority of investors happen to be thinking. Built upon the foundations of odd-lotters' theory (that small investors are always wrong in their evaluation of the market trend), the contrary-opinion theory has the objective of keeping the investors' minds flexible and open to a variety of attitudes on which to base buy-sell-hold decisions.

Since I firmly believe that the contrary-opinion theory is a dangerous market theory to follow, I should caution you against the somewhat novel idea that it is advantageous to ruminate and think contrarily. In the following paragraphs, I will outline some of my major objections to this theory.

According to the contrary-opinion theory, since small investors are almost always believed to be wrong at the top and bottom of a market, it is wise to act in opposition to general opinion only at these market turning points. In most instances, however, the public is right in the middle of a market trend, and the contrary-opinion theory is totally ineffective during these periods of continuing trends. An objective contrarian should first determine the stage of the trend and how long it will be before it is reversed. He should then ignore public sentiment except at turning points.

Another difficulty in using the contrary-opinion theory as an effective investment tool arises from the fact that it goes against psychology to think differently from the majority. It takes stern discipline to train the mind to be objective and at the same time to oppose popular sentiment. Only with constant practice can contrary thinking become a profitable habit.

Thinking in opposition to the majority is difficult not only for the general public but for the contrary-opinion theorists as well.[40] At their 1966 conference, a few days before the market bottomed out, a group of expert contrarians decided that the future market trend was bearish; they were wrong. In 1968, when the Dow was spurting up, 80 percent of the contrarians said that the Dow would rest between 1,000 and 1,100 in October, 1969. In 1969, 43 percent said the Dow would be around 900 during 1970, 31 percent said that it would be 700, and only 13 percent said it would be about 800. All these predictions were mistaken. James Fraser, who ran the conference and who writes a contrary-opinion advisory column, viewed the contrarian survey as a possible signal for him to consider the reverse. As he put it, "Almost everyone is predicting the market for the next year will be under the influence of sharp swings. The natural and contrary thing to consider is how to invest if there are no swings at all."

The latest contrary forum, held during the weekend of October 8–11, 1970, at Manchester, Vermont, was most interesting since, in the words of James Durgin, "The Contrary Opinion Forum reached a new pinnacle of contrariness this year."[41] All of the 200 contrarians who attended the forum were polled twice, once on arriving and again just before their departure, on their estimate of the outlook for stock prices. In the first poll, 51.8 percent indicated that in six months the DJIA would be between 800 and 950. A whopping 70.5 percent believed it would be in the same range within one year. After the conference was over, the collective estimate for the next six months was unchanged: 51.5 percent expected the DJIA to move to the 800–950 range. However, only 55 percent now thought it would be at the same level after a year, and 18.8 percent predicted that before October, 1971 the market will hit a new low under 600.

Still another hazard associated with the use of the contrary-opinion theory is that it is not always possible to detect exactly what the popular opinion is. Until that can be effectively done, taking a positive step in what *appears* to be a step in the right direction might be just the wrong thing to do.

Defensive and Offensive Actions

You may have noticed that trading in the stock market is often referred to as "the market game" or "the money game." Investors do play a game in the market according to the rules laid down by Wall Street and federal government regulators. The losers lose money, while the winners fatten their billfolds.

"Games, games," you say. "It is nonsense to talk about games while I put my hard-earned dollars on the line." That's right. Yet I do talk about games, and I do it with a serious purpose. Games best demonstrate strategy, and without well-defined strategies you are liable to get lost in the market.

There is a celebrated strategy to which the economists give the label of *game theory*. This complicated theory was first propounded in 1947 by John von Neumann and Oscar Morgenstern. They explained their theory with acuity, applying higher mathematics, complicated formulas, and statistical logic to selection of strategies in warfare, economics, and sociology. I will describe here in simple terms the fundamental principles of strategy in the game theory.

In any game, be it a businessman's market game or a poker game, every player must face the vexing and persistent problem of outguessing his rival. If he could guess, or make a rational calculation in advance, what his competitor will do, his actions would be far more effective and timely.

Notice I said that each player must attempt to guess his opponent's actions in advance. This implies that a player must determine his own actions under the constraints of possessing incomplete information, since his opponent tries to cover his plans with secrecy. Every player must therefore draw heavily upon his experience with his competitor's past behavior. The competitor, for his part, must avoid too obvious a pattern of countermoves in order to keep his opponent guessing.

It should be clear that the outcome of a game depends upon the *joint* effect of the players' moves. An experienced player does not plan each move independently of the others; rather, he determines each move on the basis of the collective effect that all the moves will have during the course of the game. Thus, he first adopts a broad strategy and then makes individual moves according to this strategy. This is the essence of the theory of games.

Game theory can be applied to poker. A good poker player knows that to be the winner at the end of an evening's game he must develop two diverse strategies. He must play defensively and cheaply whenever he gets ordinary or poor hands. But when he gets good hands he must play aggressively and at the same time convince his opponents that his hand is only mediocre.

A safe way to play any game—be it poker or betting on the races—is to play it defensively. Another way of expressing the same thought is to say that as an intelligent player you must never lose sight of the possibility of incurring losses, and you must carefully design your defensive actions to minimize the losses when they occur.

Offensive actions also play an important role in winning games. However, they are to be taken only *after* you have designed a defensive strategy. That is to say, you should attempt to minimize your losses by *careful design* and then win by *planned* offensive action.

I am sure you are anxious to know whether there is any close relationship between game theory and buying, selling, and holding stocks. The relationship between playing a game and playing the stock market is very close. As I mentioned above, in poker you minimize your losses by carefully designing your strategies, whereas you make money by pure chance. In buying and selling stocks, too, your primary objective should be to take every conceivable measure which offers the least chance of losing and the greatest chance of minimizing your prospective stock market losses. Having carefully designed your defensive actions, you may then proceed to map out what I have called planned offensive action. In my judgment, this combination of defensive and offensive actions constitutes one of the best market strategies.

PICK A STOCK OF VALUE

One of the interesting things you have learned from our discussions of the market is that a successful operator buys stocks at low prices and sells them when the price is high. You have also learned that it is only rarely possible to buy at the bottom and sell at the top, and then only by accident. Therefore, you need a somewhat different approach to buying and selling stocks: you should buy a stock when its present value is higher than the price ruling in the market; likewise, you should sell a stock when its present value drops below its current price.

The idea of purchasing a stock on the basis of its "value" is as old as the investment art itself. Over the years, investors have employed a wide variety of different fundamental concepts and techniques in making their investment decisions, subject, of course, to their individual investment and performance goals. A little probing into this matter indicates that, although a variety of techniques has been used, the concept of "value" has permeated all of them. Some have used "comparative" values as the basis for stock selection; others have depended more on "normative" and "intrinsic" values. I will not discuss these kinds of values, since I prefer to concentrate on a different type of value concept.

In the past decade and a half, the present value theory has rapidly gained attention as an aid in valuing common stocks. The underlying idea behind this theory is to compare the theoretical present value of the future dividend stream of a stock with its current market price in order to determine whether or not the stock is within a profitable buying range. Implicit in this approach is the fact that an established technique permits an investor to calculate the present value of a stock under certain assumptions as to growth and discount rates with relative ease and that the resulting approximation of the stock's true value will not vary as widely as the market price of the stock in question.

According to the present value theory, the worth of a common stock is the present value of all the future dividends which the company is expected to pay. The concept of present value is quite simple and can be best explained with the help of an illustration. Suppose your friend wants to borrow some money from you which he promises to return to you after a year. Since you deprive yourself of your money by lending it and you also assume a risk in doing so, you are entitled to some remuneration for your sacrifices. Let us assume that you will be happy with a 4 percent annual rate of return. This 4 percent is called the rate of discount.

Now, the next question is: Given the fact that you desire to have a 4 percent rate of return, how much money should you lend your friend if he promises to return $10 to you a year from today? The answer is $9.62, because the $10 which you expect to receive next year provides $0.38 interest, which is 4 percent of a $9.62 loan. So that, given a rate of discount of 4 percent, the present value of $10 payable after one year is $9.62.

But suppose you change your mind about the rate of return you expect, and you say that you will not be satisfied with a return of less than 10 percent, Should the present value of the $10 loan still be $9.62? Obviously not. Given a 10 percent rate of discount, the present value of $10 payable after a year would work out to $9.09, because the $10 paid next year provides $0.91 interest, which is 10 percent of a $9.09 loan. So, you see, the higher the rate of discount, or the rate of return you desire, the lower is the present value of a given sum of money you wish to receive in the future.

To apply this rather simple present value concept to the valuation of a single stock, however, is not so easy. As mentioned, the theory holds that the worth of a company's stock is the present value of all future dividends the company will pay. To arrive at this figure requires a long-term (say, 50-year) projection of the dividend stream of the company under certain assumptions as to growth rate of the company and discount rate required under varying conditions of uncertainty. One has to estimate what the dividend rate may be over each decade of the 50-year period depending on the company's rate of growth; then one must estimate what discount rate would be appropriate during the successive phases of growth and arrive at an average discount rate for the period.

Once these assumptions have been made, and admittedly they are far from exact ones, a 25-year dividend schedule can be set up in one column and opposite it can be entered in another column the present value of each dividend under the assumed average discount rate. The sum of these values gives the present valuation of the future dividends of the company up to 25 years. To extend this beyond 25 years requires making additional calculations and assumptions as to further long-term growth and discount rates and employing a multiple applied to the dividend estimated to prevail at the end of the 25-year period. Finally, one arrives at what is to be accepted as the true value of the stock—the present value of the entire future stream of dividends.

Making valid assumptions as to the average rate at which any company's dividend rate can be expected to grow and what average discount rate the market will demand over a long period of years is obviously very difficult; nevertheless analysts regard the effort as being worthwhile.

Fortunately, there are a few elements in applying present value theory that reduce somewhat its complexity. A relatively simple formula for calculating the present value per dollar of dividends at any given time of perpetual growth at any given discount rate and growth rate has been worked out. By using this formula, analysts arrive at a multiple that can be applied to each dollar of current dividends to arrive at an estimated value for the stock in terms of its future dividend stream under the assumptions made as to growth and discount rate.

Furthermore, the proportion of total value over, say, 50 years represented by the years after the first decade diminishes rapidly. Accordingly, the need for accuracy lessens in the later decades.

To further reduce complexity, books of tables are available today to assist in making calculations. These tables show how many dollars can be paid for a stock per dollar of today's dividends (the multiplier) given certain assumptions as to growth rate and discount rate. The tables even allow for variations in these rates over the period forecast.

Even so, these tables can only take account of a limited number of such variations. But today, analysts are using the computer to extend the variety of assumptions that can be made.

After you have made your own assumptions as to growth rate and discount rate and have calculated the present value of a stock by referring to the appropriate tables, compare the result with the current market price of that stock. If the former is higher than the latter, buy the stock or hold it if you already own it. Conversely, if the present value is lower than the current market price, sell the stock or decide against buying it.

P/E Ratio Strikes Again

In a previous chapter I discussed ways to use the P/E ratio as an investment tool. Here is more food for thought along the same lines.

It is generally believed that a low P/E ratio is preferable to a high one. An interesting study conducted a few years ago by Nicholas Molodovsky[42] sheds some new light on this issue. According to him, if you invest in a group of stocks with low P/E ratios and reinvest in these stocks at periodic intervals, the quality of your investment will be strengthened because over a long period of time, weaker stocks will gradually be replaced by stronger ones, and the capacity of the investor to withstand falling prices in a downward market will be greatly enhanced. In the opposite case, if you embark upon a continuing investment program in high P/E ratio stocks, you wind up purchasing those stocks which become increasingly vulnerable to a price setback. Individual exceptions will, of course, occur in both the low and the high P/E ratio groups, but they are not likely to alter materially the situations described above.

The reason for using P/E ratios as a decision tool should be clear. Since the value of a stock is closely related to the earnings potential of that company, other things being equal, one should purchase those stocks which are selling at low earnings multiples. Likewise, stocks which reach a predetermined high P/E multiple should be sold, since the risks of holding them will tend to exceed the acceptable limits.

Let there be no misunderstanding. What I have said should not be interpreted to mean that all low P/E ratio stocks automatically grow stronger and all high P/E ratio stocks automatically grow weaker. My advice is that if you discover two stocks, both of which look equally attractive, you should buy the one with a "low" P/E ratio, simply because it is less vulnerable to price declines.

While the P/E ratio is a very valuable investment guide, I must warn you against the dangers in using it as the *sole* investment criterion. P/E ratios have no existence of their own. They are merely quotients reflecting any of the several possible combinations of the numerator and the denominator and should be used with caution. The P/E ratio is a number calculated on the basis of independent fluctuations between the price and the earnings of any stock. Consequently, such a ratio will increase if (1) the price rises faster than the earnings, (2) the price rises while the earnings remain stationary, (3) the price rises while the earnings actually decline, (4) the price remains stationary while the earnings decline, or (5) both the price and the earnings decline, but the former declines more slowly than the latter. Similarly, a P/E ratio will decline when the combinations are reversed. Also, a P/E ratio will remain constant under any of the following three situations: (1) when the price and the earnings both increase at the same speed; (2) when the price and the earnings both decrease at the same speed; or (3) when both the price and the earnings remain constant.

I have set forth the conditions under which the P/E ratio will move up or down or remain stationary, hoping to deter you from the all-too-common error of assuming that a declining P/E ratio is always a buy signal and a rising P/E ratio is always indicative of something bad happening to the stock. While a low P/E ratio is generally preferable to a high one, you must analyze the reasons for the change in the ratio before using it as the basis for investment decisions. You should examine critically the statistical data from which prices and earnings are calculated. Each of these two variables is affected by a set of complex economic forces, some of which are difficult to analyze. Since very different economic conditions can govern stock prices and corporate earnings even when their ratios are identical, care should be exercised in comparing P/E ratios.

In all discussions so far, I have attempted to express my conviction that the P/E ratio is one of the important investment instruments. In honesty, I must admit that not everyone shares my view. For instance, John Hammel and Daniel Hodes[43] studied the factors influencing P/E multiples and reached the following conclusions. First, in determining the price they are willing to pay for a given stock, investors tend to be influenced much more by their expectations of the future growth in a company's earnings per share than by a company's current earnings or its record of earnings in the past. Second, companies with a history of highly volatile earnings tend to trade at lower P/E multiples than other comparable companies whose growth in earnings have been more stable around a basic trend. In a more recent study, Robert Levy and Spero Kripotos[44] surprisingly concluded that P/E ratios are of comparatively little use as a primary method of selecting securities or as a means of further refining a list of stocks initially selected by either relative price strength or earnings growth. On a somewhat different level, Joseph Murphy[45] examined the correlation between relative rates of growth of earnings per share in successive periods between the years 1950 and 1965. His examination showed no significant correlation between relative rates of growth of earnings per share in one period and the next. Only rarely did companies which recorded superior growth in earnings per share in one period show more than an even chance of recording above average growth in the next. In essence, the Murphy study rejected the concept that P/E ratios have any importance as an investment tool.

In passing, I would like to mention that rising earnings per share, or a decreasing P/E ratio, would tend to make a stock price rise. But few understand that in some cases, such as computer leasing and the conglomerates, the converse is true, too: a rising stock price can give the company the means of increasing earnings per share. This combination is what some security analysts call "a self-reinforcing cycle," and it can often send a stock up like a high-powered rocket.

In my opinion, relative price strength and earnings growth are of major significance for purposes of security selection, and careful use of the P/E ratio—but watching for its pitfalls—constitutes an effective use of this tool as an investment guide.

THE WEEDING-OUT PROCESS

During an ordinary trading day, some 1,400 issues are traded on the NYSE. Even if the stocks traded on the ASE, over-the-counter, and on the other regional exchanges are not taken into account, one must conclude that it is almost impossible for even the most ambitious and resourceful investor to analyze critically such a large number of stocks before making a rational investment decision. A method for weeding out the less attractive stocks is needed to allow the investor to focus on a relatively few "good" stocks. Fortunately, the so-called *filter approach* to stock selection has now been developed; by using this approach, you can select from a large number of stocks only those that merit further investigation.

The developers of the filter approach are Alex Gould and Maurice Buchsbaum. They have explained their approach in the following manner:

The central assumption underlying the filter approach to earnings selection is that in the light of public information reported in financial statements, it is possible to observe patterns in the data which can be used to forecast stock price changes. The purpose of this paper is to test the predictive ability of one such criterion, the earnings relative.[46]

The cornerstone of the filter approach is the idea that it is *relative earnings*, not historical earnings, that should be used to judge the future performance of a group of companies. The reason is that, since the current earnings of a company are closely related to its historical earnings record, the earnings relative (calculated as a ratio of annual per-share earnings to a five-year moving average of earnings) must be considered the best indicator of the direction of price movement of the related stock.

Gould and Buchsbaum first made a list of a randomly selected sample of 200 companies and collected data from published sources relating to their earnings during the period 1948–67. They then wrote suitable computer programs for examining the relationship between annual risks and investment returns in these companies. They discovered that the low-earnings-relative group consistently outperformed companies in both the high-earnings-relative group and the low P/E ratio group. Gould and Buchsbaum therefore concluded that the (earnings-relative) filter approach could be a useful device for reducing the number of securities one would like to consider for purchase or for sale.

The Technical Approach: Some Neglected Aspects

In Chapter 10 I explained the technical approach to common stock selection and compared it with the fundamental approach. Now I will discuss some of the neglected aspects of the technical approach.

One of the more significant recent developments in the area of technical approach is the unlimited possibilities of applying computer-oriented methodology to solving financial problems. Presently, over 50 organizations reportedly spend approximately $3 million collectively every year on improving quantitative investment techniques. Much of their efforts are directed toward information retrieval and routine data processing; that is, toward machine calculation of material which could previously be calculated only manually. A sizable portion of these calculations are currently undertaken in the belief that quantitative methods can improve the quality and consistency of investment decision making. Great improvements are also being made in common stock selection methods or, more specifically, in the methods applicable to the determination of common stocks for purchase and sale.

Let us move on to the problems encountered by an investor in trading in a particular stock. Before making a decision to purchase the stock of, say, XYZ Company, every investor must answer two questions: "Should I buy the stock of XYZ Company?" and "When should I buy the stock of XYZ Company?" The investor who asks the first question is taking a fundamental approach to the problem; when he asks the second question he is seeking a technical solution to the problem.

In analyzing the attractiveness of a stock, a fundamentalist concerns himself with the company's financial statements, history, quality of management, earnings, dividends, popularity of its product, and its relative position in the industry. The technical analyst, on the other hand, works with the relative forces of supply and demand operating on the stock of that company. He analyzes the degrees of accumulation and distribution which must take place before a stock makes a major move in either direction. Let me elaborate this point.

Practically all stocks make substantial moves at one time or another. Before a stock begins to move up, it sometimes goes through a period of accumulation by *insiders* (those who have restricted knowledge about the future prospects of these companies); that is, it passes from "weak hands" into "strong hands" until demand exceeds supply. Then the stock takes a big leap upward. Conversely, before a stock drops in price, it goes through a period of distribution by the same insiders; that is, it passes from strong into weak hands. When support is withdrawn, supply overcomes demand, thereby initiating a panicky downward move. The technical analyst is concerned with the right time to buy and sell, and the right time to sell short. He attempts to determine the moment when either supply or demand has taken control. He is an "outsider" making use of various techniques to determine what the "insiders" are doing.

The above discussion stresses the fact that a stock reaches the buying range when its demand exceeds supply. A more sophisticated statement would be that a stock should be bought when (1) the general market is in an uptrend, (2) the industry group of which it is a member is in an uptrend, and (3) the stock itself is in an uptrend. In this context, the word *uptrend* refers to price: the price of a market average, the price of the industry group index, and the price of the stock itself. Similarly, a stock should be sold short when (1) the general market is in a downtrend, (2) the industry group of which it is a member is in a downtrend, and (3) the stock itself is in a downtrend. Here again, the term *downtrend*, refers to price only.

The tools a technical analyst uses in deciding whether to buy a stock or sell it short consist primarily of charts: charts of a particular stock, charts of an industry group, and charts of a market average or index. As you know, there are two major types of charts, vertical line or bar charts and point-and-figure charts. These charts are discussed, and an explanation of how charts and graphs can be used to predict the future price trend of a particular stock is given, in Chapter 11.

A relatively new dimension of the technical approach was recently discussed in *Business Week*.[47] In recent years, a number of mathematically oriented and technically expert investors have used a unique and immensely complex approach to analyzing the market. Each year a few more computer experts, loaded with statistical tools, test their methods against the most complex game of all—the stock market. These men dream of the day when they can teach their computers to predict every turn in the market. However, so far their dreams have not materialized. Many investors doubt that the emotionalism of the marketplace and the myriad forces at work upon it can ever be quantified. But there are many experts who are not about to give up. Two such men are Frank Peluso and Howard Odzer, operators of an advisory service called MarkeTiming. Their record as market predictors has been so impressive that their service has a growing reputation, attracting such clients as an aggressive group of Boston funds, a bevy of hedge funds, at least one trader with his own seat on the NYSE, and some big private accounts.

Peluso is a research physicist with uncommon mental equipment. His goal is to express the dynamics of the entire market in terms of oscillator theory, a body of high-powered mathematics used to describe in minute detail such phenomena as nuclear and celestial spins and biological time clocks. In a sense he is transcribing into interrelated equations the intuitive, often unvoiced observations that many ordinary investors have about market movement.

The magnitude of Peluso's project is almost unimaginable. So far he has spent eight years developing his own expression of the energy (money) that constitutes the momentums and restoring forces battling one another in each of five cycles. The cycles—from one and a half years down to a few hours, which Peluso calls his "short wave"—are all interacting in the market at any given moment. Other cycles exist in the market, but they are either too short or too long for his purposes. Twenty-eight equations identify each cycle, and the computer keeps busy recalculating their shifting influences on each other. Peluso already has used up all the storage space that IBM's New York service bureau allows each customer on its 7040 time-sharing machine—about 36,000 words—and so far he is able to follow only the Dow Jones Industrials, a glamour index of his own, and 50 individual issues, which include Burroughs, Control Data, IBM, Polaroid, and Xerox. He has recently added another 150 stocks and hopes to begin to set up readings on other broad indicators.

At the heart of MarkeTiming's high hopes is Peluso's passion for high-level technical analysis. "Technical analysis up to this juncture has been empirical," says Peluso. That is, technicians watch for price patterns that are known to repeat. Because they merely try to correlate statistical observations, their highest achievement so far has been the formulation of the principle that a stock going in a certain direction will continue in that direction—for a while. Investors who follow such a "relative strength" approach regularly miss the beginnings and ends of price swings and have to be content with middles. They can also be trapped by anomalies and new patterns. Peluso, on the other hand, tries to deal with the forces that produce the patterns and thereby anticipate them before they appear. "MarkeTiming does not depend upon a particular pattern having been seen in the past to be predictable," says Peluso. "The chartist," continues Odzer, "sees the pattern as cause; Frank sees it as result." The laws of oscillator theory, in fact, are so complete—derived as they were from decades of experiments with electromagnetic waves—that Peluso has the tools to predict even changes in the forces. Thus, he expects to catch price links, both large and small and from bottom to top or, in the case of short sales, from top to bottom.

Summing Up

In this chapter I have discussed at length the ways in which you may approach the buy-sell-hold problem. At this point you might be curious as to whether or not you could let someone else manage your money. I plan to satisfy your curiosity in the next chapter.

ACT IV

THE ELUSIVE BONANZA

*Most people say that Mutual Funds are hard to
understand. But then, most men say the same thing
about women.*

—FRANCIS I. DU PONT & COMPANY

16

The Fallible
Investor's Investor

SEEKING EXTERNAL HELP

In Chapter 1 I discussed the problem of inflation which all of us face
today. I mentioned there that you *cannot* prevent inflation, but you *can*
protect your money against inflation by investing your money in good
common stock. It is worth emphasizing that while the dollar has lost one
third of its purchasing power since 1946, the S&P's Index of Common
Stocks has shown a fivefold increase over the same period. However, if you
do not have the time or the patience necessary to be a successful investor,
you may let someone else manage your money. Before we discuss that
approach let me say this: Anyone who can manage your money can also
mismanage your money. So it pays to be careful in this matter.

To my way of thinking, there are at least two very good reasons for
seeking external help. Despite all the background in the stock market
which you now have, you may still feel insecure and may therefore want
someone to manage your investment portfolio on a full-time basis. But,
more importantly, you may wish to join other small investors in filling the
pot so that collectively you are able to invest in a big way. Both reasons are
sound. But there are also other advantages and some pitfalls in this line of

reasoning. Let me point out to you the benefits and dangers of letting someone else handle your money.

LITTLE GUYS' CLUB

Suppose you are able to join forces with a group of people who are keen on beating inflation by investing in stocks but who feel totally inadequate to do the job on their own. All of you decide to form a club called VIP (Virtual Inflation Protection). Each member agrees to contribute $100 a month to a common fund. You also agree to hire a sharp, clear-thinking, zealous money manager named Zelloway, who is charged with the responsibility of buying stocks which he thinks will enjoy an appreciable increase in value in the future. You can now sit back and relax: your money is working for you just the way you had hoped it would.

Let us see how your VIP club might live up to your expectations in the long run. Assume the club has 50 members, each contributing $100 per month; the club will, in this way, accumulate an impressive $50,000 every year. If Zelloway is worth his salt he will ingeniously buy those stocks which will rapidly increase in value. If he is able to show an annual increase of 20 percent in the value of the club's net assets, he will keep all of you very happy.

But what if Zelloway turns out to be incompetent, making so many bad investments that the net asset value of the club actually declines? And what if the market turns against him and provides little opportunity to make profits? In such instances, you will have no recourse but to watch your hard-earned savings shrink under your very eyes because, under the agreement, you have no power to influence the investment decisions of Zelloway. Since the possibility of your losing money will always exist, you owe it to yourself to investigate before you invest your savings in any VIP club.

Investment clubs, similar to our VIP club, usually consist of business associates, friends, or neighbors who get together periodically to invest in the market. Every club appoints one person to act on behalf of the club. The performance record of investment clubs has been quite impressive. For instance, the National Association of Investment Clubs, founded in Detroit in 1951, has a membership of about 14,000 clubs, with stock portfolios valued at over $360 million. The average club has about 16 members and holds a portfolio of more than $26,000. In 1969, the rate of earnings for clubs in the Association averaged about 22.4 percent compounded annually.

The Detroit club is one of several in the country. It is estimated that there are about 60,000 investment clubs scattered throughout the United States, all of which cater to the needs of persons who have investible funds which are really too small for the large brokerage firms to be interested in.

Open- and Closed-End Companies

There is another route which a small investor might take. Instead of putting his money in an investment club, he may obtain the advantages of professional investment management by purchasing shares in an investment company. Although still relatively small compared with life insurance companies and banking and trust companies, investment companies have grown rapidly in recent years.

All investment companies fall in two major categories, open-end and closed-end. After the initial public offering, a closed-end company may offer a new security issue to the public, but usually does not do so, and its capitalization generally remains unchanged. These security issues are bought and sold on the NYSE and in the OTC market in the same manner in which other shares are traded.

Just as the price of popcorn or flowers reflects changing market conditions, the price of a closed-end company share reflects the ups and downs of the securities it represents. The net worth of the shares of the closed-end companies is determined by the relative forces of the demand for and the supply of the stocks the company holds. It is therefore conceivable that the price of a fund's share may fluctuate from day to day.

Unlike a closed-end fund, an open-end company—popularly known as a mutual fund—continuously offers new shares. It guarantees to redeem its shares at net asset value at any time. This value is calculated at least daily and typically more often, by obtaining the current market value of each security in the fund's portfolio, adding this up, subtracting liabilities, and dividing this figure by the number of shares of the fund's stock outstanding.

Statistics show that since the 1950's mutual funds have grown by leaps and bounds. The total value of securities owned by mutual funds was only $2.5 billion in 1950; it increased to $9.2 billion at the end of 1957, to more than $20 billion in 1960, and to $53 billion in 1970. Approximately 8 million investors in the United States today own shares in mutual funds. Several individual funds currently have assets of over $1 billion each, and a total of 182 funds are members of the National Association of Investment Companies. What is more interesting is the fact that within the past two years, mutual funds have been formed by dozens of insurance companies, including well-known ones such as Travelers, John Hancock, Connecticut General, Mutual of Omaha, Fidelity Mutual, and Allstate. Because of their extreme popularity I will confine my discussion primarily to mutual funds, with occasional references to closed-end funds where I deem the reference necessary.

The Basic Idea

The only business of a mutual fund is the proper investment of its shareholders' money in common stocks, preferred stocks, bonds, or other investment media. The basic objective is to combine growth and risk and income in the hope of achieving a specific investment goal. This implies that a mutual fund attempts to diversify its holdings—thus reducing risk and increasing growth potential or income. It also attempts to provide expert supervision in the management and administration of its investments, for which it receives a percentage of the net asset value. In effect, a mutual fund is a single, large investment account owned by many individuals, who share its income and expense, its profits and losses, in proportion to their individual shares in the account. It is a unique method of providing for any investor, small or medium, the same advantages and safeguards that wealthy people with large holdings normally enjoy.

A mutual fund issues shares of its own stock. Each share represents the same fractional interest as any other share in the investment portfolio of securities. The buyer participates in the growth of the fund by an appreciation of the shares he holds and in the dividend income after a deduction for management expenses and fees.

Not all mutual funds have the same objectives and performance records, however. Some bank upon rapid growth and are known as "go-go funds"; others are established on more solid, long-term grounds. Some companies emphasize safety of capital and payment of current income rather than growth. Some try to keep a balance between the major investment objectives. Some mutual funds invest heavily in common stocks; the portfolios of others are made up wholly of preferred stocks and bonds. Some diversify broadly; others specialize in a small number of companies or in a couple of industries. Some even go into the real estate business.

What Do Fund Shares Cost?

When you buy shares in a closed-end investment company, you pay the same brokerage fees you would pay for any other stock, say, AT&T. Not so with open-end or mutual funds. Here you pay, in addition to net asset value, a fee (generally 7 to 9 percent of the selling price) to compensate the sellers of the share. This is called the "loading charge." There are a number of "no-load" funds that sell their shares directly to the public without adding this sales charge. You can tell the no-load funds in the listings on a financial page in the newspaper because the "bid" price per share is the same as the "asked" price.

In addition to the sales charge, every fund customer must pay for the operating expenses of both open-end and closed-end companies. A major item of expense for most mutual funds is the payments the companies make to investment advisors. This expense varies from company to company, and three fourths of 1 percent of net asset value, deducted annually, might be a fair average. This cost is divided pro rata among all the shareholders of a fund.

What Do You Gain?

Mutual funds provide several advantages. First, by providing a suitable outlet for savings, these funds help you and the average investor in becoming investors. Participation in ownership of the nation's great productive enterprises by people in all walks of life is no longer a dream—it's a reality. "People's capitalism" is here to stay.

Second, buying mutual fund shares offers the average investor the only practical means available for him to take advantage of the techniques of professional management. One of these techniques is broad diversification. With your limited savings (say, $100 or even $200 a month) you could hardly buy shares in one company, let alone buy stock in many companies. Buying shares in only one company is like putting all your eggs in one basket: if you lose one you lose all. By participating in a fund, however, you are spreading those eggs over a number of baskets because you own an interest in all the varied stocks the fund owns. If one hundred people like you each put $100 in the fund's treasury, you will have, collectively, $10,000 every month or $120,000 every year to invest. If this is invested in a conservative balanced fund, for example, the money will be used to buy some blue-chip stocks with a good record for conservation of capital, price stability, and dividend payments; some shares providing reasonable income; and some with good potential for price appreciation. In effect, you will buy the protection the conservative balanced fund affords you through its diversified holdings.

Third, in buying fund shares, you embark on a pay-as-you-go investment plan, without your having to pay those heavy commission charges for making a large number of odd-lot purchases. This method of periodic investing will undoubtedly encourage in you the healthy habit of putting aside something out of income. It will enable you to accumulate, over a period of time, securities that you might not otherwise own if you had to save up and buy them all at once.

What I have just said might lead you to the erroneous conclusion that by joining the fund you engage in buying some securities "on time." That is simply not true. You pay as you go. There are no down payments, you don't owe any "balance," you are not charged any interest, and you are not indebted to anyone. You are actually the owner of the shares you have purchased. Your account is credited with both full and fractional shares.

Fourth, mutual funds provide the advantage of ready marketability. By

choosing to be a long-term investor, you do not firmly commit yourself to
hold on to your fund shares indefinitely. At any time you can ask your
broker to sell all or any fraction of the shares you hold. He will carry out
your order and send you a check for the proceeds. This easy and quick
redeemability feature of mutual funds is a distinct advantage in buying
fund shares. However, caution in this connection should be exercised.
When you sell your fund shares, you get the market value of your shares,
but the 7 to 9 percent charge which you paid to acquire the shares is not
refundable. You should also be careful in redeeming the shares of the so-
called "front-end load" funds. These funds apply up to 50 percent of the
total amount of your first 12 payments to the sales charges rather than to
your working capital; consequently a short-term selling of your shares
would result in a loss of all payments made for sales charges.

Fifth, unlike banks, insurance companies, and pension trusts, mutual
funds have no liability to speak of and thus cannot become insolvent. It is,
of course, true that the shares of a mutual fund are redeemable on demand. However, since they are redeemable at the current net asset value,
the risk of insolvency is virtually eliminated.

To sum up, by charging your fund manager with the responsibility of
investing your money you are in effect benefiting from his professional
management skills and also from the valuable insights he has gained from
his long market experience. Also, he is capable of prying information out of
corporate executives, which is a valuable asset to an investor. As against
this, the counsel you might get from your broker is certainly a poor substitute. If you are a small investor, the broker cannot be expected to give you
much personal attention and assistance, since he does not get enough
commissions by handling your miniature account.

How Much Can You Lose?

While your fund provides many advantages, it certainly does not provide you with a panacea for all problems. No mutual fund, no matter how
large and well managed, will protect you from losses in a declining market.
As a matter of fact, no one could tell you a priori how stable a fund will be
in a period of economic stress. This is a legitimate concern because in the
general philosophy of such funds there is one contradiction that can spell
disaster.

As a general rule, mutual funds are most popular when the market is
strong, since that is the time when they attract the largest number of
investors. And yet, since stock prices in a strong market are already too
high, that is precisely the time when it is most difficult for the fund
managers to invest wisely the new capital pouring into their treasuries. The
situation worsens in a declining market. In such a market, small investors

desperately try to convert their shares into cash. Faced with heavy demands for cash, the funds are forced to lighten their stock portfolios, often at a considerable loss.

The argument that mutual funds are always in the hands of sound, professional management is also not entirely true. Part of the problem lies in the public's penchant for buying mutual fund shares on the basis of raw performance. More often than not, the tendency of individuals is simply to check the lists and buy shares of that fund which in the recent past has increased its net asset value faster than other funds. This puts tremendous pressures on fund managers, many of whom thoughtlessly choose glamorous issues which are likely to participate in speculative fervor in order to display a box office performance.

It is important for you to be aware that much of the money invested in these funds is so-called "greed money"—money which flees at the first sign that the fund is faltering. This fear may become even greater if you remember that a bad market is really the test of the quality of a fund's investments. These fleeing funds may necessitate additional selling which results in the fleeing of more funds, thus creating a snowball effect.

Besides glamorous and speculative issues, some mutual funds have a vested interest in newly offered securities with dubious futures, which cannot be easily sold in the market. Brokers are often eager to give these funds a substantial amount of shares in a new issue because there may be an implied promise that the funds will channel some of their business through the cooperating brokerage houses. The main criterion for selecting new issues may, therefore, be the brokers' eagerness to sell these shares, not their inherent worth. Other problems which plague the funds are buying shares of obscure companies, where the shares available in the trading market are relatively few, and investing heavily in a handful of companies or in one industry.

Another minus factor against mutual funds is that they are not designed for short-term buying and selling. I think you are aware that there is no such thing as permanent investment. Changing market conditions may induce you to change your portfolio to take advantage of stock fluctuations; however, if you are a member of a fund you cannot do this directly. You must rely solely on your fund's manager, even if you do not approve of his policies or actions.

HEADS YOU WIN, TAILS YOU LOSE

I hope you are convinced, as I am, that mutual funds cannot *guarantee* success. Sometimes they outperform the average investors as measured by the records of stock used in the DJIA, S&P, or other averages. At other times, their performance fails to meet this test.

Recent business records of mutual funds appear to underscore this conviction. Thus, in 1968, the 172 U.S. mutual funds in *Barron's* Quarterly Record scored an average gain of 11.8 percent in per-share value (market appreciation, plus realized capital gains). This advance was a little less than three times the 4.3 percent gain in the Dow Jones Industrial Average. Furthermore, the per-share values of 25 funds appreciated by more than 20 percent. In 1969, however, less than 50 percent of the mutual funds came out ahead of the Dow. The latest Quarterly Record, published in the November 2, 1970, issue of *Barron's*, unfolded similar facts. During the third quarter of 1970, mutual funds scored a gain of 10 percent, equal to the percentage gain in the Dow. However, during the year ending September 30, 1970, the 170 U.S. funds posted an average decline of 13 percent in per-share value (market depreciation, offset by realized capital gains). This decline was more than double the 6.4 percent decline in the Dow-Jones Industrial Average. On the basis of past performance, it is possible to conclude that mutual funds do not have a monopoly over success. Sometimes they perform very well; at other times their performance leaves much to be desired.

The Go-Gos Are Gone-Gone

So far I have been talking about mutual funds in general. Now I will single out a special group popularly known as "go-go" funds. In a good market they perform very well and are extremely *popular* among fund investors. But when the market turns against them, their net asset values drop precipitously, resulting in millions of dollars of losses for their investors.

The performance of the go-go funds was recently surveyed by *Business Week*, and the accompanying table and graph (Table 16–1 and Figure 16–1) were used as the basis of the survey. The article pointed out that during 1969 the funds had fallen slightly less than the DJIA. Even the most aggressive group, the growth funds, lost only 15.7 percent in net asset value per share, just a bit more than the Dow. During the first five months of 1970, however, the picture changed dramatically. While the DJIA declined by 17 percent, the mutual funds dropped more than 25 percent.

It is nothing new for go-go funds to do worse than the Dow in a bear market—traditionally by about 80 percent—the article pointed out. But the market clout these funds now suffer from is unparalleled. The article concluded:

. . . the go-gos are selling what they can and moving into cash. They are realizing too late that many of the small, less marketable securities they hold may never bounce back to their high-p/e gravy days. . . . The trouble the go-go funds have had with small, highly volatile stocks obviously will make

TABLE 16–1

How the Growth Stock Mutual Funds Performed

Fund	Assets in Millions of Dollars	% Change 1970 to Date*
The top ten		
Davidge Fund	$ 1.4 ...	− 3.93%
Apollo Fund	0.3 ...	− 5.41
Over-the-Counter Sec.	4.1 ...	− 8.39
Bank Stock Fund	0.2 ...	− 9.11
Alliance Growth Fund	0.2 ...	−10.57
Templeton Growth	7.4 ...	−10.81
Pension Capital Gr.	1.3 ...	−12.23
Contrafund	29.9 ...	−12.27
United Fds. Can. Intl.	10.2 ...	−12.71
O'Neil Institutional	1.8 ...	−13.83
The bottom ten		
Gibraltar Growth	83.0 ...	−58.05
Investors Indicators	15.7 ...	−57.58
Pennsylvania Mutual	21.6 ...	−56.44
Wincap Fund	15.0 ...	−54.24
Doll Fund	0.5 ...	−54.06
Fundex	3.0 ...	−53.28
Ocean Technology	2.3 ...	−52.69
Market Growth Fund	3.9 ...	−51.18
Samson Fund	0.8 ...	−51.94
Afuture Fund	11.4 ...	−51.73
The biggest		
Dreyfus Fund	2276.3 ...	−24.09
Mass. Investors Gr. St.	1173.0 ...	−29.30
United Accumulative	1172.3 ...	−26.71
Fidelity Trend	1039.1 ...	−25.85
Investors Variable Payment	976.9 ...	−30.71
National Investors	772.7 ...	−28.22
Putnam Growth	667.9 ...	−19.92
Enterprise Fund	665.1 ...	−36.91
Technology Fund	622.0 ...	−23.04
T. Rowe Price Growth Stock	607.6 ...	−26.90

* As of May 21, 1970.

Source: Business Week, May 30, 1970, p. 86.

them gun shy for some time. It may also have a long-range effect on the public's psychology. . . .[48]

Before I leave this topic let me emphasize that, before selecting a mutual fund, you should not only examine its performance both in good and bad markets, but even after that you should stay away from any so-called go-go fund which makes daring commitments to highly volatile speculative stocks for quick profits.

FIGURE 16–1

PERFORMANCE OF GROWTH FUNDS

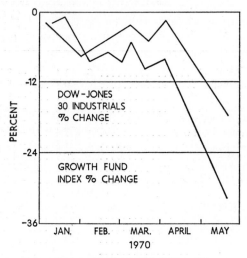

Source: Business Week, May 30, 1970, p. 86.

RISE AND FALL OF A FUND MANAGER

It is generally believed by investors—and there is a good deal of truth in it—that the success of a mutual fund depends primarily upon the investment fund manager. The story I am about to tell you corroborates this belief. Here is the story of the rise and fall of Fred Carr, who won the title of "Fund Wizard" when he managed the famous mutual fund known as the Enterprise Fund.

Fred Carr joined the Enterprise Fund in 1963 as their chief portfolio manager. In that year the assets of the Fund were about $20 million and the net asset value per share was about $4. In 1967, the asset value of the Fund increased by a whopping 116.3 percent with a further increase of 43.6 percent in the following year. By the end of 1968, the Fund's assets had reached the billion dollar mark and shareholders' assets per share had crossed the $12 level.

Carr's secret of such grand success lay in his discovering the emerging growth situations. In addition, Carr was one of the first money managers to realize that, beginning with the Fall of 1967, go-go funds were going to get heavy publicity and he was successful in capitalizing on this idea.

Interestingly, the fall of Carr the Fund Wizard was no less spectacular than his rise. Toward the end of 1968, when the Enterprise Fund was still enjoying a glorious success, Carr relinquished the reins to a group of five portfolio managers. During the following nine-month period, ending in September 1969, the assets of Enterprise dropped 23.99 percent. Furthermore, on November 10, 1970, after the market had made a major move, the price of an Enterprise Fund share was 5.67 bid, well below the level reached in 1968.

With the turn of the year 1969, Carr became active in the Shareholders Management Company (known colloquially as the "Fletcher Group" of mutual funds), and in May 1969 took over its presidency. The Fletcher Fund had climbed 103.4 percent in 1967 and another 12.5 percent in 1968. With Carr at the top, everyone wondered as to whether a whiz of a portfolio manager would be quite as successful in running a fast-growing company.

Fred Carr did not give people much time to speculate. In his estimate, sales of the Fletcher Fund in 1969 were going to be around $500 million compared with $1.1 billion in 1968; likewise profits were also going to be sharply lower. Instead of taking this as a professional challenge, in November 1969 Carr resigned from his job, saying, "I've had enough." After his resignation, the parent company's stock took a serious beating—from a high of $27 in early 1969 to a low of $9 at the end of that quarter. On November 10, 1970, it was quoted at $5.01 bid.

THE IMPECCABLE FUND MANAGER

In the discussion of Fred Carr and in most of the previous discussions, I assumed that fund managers are better qualified to manage your money than you are. Interestingly, in a book entitled *Mutual Funds and Other Institutional Investors*, authors Friend, Blume, and Crockett find major deficiencies in fund management.[49] On the basis of an examination of the records of 299 leading funds for the years 1960–68, the authors discovered that the average performance of these funds produced a smaller return than would have been produced by an investment spread equally over all the stocks listed on the NYSE. They detected no correlation between performance and the size of the fees charged to shareholders. They found that fund managers were less likely to anticipate market trends than to follow them. The authors also argued that fund managers caused fluctuations rather than stabilized the market and that conflicts of interest were built into the structure of the business.

Studies such as this one have an important impact in Congress. In April, 1970, for instance, a House commerce subcommittee reached tentative agreement on a compromise bill to regulate mutual funds. The bill, if passed by both Houses, would regulate management fees and sales commissions, and it provides for imposing tighter controls over fund operations. The bill has already passed the Senate, and is now before the House Interstate and Foreign Commerce committee. However, even if the bill is passed, and more studies critical of mutual funds are undertaken, people will not be altogether discouraged from buying fund shares. As Seligman says:

. . . there is actually nothing in the findings that should lead investors to back away from mutual funds. For anyone in the stock market, diversification will doubtless continue to be a superior strategy, and mutual funds will continue to be—as there is no doubt that they have been in the past—a uniquely efficient way to diversify. They seem, in fact, to be the cheapest way to latch onto those random returns.[50]

The Toughest Job of Block Trading

Before I conclude this discussion of fund managers, let me tell you about the tough job of *block* trading that some portfolio managers have to perform. Following is the biography of Jay Perry of Salomon Brothers and Hitzler (SBH).[51]

Nonchalantly, the caller in SBH's branch office explains that his fund's portfolio manager wants to sell 100 AT&T (100,000 shares of AT&T). The trader specifies that there must be no discount (the market is 40½) and no exposure; if short sellers hear of this deal they will force the price down. Instantly, the branch man puts in a direct call to Jay Perry in New York, and the drama of giant block trading begins to unfold.

When the call comes, Perry instantly reaches for his notebooks containing interest indications from institutions in every conceivable stock, reports on fund holdings, and reams of data about past trades collected by Perry's men on the exchange floor after every trading day. Simultaneously, he checks with the expert on AT&T about supply and demand in that stock. A 120-key console on his desk connects him by direct lines to major funds all over the country, and he begins calling key clients for rumors. He is not just searching for possible buyers; he must discover whether there are other big sellers for that stock.

With Perry's message in hand, everyone in the trading room starts feeling out prospective buyers on AT&T. Finally, after very delicate bargaining, Perry is able to dispose of 100,000 shares of AT&T, maybe at 40.

The principal danger in institutional trading, as Perry puts it, is "getting run over by a Mack truck while you're trying to start your VW bug." Perry must make sure that the fund selling 100,000 AT&T does not have another 300,000 coming along behind through another broker. Further, a big block coming from another quarter could torpedo Perry's deal before he could package it, or sandbag his buyers afterward by driving down the market. A clean-up protects all the buyers. And that's where the expertise of giant block trading portfolio managers comes in.

I have undertaken this brief discussion of a portfolio manager's assignment in the hope that you will learn to appreciate the difficulties under which he operates and that you will take this into account when you buy investment company shares.

Which Fund for You?

An important question you may want to ask is: Which mutual fund is right for me? After all, you are not just anyone seeking to pocket some quick profits. You are a very special person with a unique savings record, independent investment objectives, and fascinated with some types of stocks. So you wish to join that mutual fund which is tailor-made for you. Unfortunately, all your wishes cannot be fulfilled, since that would imply the formation of as many funds as there are investors interested in joining them.

While you may never have the good fortune of joining a fund established just for you, you do have the opportunity to buy the shares of the type of mutual fund that best meets your objectives. Let me caution you, however, that this business of categorizing mutual funds has serious limitations, since no two funds are exactly alike. The holdings of some funds consist primarily of a diversified selection of common stocks of good growth quality. Other funds buy only preferred stocks and high-yielding bonds. Some funds traditionally buy high-flyers (that is, those stocks which move quickly relative to Dow Jones stocks), while many others specialize in the common stocks of a specific industry, such as aerospace, electronics, or defense. Bearing in mind these limitations, let us classify all mutual funds into five broad categories.

Assume that your investment objective is a sizable return on your money and a hope for some future growth. In this case, you should buy shares of *current income funds*, which basically favor securities with good current income potential, although growth possibilities are not ruled out. However, if future benefits of long-term capital growth are more important to you than immediate returns, then *growth funds* are for you. The main objectives of these funds are long-range capital appreciation and capital gains distribution. Their investments are largely made in established companies which have demonstrated their ability to expand faster than the nation's economy as a whole.

In the event that your objectives are conservation of principal and reasonable income return, as well as some growth of your principal and income, then you should opt for *balanced funds*. These kinds of funds invest in a broadly diversified list of both stocks and bonds. Their investment policies tend to be conservative, with preferred stocks and bonds serving to stabilize the funds' principal, while the remaining resources are spread among common stocks for the purpose of producing income and capital gains.

At this point I should like to bring to your attention the existence of what is known as *performance-fee* (P-F) funds. The objective of these funds is long-term appreciation of capital. Managers of these funds earn extra money for superior performance but are forced to pay a penalty for a poor show. Their performance is measured against Standard and Poor's Industrial Index of 425 stocks. Because of this "built-in inducement" feature of P–F funds, managers usually deal in smaller companies where the potential rewards (and risks) are greater. In recent years P–F funds have gained considerable popularity among investors. In 1967, there were only 16 P–F funds; today the number has risen to 145. Some of these funds are relatively small; others handle portfolios running into hundreds of millions of dollars.

I should also mention here that if you are a fan of particular industries, such as electronics or utilities, then you will find *specialized funds* most suited to your needs. This is a highly diverse group of funds which concentrate their investments in particular industries.

In concluding this section, I would like to point out that one of the best ways of deciding which mutual fund is suitable for you is to try to answer the following nine questions. These questions adapted from *Investment Companies*[52] may help you evaluate your investment objectives vis-à-vis mutual fund investing:

1. Do you want the whole job of investment management done for you?
2. Do you prefer to establish the broad divisions of your account yourself, as among bonds, preferred stocks, and common stocks of different types such as maximum appreciation (and risk), long-term growth and income issues?
3. Are you investing for a long time—or are you likely to want to cash in your holdings on short notice?
4. Can you look at "paper losses" with equanimity?
5. How great is your true need for current income?
6. If you don't intend to spend current income, do you want to be certain it is used to build up your account through the purchase of additional shares?
7. Would you now, or at some future time, find a formalized monthly withdrawal plan convenient and useful?
8. How important to you are taxes and possible ways of reducing or temporarily avoiding them?
9. Do you want to use investment company shares in lieu of a speculative account in individual stocks?

Good luck with your self-evaluation plan.

Mutual funds have developed at least three purchasing plans to conform to your savings and spending pattern. If you are among those persons who detest regimentation, you may wish to buy fund shares whenever it pleases you. In that event, the *Direct Outright Purchase (DOP) Plan* is for you. Under this plan, you receive a certificate for each purchase indicating your shareholding interests in the fund's securities, and you agree to accept in cash all dividends and capital gains distributions.

If you are like most people, the DOP Plan will seem unattractive or it may be beyond your reach. In that case, what you would prefer is something like a "pay-as-you-go" systematic plan, called in technical jargon *Voluntary Accounts* (VA). Since this plan is very popular, let me outline it.

A small initial investment of, say, $200 buys your original nest egg of shares at the prevailing offering price per share on the day your order is received. As soon as you join a fund, you indicate to the manager the amount of money you wish to remit at regular (monthly or quarterly) intervals. The fund agrees to invest your money as soon as it is received so that it will not lie idle. As a general rule, the fund does not charge for holding your shares in trust or for making available the opportunity for continuous and systematic investment.

There are some other features of this plan which deserve to be mentioned. You may at any time remit more than the stipulated amount. Failure to make a regular payment is not penalized. Also, you may withdraw your shares at any time without penalty. Finally, most plans have provisions for automatic reinvestment of dividends or gains distributions.

The DOP and VA plans give you varying degrees of freedom in setting up your own investment pace. However, if you are afraid of failing in your investment objectives unless you are *forced* to save and invest, then the *Contractual Plan* (CP) is for you. This plan requires you to agree to make periodic payments (usually monthly) of $10, $15, $25, or more, over a period of years toward the goal of a specific sum. However, you can terminate the agreement at any time, since it is essentially a promise to yourself.

In the Contractual Plan, up to 50 percent of the total amount of the first 12 payments is applied to sales charges rather than to your working principal. This feature, sometimes called the "front-end load," makes the plan a long-term program, since a short-term selling would result in a loss of all the money paid for sales charges.

Stick to a Mutual Fund: A Sticky Question

If you are convinced that you would like to play the mutual fund game and have chosen the fund which most appeals to you, you may wish to know how long you should remain faithful to this fund. This is a loaded question and is not amenable to an easy answer; a rational decision to stick to the same fund or change to a new one should be based upon a special kind of statistics. And such information, as you know, is hard to acquire. But the situation is not hopeless.

When the men who manage mutual funds arrive at their offices each

Monday, they find on their desks a three-section, 12-page report that the public rarely sees but that is instantly recognizable by its yellow-striped paper. This report, for which the fund managers pay a $500-a-year subscription fee, makes for fascinating reading about triumph, mediocrity, and despair in the fund business. Entitled the *Mutual Fund Performance List*, but known colloquially as the "Lipper List," it spells out the rises and falls in the fund empire. The form in which statistics are presented is simple. An example of how the information is offered is the following:

. . . Putnam Growth Fund, 157th, is down 12.16% so far this year, . . . [slightly above] the Dow-Jones industrials but better than the industry average by 2.28%. Last year's star, Neuwirth Fund, is off 19.83% even more than the American Stock Exchange index. Last week, it looked as if Shiff Hedge Fund was beginning to move but this week it faded and remained off 29.11%. Templeton Growth Fund scored the biggest gain of the week (3.08%) and heads the field with an 11.08% increase on the year. Among newer outfits, New York Venture Fund is up 6.11% since February, while Diamond Growth Fund, started barely four months ago, has already managed to lose more than a fifth of its shareholders' money.[53]

But this is not all. This advisory service also produces daily portfolio pricing, investment and shareholder accounting, and trust custodial services. Another weekly report sums up such investment data as changes in corporate earnings and profit margins, the totals of new highs and lows on the exchanges, and the Big Board stocks "with inexplicable performance based on published data."

An exceptional feature of this service is the valuable information it puts out under the supervision of Harold Oberg, one of the company's directors. Using data collected from funds' annual and quarterly reports, prospectuses, and forms filled with the Securities and Exchange Commission, Oberg measures how—and suggests why—one fund performs better or worse than others with similar investment objectives. Called "Portfolio Performance Perspective," the service uses devices that, among other things, measure the quality of portfolio holdings against their liquidity, scrutinize turnover ratios and the purposes to which commissions are directed, and eventually try to assess the tendencies and weaknesses of individual portfolio managers. In short, this service attempts to produce a statistical analysis for funds.

At this point you must surely be asking: If I have to go through all this rigmarole, will I not be better off in starting a mutual fund myself? Well, you may be right. But I am not suggesting that you kick over your job and start studying the Lipper List. What you need is to be aware of what this advisory service has to offer. Once you are familiar with it, you may then periodically check with your broker to determine whether or not you should stick with your current mutual fund.

Are Mutuals and You Mutually Consistent?

Of the more than 24 million Americans who own stocks, about one in every five now uses the services of mutual funds. Those who avail themselves of these services are the kinds of people who should not manage their own investment portfolios. Who are these people?

First, there are those people in situations which militate against their success. A person should not manage his investments if his spouse or employer is strongly prejudiced against it. In addition, people who do not have the financial ability to assume market risks should stay away from buying and selling stocks. Finally, those persons whose mental and emotional qualifications are not suited for stock market operations should under no circumstances be active in the market.

Those people who cannot and should not operate in the stock market on their own may, nevertheless, own a stake in our country's economic future. This is possible only because millions of Americans who used to consider stock ownership inappropriate to their circumstances can now participate in the market by owning stocks of mutual funds.

While mutual funds provide investors with excellent investment opportunities, they carry with them several disadvantages and risks. It is therefore imperative that you study thoroughly the advantages and disadvantages of purchasing shares in investment company funds such as those discussed above before you decide whether or not this would conform to your investment philosophy and help you meet your investment objectives.

Money doesn't bring happiness, but it calms the nerves.

—FRENCH PROVERB

Be Rich and Bewitch

ON LEISURE

Leisure, as defined by *Webster's Third New International Dictionary* is "freedom or spare time" during which one may follow his interests at his convenience. Surprising though it may seem, the number of leisure hours of an average American are only exceeded by the number of subsistence hours: the average time needed for eating and sleeping. According to the most recent estimate, more than one third of the lifetime of most Americans is composed of free, unoccupied time, and the number of ways in which this time can be used is limited only by the inventive capacity of the human mind.

What do most people do with their leisure? As a publication of a leading brokerage house puts it succinctly:

They watch television, listen to the radio and phonograph records; they read newspapers, magazines, and books; they work around the house or garden, sew, and entertain at home; they go for drives, visit family or friends, and go out to dinner. They go to movies, plays, concerts, and operas; and they visit museums and art galleries, or go back to school. They walk, fish, swim, surf, sail, bowl, golf, ski, ride, and fly; they play basketball, football, baseball, tennis, and squash. They paint, sing, dance, and play musical instruments. They travel in the United States and abroad; they picnic, camp, and visit the national parks and forests. They watch sporting events, play cards, and place bets at racetracks; they collect art, coins, and stamps; they take pictures, keep pets, and play slot machines. At times, they contemplate or simply do nothing.[54]

174

Notice that this long list of leisure-time activities does not include the hobby of making money and becoming rich. Participating in the stock market can be a source of much pleasure. However, you should realize that if you make too much money you might make some of your friends jealous. Assuming that you are interested in exploring the possibilities of enjoying the leisure that making money on the stock market can provide, let me supply you with some information that will help you undestand how to make more or lose less money, the shortcuts for making money, money-saving techniques, the tricky manipulations with handsome payoffs, and so on.

Honest Money

There are some honest ways of making money in the stock market about which the average investor may be uninformed. One of them is buying tax-free securities. Such securities have special appeal for investors in the higher tax brackets, since not having to pay tax on the income from these stocks means a greater saving to them than it does to those in the lower brackets.

Generally speaking, municipal bonds, which are floated by states, cities, and other local governments to build public works such as schools, highways, and parks, have a built-in feature of tax exemption. In effect, a municipal bond is a promissory note issued by an authorized public body in return for borrowed money. The issuer pledges to repay on each bond to the lender a given sum (usually $1,000 face value on each bond) in a certain number of years. Moreover, the purchaser of the bond receives a promise of getting a specified rate of interest each year for lending his money.

The most important reason for investing your money in these bonds is that they provide dependable tax-free income. Here is a specific example. If you earn between $55,000 and $64,000 a year and you receive income from 4.75 percent tax-free municipal bonds, you would have to earn 12.5 percent on a taxable security to match the tax-free income. Another way of looking at this source of income is that for anyone who pays 70 percent in federal income taxes on his top dollars, the rate on a 6 percent tax-exempt note is equivalent to a rate of about 20 percent in taxable interest. Even if you earn a modest $12,000–$14,000 a year, you still have an edge when you buy municipal bonds. For instance, you must earn 7.42 percent on a taxable security to match the tax-free income earned from a 4.75 percent municipal bond.

Besides tax-free income, municipal bonds generally provide you with security of principal and interest. Also, by purchasing municipal bonds at appropriate intervals, you may set up a "planned income" program in order to realize a fixed income during the next 5, 10, 25, or more years.

In addition to municipal bonds, stocks of certain public corporations provide a source for making money. Dividends of some *public utility companies* are partially free of income taxes, for the reason that these companies (for example, Arizona Public Service, Cascade Natural Gas, Central Louisiana Electric, and so on) are allowed by law to depreciate their assets at an accelerated rate.

Another kind of security which provides the possibility of substantial price appreciation is known as a convertible bond or convertible debenture. A bond may or may not be secured, but a debenture is backed only by the general credit of the corporation and no asset is attached to it. Since this type of security is likely to be only moderately attractive, many corporations "sweeten it" by making it convertible into a specified number of shares of common stock. Occasionally, interest paid on a convertible bond or a convertible debenture is tax-free, which makes such a bond or debenture even more attractive than a municipal bond. Examples of convertible debentures are Allied Stores 4½, 1992; Chase Manhattan Bank, 4⅞, 1993; and United Aircraft, 4½, 1992.

In addition, there are several reasons why convertible bonds should occasionally be more attractive than common stocks. One reason has to do with the amount of money you have to put up as down payment in order to buy convertible bonds. As explained, a convertible bond carries with it a claim on stocks. At the present time, to buy stocks would require you to put up 65 percent of the purchase price as margin. To buy the bond, the purchaser would need to put up only 50 percent. Another advantage of buying convertible bonds is that they offer stable income as opposed to the variable income of common stock. But the major advantage of buying a convertible bond is that quite often its price moves up much faster than that of the related stock. Consequently, it is possible for a convertible bondholder to benefit from larger price fluctuations while at the same time retaining his convertible option.

SHORT-TERM PAPER

If you are temporarily disillusioned with the stock market and for some reason do not care to buy municipal or convertible bonds, you have another choice. You can take refuge in short-term paper. Every refuge has a different appeal, depending on your objectives. Let me elaborate on this point.

The following news item illustrates the appeal of short-term paper:

On last January 5 [1970], a Monday, some two hundred people, a record number, ventured resolutely into the Wall Street area quarters of the Federal Reserve Bank of New York to buy some of the three- and six-month U.S. Treasury bills that were sold at auction that day, as on every Monday, in denominations of $1,000. Most of the crowd knew only that the return on Treasuries was sufficiently higher than the rate on their savings-and-loan accounts, currently a maximum of 5¼ percent, to make the trip to lower Manhattan eminently worthwhile. At the auction a week earlier, the discount on three-month Treasuries had risen to over 8 percent for the first time in history. While most of the prospective buyers had only a few thousand dollars to invest, several of them filled out the "tender" forms for over $50,000. One gentleman tendered for $116,000.

Had these better-heeled investors only known it, they could have got an even higher yield by investing in federal agency notes, or, if their incomes were high enough to warrant it, in tax-exempt state or local notes.[55]

The news item clearly states that short-term paper is a distinct form of investment. As a matter of fact, during the long 1968–70 bear market, the matter of short-term investment has assumed increased importance for individual investors of all stripes. In general, every investor who has some funds to invest should decide *where* he should put his funds on the basis of three factors: (1) the amount he has to invest and his tax bracket; (2) his desire to have liquidity; and (3) his willingness to take risk. Within this framework, an investor can make up his mind which of the alternatives shown in Table 17–1 is best for him.

TABLE 17–1
THE TERMS FOR SHORT-TERM MONEY

Invested in:	Yield 1.9.70	Tax status of interest
Municipal notes	5.25–6.00	Exempt from federal taxes (also from state and local income taxes in issuer's state and locality)
Eurodollars	10.50	Fully taxable
Commercial paper	9.34	Fully taxable
Bankers' acceptances ..	9.18	Fully taxable
Prime certificates of deposit	9.13	Fully taxable
Federal agencies	8.30	Exempt from state and local income taxes except for Fannie Mae issues, which are fully taxable
Treasury bills	8.02	Exempt from state and local income taxes

Source: Fortune, February, 1970, p. 181.

MONEY-SAVING TECHNIQUES

It is a commonplace that money is the seed of money; you need money to make more money. Consequently, the techniques which enable you to buy more for less should be of special interest.

One such technique, *margin trading*, is the practice of buying stocks with borrowed money. Borrowing money for stocks is much simpler than borrowing money for almost anything else you can imagine. When you buy stocks of a certain value on margin, the broker tells you how much money to put up; he supplies the rest at a specified interest rate. In short, he grants you a quick loan without your having to apply for one. The portion of the total purchase price which you are asked to put up is not arbitrarily determined by the broker. Depending upon the degree and nature of speculative buying of stocks, the Federal Reserve System determines this portion, which is known as the *margin requirements*. If you buy shares worth $10,000 and are required to put up $6,500 of your own, your margin is $6,500, and the margin requirement set by the Federal Reserve is 65 percent. Your broker lends you $3,500 on which you are required to pay, say, 9 percent interest. The possibility of trading on margin thus enables you to buy stocks worth $10,000 by putting up only $6,500.

But what happens when you sell securities bought on margin? Do you get your money back? Who keeps the profit? Does your broker gain anything? Let me answer these and related questions.

Suppose a month ago you purchased 100 shares of Terox Corporation at $100 per share, or $10,000 worth of stock. You bought the shares at 65 percent margin, putting up $6,500 of your money and borrowing $3,500 from your broker. Assume that you made the right decision and that your stock is worth $15,000 today. If this stock now appears to be overpriced, you would undoubtedly call your broker and ask him to sell it at the market. When the stock is sold, you will receive the sale price less the amount of your loan. In this case, you will receive $15,000 minus the borrowed $3,500 (less commission and interest charges, of course). In essence, you will get approximately $11,500 or $5,000 more than you put up originally. Isn't it wonderful that you put up only 65 percent of the purchase price of your stock at the time of purchase but that you get to keep all of the net profit (less commission and interest) when the stock is sold?

Let me now recreate the scene with a slight modification. Suppose you bought the same stock at the same price but without borrowing any money. Since you only have $6,500 to invest, you are able to buy 65 shares (ignoring commission) of Terox at $100 per share. When you sell these shares at $150 per share, you get approximately $9,750; your net profit is only $3,250, which is $1,750 less than the profit in the previous example.

But what if the price of your 100 Terox shares bought on margin goes down by 50 percent instead of increasing by that percentage, as we assumed in the previous example. If you sell your stock at $50 per share, you will get only $5,000 less $3,500, or a net amount of $1,500. Since you originally put up $6,500 of your money, your loss is $5,000. Notice that you must assume 100 percent of the loss. Also note that if you had bought the stock with your own money, your loss would have been only $3,250.

The implications of buying on margin should now be clear. If you buy on margin, you receive all the profit if the price of your stock goes up, and you assume all the risk of loss if the price drops. The advantage in buying stock on margin is that you make *more profit* if your stock increases in price. Of course, you *lose more* if the price drops.

Let me point out another risk in margin trading. Assume you purchased 1,000 shares of Terox Corporation at $100 per share at 65 percent margin. Should the price subsequently decline, your margin (the ratio of your equity to the value of your collateral) would shrink, since your borrowing would remain stationary. At a price of $90 your margin would be 61 percent, at $80 it would be 56 percent, at $70 it would be 50 percent, and at $50 it would be 30 percent. At prices lower than 35 your debt to the broker would actually exceed the value of your collateral. If that happens, in order to protect himself the broker will give you a margin call; that is, he will demand an extra margin adequate to absorb any reasonably expected losses. He must also set a minimum limit below which your margin must not be permitted to fall. As your margin approaches this lower limit, you will be asked to deposit additional cash. Failure to do so can result in your stocks being disposed of by your broker. The most regrettable aspect of this situation is that you are likely to be called upon to advance additional cash only when the market suffers a major setback and you are least able to bear this additional burden. Despite this risk, however, if caution is exercised, the technique of margin trading can be used to your advantage.

Another money-saving opportunity is provided by *stock rights*. As the name suggests, a stock right is the privilege granted a stockholder to buy more shares in his company when it needs to raise more capital. Let me explain how stock rights originate and how they offer you a means of saving money.

Assume you purchased 1,000 shares of UAL Incorporated, with 100,000 shares of common stock outstanding. You have acquired a one-hundredth part of control of the company, a one-hundredth part of net earnings available for dividends on the common stock, and a one-hundredth part of the corporation's net worth. As the company grows, its earnings potential and net asset value are likely to grow, and as a stockholder you expect to maintain your relative share of control, earnings, and assets.

Assume now that UAL needs additional funds to finance its expanding business. The two most common methods of raising funds consist of floating bonds and issuing new shares. If the decision is to issue new shares, the company must offer the first rights to purchase these shares to the existing stockholders. Two special steps need to be taken. The new shares must be sold at a slightly reduced price to make the new-share price consistent with the current market price, since at a subsequent date the latter price is more than likely to decline as a result of dilution (that is, a reduction in each shareholder's claims because of the larger number of stockholders participating in the company's earnings and assets). Also, if a stockholder does not wish to purchase additional shares, he must be given the opportunity to sell his option in the market.

Within this framework, UAL may raise additional funds by giving you and other stockholders the "privilege" of subscribing to additional stock at a price lower than the current market price. This privilege, reflected in stock rights, is given in proportion to your existing holding. Thus, if the number of shares of stock is to be increased by 25 percent and you hold 1,000 shares, you will be entitled to rights to purchase one share for each four shares you hold. In addition, you will be given the option to sell your rights in the market should you decide against exercising your option.

Here is how to use stock rights to your advantage. If you own stock rights, you may sell them to make some quick profit. Like highly speculative stocks, prices of stock rights fluctuate widely, sometimes going up as much as 100 percent or more within a short period. If you play your cards right, you may make a substantial profit by selling them when the price rises as a result of considerable interest in these rights.

While selling rights at higher prices appears to be a straightforward deal, a word of caution is in order. "Stockholders should sell rights early" is an old Wall Street belief. It is a commonplace that stock rights reach their maximum price shortly after the start of trading. They decrease in value as the subscription date (the date of expiration), draws to a close, and finally become worthless on the subscription date. There is a simple reason for this belief. In the initial period of the issuance of stock rights, the holders of stock rights generally adopt a "wait-and-see" policy, hoping to make substantial profits at a future date. However, as the subscription date approaches, rights holders begin to dump their rights in the market in a desperate effort to get as much as possible from their soon-to-be-valueless rights, thereby forcing prices down. You might be interested to know that earlier studies made by Arthur Stone Dewing and George Leffler showed that, more often than not, rights obtained their greatest values in the initial third of the subscription period. However, a more recent study conducted by Robert Soldofsky and Craig Johnson disagreed.[56] According to their study, those rights which reach peaks in the middle period also reach identical peaks in the first and/or last periods. Furthermore, a slight advantage might be gained by selling rights in the initial period if they are traded "normal." On the basis of these observations the study concluded that, as a general rule, one should not sell rights in the middle of the subscription period. Whether you believe in the later study or the earlier one, it would be advisable for you not to hold stock rights until the last moment if you desire to trade them. You should never lose sight of the fact that upon expiration these rights become valueless; hence their prices might experience sharp breaks as the date of expiration draws near.

Perhaps at this point you would like to ask: "But what if I don't own stock rights? Couldn't I still trade in them and make a profit?" The answer obviously is yes. If you do not own rights, there are at least two ways in which you may take advantage by trading in them. One advantage stems from the fact that the prices of stock rights do not always maintain a fixed ratio with the prices of stocks they represent. Let me give you an example. Assume a corporation whose stock was selling at $110 a week ago issues rights on a 4-to-1 basis at $100 per share. Assume further that after the rights are issued, the current market price drops to $108. Since the value of each right is the difference between the market value of the shares before the new ones are sold ($110) and their market value after the new ones are sold ($108), on a 4-to-1 basis the price of each right should be $2. Now if the current market price of rights drops to 1¾, you may take immediate advantage of the situation by trading in these undervalued rights. Suppose you buy 400 rights at $1¾ and sell short 100 shares (sell 100 shares now and promise to buy them later for delivery) at $108 per share, planning to deliver them as soon as the new shares are issued. You have received $10,800 for the shares you sold and have purchased rights for $700. These rights have given you the option to buy 100 shares at $100 per share. You have thus technically made a profit of $100 ($10,800 less $10,000 less $700), not taking into account transfer tax and broker's fees.

Another advantage in dealing with stock rights, which is by no means a small one, is that if you own the stock of a company which has issued stock rights, you are allowed to purchase these rights by putting up only 25 percent of the total value of your purchase, provided you wish to exercise them. If you are short of ready cash, this can become a tremendous money-saving proposition.

Selling Short Is a Bear's Game

Selling short is a game which only the bears should play. The rules of this game are fairly simple, and if the players' guesses are correct, they are in for big money. If they prove wrong, however, they are likely to lose their shirts.

Suppose Mr. Spengler finds out through research that the stock of Fairlane Corporation, selling at $95, is going to plummet. To take advantage of this expected price decline, Splengler *sells* 100 shares of Fairlane through his broker at $95 a share without first owning them. Since Spengler does not have the shares he sold, he borrows them from his broker for regular delivery to the purchaser. The broker required Spengler to deposit with the brokerage house 65 percent of the value of the shares ($6,175), assuming that the current margin requirement is 65 percent.

Once the formalities are completed, Spengler can sit back and relax until the Fairlane price drops sufficiently to yield the desired profit. There is no time limit within which he must buy back the shares, so that Spengler is in no hurry to place his buy order.

If Spengler's prediction is correct, the price of Fairlane Corporation will drop. If the price declines to, say, $75, and Spengler decides that the stock has bottomed out, he will buy 100 shares of Fairlane for $7,500 and make a clean profit of $1,325. But what if the prediction proves wrong and the price of the stock shoots up to $130, $200, or $500? After all, there is no limit to how far the price of a stock may rise. If that happens, Spengler will be in real trouble, won't he?

In a very real sense, selling short *is* potentially more risky than buying long (purchasing stock expecting the price to go up). When you buy a stock, there is no limit to the amount of profit you may make if the price rise is substantial. Furthermore, no matter how much the price drops, you can lose no more than your initial investment. On the other hand, if you sell short you may be forced to take a loss much greater than your initial investment if the price more than doubles. Moreover, you can never do better than double your money, since the price of a stock cannot decline below zero, and you can only do that if the stock becomes completely worthless.

Because of the risk involved, short selling has never been a popular investment tool among common investors. Indeed, during the course of a year, short sales account for only 2 to 3 percent of the public's trade on the New York Stock Exchange. However, there are some exceptions to this general rule, as will be seen from the following paragraph.

Richard Martin tells the story of one Meyer A. Berman, who invested lots of money in losing stocks but never once regretted his decisions:

Meyer A. Berman's mother wanted him to become a rabbi, a doctor, or a lawyer, and—at first glance—maybe she was right. He became a stockbroker, and, among other moves, he put his customers into Acme Missiles at $38 and watched it fall to $5. He got into Gale Industries at $26 and it went to $2. And he got on the National Video bandwagon at $120—and it promptly fell to $12.

But Meyer Berman isn't really a bad broker. In fact, he's an expert. When Mr. Berman got into these stocks, he got in as a short seller. . . . Despite his success, he says, "my mother is still a little disappointed in me." His mother, he says, "still tells me that she knows a medical school in Switzerland where I could get in."[57]

On the basis of this story I will have to admit that Berman is a pretty smart short seller. However, as I mentioned above, the success story of Berman is not common, and short selling remains an esoteric investment tool to most investors.

Whether or not you like short selling as an effective investment tool, the fact remains that if you intend to use it as a tool, you must first make sure that you know what to look for. In a book entitled *Hedgemanship: How to Make Money in Bear Markets, Bull Markets, and Chicken Markets while Confounding Professional Money Managers and Attracting a Better*

Class of Women, Conrad Thomas has given some important guidelines. Commenting on this book, Thomas writes:

The quality that is desired in a short sale candidate is the ability to subside gracefully, without sudden flare-ups to annoy and confuse the short seller. Volatility should be fairly low for two months or so before the short sale. . . . Recent daily volume should be moderate. . . . The stock should already be headed down, and there should be nothing in the fundamentals to indicate any reason for a reversal in the trend . . . the gliders, or the shot-down high-fliers, are much preferable to the active high-fliers, as short sale candidates. This is because there is some fundamental logic behind, some factual basis for, the behavior of the gliders, while there is literally no way to predict to what peaks emotional . . . trading will push a popular stock, nor what the extent of the wild gyrations will be for either the ascent or the descent which will follow.[58]

Before leaving this subject, let me call attention to a recent study in which Richard McEnally and Edward Dyl concluded that, contrary to common belief, short selling does *not* appear to be highly risky.[59] They suggested that investors should make short selling an important part of their management strategy. By all means accept this suggestion but remember to exercise extreme caution in dealing with the tool of selling short.

Puts and Calls

One of the shortcuts to making money in the stock market is the technique of *puts* and *calls*. However, it appears that most investors do not know a "call" from chartreuse nor a "put" from pithecanthropus. There is actually no reason for this confusion, since the concepts are fairly simple. A *call* is simply an option to buy (or "call for") a specified number of shares (usually 100) at a given price within a specified time. The purchaser of a call pays for the privilege of getting the option to buy a stock at a specified price. He makes a profit if the price of that stock goes up sufficiently by the specified date, and he loses his money if these expectations are not realized. Conversely, a *put* is an option to sell (or "put") at a specific price within a specified time limit. When a person buys the privilege of selling a certain number of shares at a specified price, he expects the price to go down substantially so that he may buy these shares at a lower price and sell them at the contractual (higher) price.

As stock market instruments, puts and calls are in some ways similar to commodity futures, which are very popular among the more affluent investors. Commodity futures offer the opportunity to make sizable profits with limited risks. An explanation of how to deal in commodity futures will expose you not only to an important trading instrument but will also pave the way to a better understanding of puts and calls.

Assume that a trader signs an agreement by which he undertakes to purchase $20,000 worth of live chickens. He only has $500 in hard cash to offer as down payment. The agreement, which calls for the delivery of the chickens three months later, is known as a commodity *future*. On the delivery date the trader must produce the balance ($19,500) to fulfill his bargain. If on the delivery date chicken prices are higher than the price prevailing on the date of the agreement, the trader will sell the agreement and make a sizable profit on an investment of only $500. If he is unlucky and the price of chickens drops, he must sell the contract at the lower price and assume the loss, which might easily run to more than his original investment.

People dealing in puts and calls also get the opportunity to make big money while limiting their risks. To investors, puts and calls are a way of reducing the risk of loss where an investment in a stock is concerned. Interestingly, speculators and small investors generally approach the option game from the buy side; that is, they buy calls if they are optimistic about the future, while puts are bought if pessimism prevails. Let me explain by means of an illustration how puts and calls work.

Suppose that for a long time you have been interested in buying 100 shares of Itel Corporation on a dip. Currently Itel shares are selling at $60 a share, and you are certain they will rise to $90 before anyone realizes it. (In this and subsequent examples I will ignore the cost of taxes and, where appropriate, brokers' commissions.) Instead of buying 100 shares in the market and investing $6,000, on January 1, 1970, for $800 you buy a six-month-10-day call on 100 shares of Itel at today's price of $60. You could have bought a call for anywhere between 30 days and one year; but you bought this one so that you could take shelter in the long-term capital gains provision of the tax code which provides that if you make a profit from the sale of stocks held by you for more than six months, you will not have to pay tax on half of that income.

If during the six-month period the price of the stock actually goes to $90, you will make a profit of $2,200 ($3,000 less $800), or 275 percent. Notice that your break-even price is around $68; that is, if the price reaches $68 when you exercise the call, you will neither gain nor lose.

But what happens if the price does not go up or if it actually declines? In that case, you can lose no more than your $800 initial investment, since there is no penalty for not exercising the call. There is another aspect of buying calls which is usually misunderstood. It is commonly believed that a call buyer will not exercise his call unless the stock reaches his break-even price. This is not true. You should exercise your call option if the price is high enough to recover part of your initial investment. In this case, if the price goes up to $62 and you exercise your option, you will not make a profit but you will certainly cut down your loss.

The implications of the above example are very interesting. Not only did you make a 275 percent profit within six months (which would have been impossible were you to buy 13 shares of Itel with $800) but you limited your risk of loss to $800. Not bad as an investment philosophy, wouldn't you say?

What I have just told you is only part of the story; the rest goes like this. If you are pessimistic about the market, you still have the opportunity to make big money and limit your risk by buying a put. Suppose, on May 27, 1966 when the economy was experiencing a recession, you bought a six-month-10-day put option for $2,000 for 100 shares of Fairfield Company, selling at $156 a share. The date of expiration of your option was thus December 27, 1966, and the *striking price*—the price at which you would break even was $136. By November 25, the price nose-dived to $101 per share. You could then buy 100 shares of Fairfield at $101 per share ($10,100) and sell them at $156 ($15,600), thereby realizing a profit of $3,500 ($5,500 less your option cost of $2,000).

Notice that if you exercised your put option within six months of your purchase, you would not get the long-term tax benefit. For that, you had to wait for a few more days, during which time the price of the stock could sneak up on you. Let me also point out that you had another option open to you: You could have sold your put option for, say, $3,000 and have pocketed a substantial profit. Had the price of the stock risen, you would have lost no more than the amount of money you spent ($2,000) for buying the put option. You could have made a much bigger profit ($5,500) had you sold 100 shares of Fairfield Company short at $156 (instead of buying a put option) and bought them back at $101. While that is true, there are three problems which are not easily detectable. First, if you participated in the short-selling transaction, you would have had to pay a federal tax on your profit at relatively high ordinary-income rates; all profits on short sales are taxed that way. Second, unlike put options, the risk of dealing in short sales is practically unlimited, and the degree of risk can never be determined. Third, if you had decided to sell short instead of buying a put option, you would have had to put up 65 percent of $15,600.

It should be clear that you buy a call when you anticipate a price rise and purchase a put when you expect an appreciable price decline. But what if you are not sure which way the price will go but are still eager to take advantage of price fluctuations? You may then buy a *straddle*, which is essentially a combination of a put and a call option into a single option. The straddle gives the holder the right to sell a certain number of shares of the specified stock at the stated price before the due date and/or the right to buy a certain number of shares of that stock at the same price before the same date. You pay a higher price for this than for a call or a put, but you also get a lot for your money. Another interesting aspect of a straddle is that you may exercise *both* the put and call options during the life of a straddle.

Suppose you buy a straddle for $800, which gives you the right to buy 100 shares of Macy Corporation at $30 and/or sell 100 shares of Macy at $30 within a period of 6 months and 10 days. If Macy drops to 16 and then rises to 50 during the lifetime of the straddle, you may first buy 100 shares of Macy at the market at $16 per share and sell to the maker of the straddle at $30. Later, when the price rises to $50, you will have the right to buy from the maker 100 shares of Macy at $30 and sell them at the market at $50.

There is another way in which you can use straddle to your advantage. Suppose you expect the price of your stock to go up and therefore wish to buy a call. It is generally cheaper to buy a straddle and sell the put portion of it than to buy a straight call. Similarly, having bought a straddle, you may sell the call portion and retain the put if you so desire.

If puts, calls, and straddles do not provide you with enough "leverage" (a chance for big profits with limited risk), there are other combinations known as strips, straps, and spreads. For instance, a spread is similar to straddle except that a straddle is a combination put and a call at the same price, whereas the spread is a put at a price below the current stock market price and a call at a price above the current stock market price. A spread is less expensive than a straddle on the same stock for the same length of time by approximately half the difference of the spread between the put and the call. For example, if a straddle at $60 costs $600, a spread of 2 points up and 2 points down would cost $400. The difference of $200 would represent half of the spread between $58 and $62.

Perhaps you are curious to know why, if puts and calls provide a vehicle to make a sure-fire fortune, there has never developed a central market for these esoteric instruments. The reason is simple. More often than not, the buyers of calls make wrong predictions about their stocks, and the maximum loss involved in buying a call or a put option becomes the normal loss. Actually, only one in five options is ever exercised profitably.

So far I have talked about buying an option. You may sell an option too, and pocket some handsome gains. Here is how to do it. Suppose that in February, 1968 you decided to buy General Motors stock, selling at $75 per share. You had savings of $7,500 and could use this money in several ways. You could buy 100 shares of GM for cash, or you could buy the shares on margin. At the prevailing margin rate of 65 percent, you would have been required to put up only $4,875 for buying 100 GM shares. Better still, you could have bought a six-month-10-day call for $750 per call, or a total of 10 calls for $7,500. But in that case the price of GM shares had to increase within a six-month period beyond the $82.50 level before you could make any profit. If that did not happen, you would have lost all your money.

Assume that you did not like any of these alternatives and decided to sell a put option instead. Let us see what this involved. When you sold a six-month-10-day put option for 100 GM shares for $500, you agreed to buy within that period 100 shares of GM at the prevailing price of $75 a share. When the broker completed the sale of your put option, he asked you to post a margin equal to 50 percent of the market value of the shares, or a total of $3,750; but since you had already received $500 by selling the put option, you had to put up an additional $3,250 only. The formalities completed, your six-month's waiting period began.

During the next six months one of two things could happen. If the price of GM shares declined below $75, you would have been called upon to buy 100 GM shares at $75. That should have been just fine, since that's what you wanted to do in the first place, but with the difference that your cost per share worked out not to $75 but only to $70 ($75 less the $5 per share you received by selling the put option). If, on the other hand, the price did not drop to $70, you would not be asked to buy your shares, and you would have made $500 on an investment of $3,250. Let me add that you could keep on writing puts on GM ad infinitum, thereby setting up for yourself a nice money-making machine.

As with selling put options, you may sell call options too, although in that case the circumstances must be different. For instance, assume that you currently hold 100 shares of Computer Techniques which you think are fully priced at $30. Instead of selling them outright, you may sell a six-month-10-day call option for $400. If within the stipulated time period the price goes above $30, you will be called upon to surrender your shares. That should not bother you, since you wanted to do that in the first place. As a matter of fact, you are $400 ahead, the price you received for selling the call option.

There are some drawbacks in embracing this strategy. For instance, if the price of Computer Techniques shot up to $75, you would have felt like retiring from the investment world. On the other hand, if the price dropped to $15 and stayed there, you would normally have held those sinking shares until your option expired. Another drawback is that the money you receive by selling options is taxable as ordinary income if the stock is called away. Of course, if the call option is not exercised for six months or more, then the call money is treated as a long-term gain.

Personalized Price Control

Although you always seek to make a large profit, sometimes you will lose part of your profit, while at other times you will incur losses. You must therefore learn how to protect a paper profit or limit a possible loss by instituting a system of personalized price control.

One of the easiest ways to limit the amount of loss is by a *stop order*. Stop orders are valuable, but need careful handling. What I mean is that a stop order is a handy tool, but you must know its limitations if you are to get the maximum benefit from it.

Before explaining the mechanics of stop orders, let me lay down some modified ground rules in case you wish to use these orders as a guide for your investment program. First, you must learn to accept the fact that sometimes your stocks will be sold simply because the price touched your stop order price and not because the stocks had become bad.

Second, stop orders are not like commodities to be used as a means for satisfaction. Rather, they are like health insurance; you do not ever wish to collect on your premium money, but you do want to be sure of some financial backing in case of illness.

Third, stop orders cannot be used successfully by depending on hunches or guesswork. The user must get involved in charting (or use some other comparable theoretical instrument) to provide himself with the essential stop-order guidelines. Bearing in mind these limitations, let me discuss the instrument in detail.

A stop order is nothing more or less than an instruction to your broker to buy or sell a certain stock when that stock sells at or through the "stop price." So the best thing is to look first at this stop price.

Assume you wish to buy 50 shares of Sklic Corporation at $22 per share, because it deals in air pollution and pollution is currently attracting attention. You cannot be sure what effect the national focus on pollution will have on the stock, so you buy the stock at $22 and simultaneously place the order "to sell at 19 stop." This will constitute your stop (sale) order. If and when the stock declines to 19, your stop order will automatically become a market order, and your stock will very likely be sold at $19 per share (or close to that price, depending upon the price at which the trade after the order takes place).

A stop (buy) order functions similarly to the stop (sale) order. In the previous example, suppose that Sklic stock is selling at $22, but you are not sure whether or not the stock will start to move up in response to the government's concern over pollution. Under these circumstances you may wish to buy Sklic only at a price no higher than $24, so you order "buy at 24 stop." Then you can sit back and relax. If the price of Sklic touches $24 (or a price close to $24, depending upon the price at which the postorder transaction takes place), you will immediately become the owner of a specified number of Sklic shares; if not, you won't buy them.

A variation of stop order is the *stop limit order*. Suppose you own 100 shares of Itel Corporation. You already know it is a volatile stock and has the habit of bouncing around between $60 and $90. Currently it is selling at $84 per share and you do not wish to ride with it down to $60. So you enter an order to sell 100 Itel at 80 *stop, limit* 80. Subsequently, the price may decline from $84 to $80½ to $81 to $80. At that point your order becomes a limit order at $80, *not* a market order. Your stock will not be sold at, say, $79⅞ (which could happen in the case of a stop order at 80) because you have ordered your broker not to accept anything less than $80.

Perhaps you wonder whether you could specify two different prices, one for the stop and one for the limit. The answer is yes. You could have entered an order to sell 100 Itel shares at 80 *stop*, *limit* 78. This implies that should Itel sell at $80 or below, your order will then become an order to sell only at $78 or higher. Since Itel is an actively traded stock, chances are that your stock will be sold at $80, certainly long before it hits $78.

Stop orders can also be used to minimize the risks involved in short sales. Control Data provides us with a classic case. It was not too long ago when, after trading in the mid-30's for a long time, the stock jumped to $65. No one believed that the stock could survive at that price level, and if you were a typical crowd follower you would have rushed to "short" Control Data at $65.

I hope you realize now what would have happened if you had engaged in that short sale and did not have the patience to wait until the 1969 market drop brought the price of that stock down to a much lower level. I remember that within a short period the stock touched base at $150, and I hate to calculate how much money you would have lost in that transaction had you been forced to cover yourself at that time.

But you didn't have to lose all that money. If you had shorted the stock at $65 and simultaneously placed the order "cover at 70 stop," you would have limited your loss to 5 points only. In this case, you would have bought Control Data at $70, and your loss would have been limited to only $500, not $8,500.

Let me recapitulate. Stop orders are, you might say, the "infallible super price watchers" which no broker can ever hope to be. They provide you with an automatic vehicle for protecting gains or limiting losses in your stock transactions. However, like fire or a sharp razor blade they must be used with extreme caution. If you know just what stop orders can do—and what they *cannot* do—you have at your disposal an effective device by which you may protect part of a profit or limit a loss. I should add that since stop orders on the AMEX are stop limit orders, even more caution should be exercised in dealing with those stocks.

In passing, I might mention that a rule of thumb which might be usefully applied to limit losses is to maintain a substantial cash position in case the market trend appears uncertain. There is always the temptation to chase your favorite issues lest they run away from you. In reality, the market rarely runs away from you, and eventually market prices of your favorite stocks settle near their *true* investment values.

GTC Order

The option of placing GTC (good-till-cancel) orders, which is open to all investors, should be mentioned here. When you give your broker a limit order or a stop order, you can specify that it is to be good for a day, or a week, or a month. However, you need not limit yourself to any specific time period. If you want your order to hold good indefinitely, you give your broker a GTC order, which will remain in effect until it is executed or until you cancel it.

Warrants Warrant More Attention

There is a relatively simple way in which you may be able to make money in the stock market, namely, by dealing in *warrants*. Perhaps it is best to say that warrants are generally issued with preferred stocks or bonds as a "sweetener" to induce investors to buy the stocks or bonds at a price higher than would otherwise be possible.

Warrants are not universally favored as an important investment tool, however. The New York Stock Exchange characterizes them as "hybrid securities that will never meet our stringent requirements for listing." Interestingly, in 1970 the New York Exchange backed off from its position on warrants and agreed to list the new AT&T warrants. Homer Budge, chairman of the Securities and Exchange Commission, argues that warrants give their owners a false sense of possessing something of value. Even some corporate executives, who have themselves issued millions of dollars worth of warrants, spitefully call them "funny money."

On the other hand, no one can deny that the popularity of warrants has been increasing. Today more than 150 warrants are actively traded in various markets (including the NYSE), against only 6 in 1950. The number of warrants listed on the American Stock Exchange has grown to 39 from 24 since 1967, and the volume of warrant trading on the AMEX increased by 176 percent between 1964 and 1968.

What, then, are warrants, and how can they be used to accumulate profits? A warrant is an option issued by a company to buy a number of shares (usually one) of its common stock at a predetermined exercise price during a set period, usually 5 to 20 years. In a small number of cases, warrants are issued for the lifetime of the corporation, or until exercised. For instance, TWA warrants must be exercised by December 1, 1973, but Tri-Continental warrants are perpetual.

Like common stocks, warrants are issued at a fixed price. However, warrants are actively traded in the market, and their prices fluctuate along with the prices of the related stocks, though not necessarily in the same ratio. And therein lies the clue to making money by trading in warrants.

Suppose Cohr Electronics, currently selling at $10 a share, issues 20-year warrants with an "exercise price" of $12, which is 20 percent above the market price of the stock. The price of warrants is determined by a combination of two important factors: the immediate profit a warrant holder can make by selling it in the market, and the premium which the holder can charge for transferring to the buyer the chance of making larger profits should the stock go up above the exercise price at any time during the life of these warrants. I might add that the dividend yield on the associated common stock and the potential dilution of the common stock resulting from the exercise of all the outstanding warrants might also influence their prices to a certain degree.

Coming back to our simple arithmetic, suppose the price of Cohr Electronics advances from $10 to $15. In that event, the price of warrants probably would be quoted at $5. Of this price, $3 would represent the immediate profit a warrant holder could make by buying Cohr stock for $12 and selling it at $15. The other $2 of the warrant price would represent a "premium," the amount which an investor would presumably be willing to pay for the chance that Cohr stock would advance in price appreciably before the warrants expired. As time passes, the warrant price would go up with advances in Cohr stock prices. Conversely, the warrant price would go down if Cohr price declined; the price of Cohr warrants would also go down as its date of expiry draws near.

Notice that, although warrant prices currently are a little less than half the stock prices, the warrants have no intrinsic value. The holders are neither part owners of the company's assets or earnings nor are they creditors of the company. The warrants derive their value purely because they are convertible into shares of Cohr Electronics.

Thus far the mathematics has been simple; thereafter it becomes abstruse. Suppose a couple of years later Cohr reaches the $30 mark, pulling up the price of warrants to $20—the $2 premium plus the $18 profit a warrant holder can now make exercising his option to buy Cohr at $12. An ordinary investor might conclude from these price changes that it is better to buy the common stock than the warrants, since the former advanced by $20 whereas the latter increased by only $15. Such a conclusion would be unequivocally wrong, since the *real* advance in the warrant prices (300 percent) is much greater than the real advance in stock prices (200 percent). It is this fact which makes warrants more attractive relative to stocks.

Actual incidents that have taken place in the recent past in the stock market reinforce the belief that warrants have some advantages over stocks. Sidney Fried, president of RHM Associates, once boasted that the 78 warrants he recommended in September, 1966 had risen an average of 161 percent by December, 1968. During the same period, the Dow Jones Industrial Average increased by a miserly 19 percent. Others have also expressed similar optimism toward warrants.

While warrants are great trading vehicles, in all fairness I must point out that warrant holders likewise risk a much greater loss when stock prices fall dramatically. A customer who traded in warrants through Moore & Schley lost 60 percent of his investment during a period in which the Dow

Jones Industrial Average declined by only 20 percent. Others have also lost a great deal of their hard-earned money by dealing in warrants in a declining market. Consequently, it is more appropriate to treat warrants as a valuable speculative instrument than as an important investment tool.

On the basis of the above discussion, it is possible to say that purchasing warrants in preference to the related stock does not necessarily give you more leverage and control. It is therefore imperative that in each instance you figure out whether to buy a stock or its warrant. Daniel Turov, an account executive with Walston & Company, has figured out a way to perform that task scientifically. He explains his technique in the following manner.

Assume that ABC is selling at $20 and that there is an outstanding warrant which allows purchase of one share within five years at $10. Theoretically this warrant should sell for $10. However, if the stock doubled to $40, the warrant would now be worth $30, or triple its former price. Since this leverage is desirable in a rising stock, the warrant has added appeal and will sell for a premium of, say, 50 percent, or $15. If five years from now the stock is selling for $40, the warrant should sell for $30.

In cases where the warrant is about to expire or where the stock is greatly above the exercise price, the warrant will sell at little or no premium, since there is neither little time nor little leverage left. If the stock does not advance to $40 in five years, then purchase of the warrant at $15 would have been less profitable than buying the stock; if the stock had gone to only $30, the warrant would be worth $20, or a rise of only 33 percent, compared to a 50 percent advance in the stock. Conversely, if the stock had gone above $40, the warrant would have yielded a higher percentage profit; at $60 the stock has tripled, but the warrant is worth $50, a gain of $3\frac{1}{3}$ times. Thus, concludes Turov:

This factor, which represents the number of times the stock must appreciate for the warrant to have a value on expiration [i.e. without premium] representing the same amount of appreciation, is a highly significant number. It is equal to the exercise price divided by the current price of the stock, minus the current price of the warrant.[60]

It is my hope that you will always make this mini-calculation a firm basis for answering the "stock or warrant" question.

NOVELTY OF NEW ISSUES

A distinctive form of investment is the purchase of a selected number of stocks newly issued by companies. Devoid of any history, new stock issues do not provide their purchasers a firm basis for arriving at their true investment value. As such they can be classified as high-risk securities. On the other hand, because the corporations which issued the stocks have not had the opportunity to prove themselves, new stock issues are generally offered at bargain prices and consequently provide investors with excellent buying opportunities.

Frank Reilly and Kenneth Hatfield studied investor experience with new stock issues, both in the short (one month) and in the long (one year) term.[61] The authors discovered that, although the number of new issues experiencing superior changes was not significant, the relative size of the gains was always substantially higher than the size of the losses. The authors therefore concluded that "although on the average the investor experiences as many relative losses as relative gains, his downside risk is relatively small while his potential relative gains are substantial."

I mentioned above that in a new stock issue the investor is required to assume high risk. Based on this observation, I am prompted to ask a related question: "Do high risks always lead to high returns?"

One of the most authoritative studies (by the Bank Administration Institute) attempting to answer this question contained the following observation:

One of the best documented propositions in the field of finance is that investors, on the average, can receive a higher rate of return by assuming greater risk. It has been found, for example, that low-grade bonds on the average produce a greater return than high-grade bonds, and low-grade stocks on the average produce a greater return than high-grade stocks.[62]

Interestingly, Lemont Richardson categorically dismissed the findings of the Bank Administration Institute study as having any major significance.[63] He pointed out the serious limitations of the empirical evidence cited by the BAI study and referred to certain inconsistencies in its logic. Richardson concluded that the notion that investors, on average, can realize higher returns by taking greater risks has no practical validity in investment decision making. While I do not support or reject the findings of either study, I must say that you are likely to gain handsome rewards if you undertake some risks, provided that you know when to assume them and how to take defensive action against them.

The Fun of Pyramid Buying

Another popular, albeit risky, way of making money is known as *pyramid buying*. Basically, pyramid buying is a way of taking financial advantage of appreciation in the value of your stocks. Here is how this method works. Suppose that three months ago in your margin account you bought 100 shares of United Company at $45 a share and put up $2,925 (to satisfy the 65 percent margin requirement) of the $4,500 cost. Let us assume that the stock advanced to $90 a share, making your total holdings worth

$9,000. Your broker would recognize the inflated value of your original investment and would accept that added value as collateral on the additional purchases. In this instance, you could sell 100 shares at $9,000, pay off the $1,575 loan, and have $7,415 left. However, instead of selling your shares at 65 percent margin, you might buy additional shares of approximately $11,400 on a cash margin of only $2,925. If you continue to be lucky, you could run your paper profits to $100,000 or even $1 million, all for just $2,925 cash.

Before you begin to think and act like a millionaire, however, let me warn you against the dangers of pyramid buying. Just as you may build an empire on paper profits, so in a sagging market your empire may collapse like a house of cards, and that may lead to bankruptcy. Consequently, you cannot be too careful with this money-making vehicle.

MONEY MAKING: A BYSTANDER'S APPROACH

So far I have talked about a number of ways in which you can make money by taking an active part in the market. Let me now tell you how you may get rich without putting in lots of money and hours of hard work. If you follow this route you do not have to make important decisions nor are you required to perform those tricky manipulations. All you need do is join the plan and promise to put part of your paycheck into stock every month. Then you can sit back and relax; your money will probably grow automatically if the market is kind to the plan managers.

This plan which I have just referred to is the *Monthly Investment Plan* (MIP). It is sponsored by member firms of the New York Stock Exchange, and it offers advantages to many investors. The MIP permits the investor to take advantage of dollar-cost averaging.

Suppose you decided to put $50 into stocks every month for 12 months, beginning with January, 1970. Assuming that the price per share fluctuated throughout the year, you would have benefited from dollar-cost averaging, as shown in Table 17–2:

In the example in Table 17–2, the average price per share is $11.01, whereas the average cost per share is $10.87. You clearly benefited from dollar-cost averaging because more shares were purchased when the price was low relative to when it was high.

Another important feature of the MIP is that it helps you accumulate stock on a regular, convenient basis and encourages you to develop the habit of putting aside some money regularly. Furthermore, in this plan your dividends are automatically reinvested for you in the stock you are buying, so that your money grows more rapidly. Of course, you should not lose sight of the fact that the MIP, or any plan for that matter, does not assure a profit or afford protection against depreciation in a declining market.

TABLE 17–2
Dollar-Cost Averaging

Investment (1)	Amount of Investment (2)	Price per Share (3)	Number of Shares Purchased (2 ÷ 3)
Jan.	$ 50	$ 10.00	5.0
Feb.	$ 50	$ 9.80	5.1
Mar.	$ 50	$ 9.60	5.2
Apr.	$ 50	$ 9.80	5.1
May	$ 50	$ 10.20	4.9
June	$ 50	$ 10.50	4.8
July	$ 50	$ 11.00	4.5
Aug.	$ 50	$ 11.40	4.4
Sept.	$ 50	$ 12.00	4.2
Oct.	$ 50	$ 11.50	4.3
Nov.	$ 50	$ 12.30	4.1
Dec.	$ 50	$ 14.00	3.6
Total	$600	$132.10	55.2
Average price	$11.01		
Average cost	$10.87		

The operating rules of the MIP are simple. A small initial investment (as small as $40 every three months or as large as $1,000 a month) buys your original nest egg of shares at the prevailing price per share on the day your order is received. With your initial order you indicate the amount of money you will be remitting at regular intervals. Thereafter, when you send your money it is invested and your account is duly credited. You become a part owner of the companies whose shares are bought by the fund. Also, like any tangible property, you may sell your fund shares at any time and receive a check for the proceeds.

Naturally, the MIP is not suitable for all types of investors. But for those who prefer something like a pay-as-you-go plan with a minimum down payment and a systematic, gradual accumulation of long-term gains, plus the big advantage of dollar averaging, this plan is ideal.

Those Tricky Manipulations

Finally, let me introduce you to some of the relatively unknown but profitable methods of making money. You will do well to remember that all of them involve tricky manipulations and therefore they require extreme caution and good judgment.

You have learned how to use call, put, straddle, and spread to your advantage. There are several other ways to use call and put profitably. Some of these are discussed in the following paragraphs.

Suppose you own 100 shares of Milo Electronics, which you bought at $50 per share, and for which the current market price is $70. You feel that the stock has greatly appreciated in value but that it still has the potential for further appreciation. In such a situation, you may sell your holdings for $7,000 and buy a three-month call for $500. If the price goes up to $90 within the stipulated period, you will make a further profit of $1,500 ($2,000 less the $500 call price). If the price drops to $60, $50, or even $30, all you lose is the $500 purchase price of the call, but you also gain $2,000 by selling your stock at $70.

Let us use the same example with the sole modification that you do not own 100 shares of Milo. You may still take advantage of the situation by selling short (that is, selling 100 shares at $70, hoping to buy them later at a cheaper price) and buying a call for $500. Here again, if the price nose-dives to $50, you gain $2,000 (for selling it short at $70) and lose the $500 call price. If, on the other hand, the price goes to $90, you gain $1,500 for buying the call and lose $2,000 for selling short. Thus, you make substantial gains if you are right, while your losses are limited if your predictions are wrong.

A third method may be applied if you hold shares of a fairly stable company. Suppose you hold 100 shares of Kenn Shops which you bought at $12 a share some three months ago. The price has fluctuated between $11½ and $13, and you expect the pattern of fluctuation to remain relatively unchanged. Under these conditions, when the price reaches $13, you may sell a three-month call for $300. You make a clear $300 profit if the price does not rise about $15. And even if the price goes to, say, $17, and the purchaser of the call exercises it, you still have $300 profit from the sale of the call.

In another instance you may wish to insure substantial paper profits by buying a put. Suppose you had purchased 100 shares of Duracel at $60 per share and the current market price is $87 per share. You think the stock will go much higher but are afraid that you will lose this profit if the market declines. So to protect your potential profits you buy a put for $400. If your intuition is borne out and the price goes to $120, by selling the stock at that price you will be ahead $2,700. This is because you gained an extra $3,300 by selling the stock at $120 rather than at $87, but you lost the $400 which you paid for the put option. If, on the other hand, the price drops to $37, and you decide to hold the shares but exercise your put option, you will have a clear gain of $4,600 ($5,000 by exercising the put option less the $400 you paid for the put, which is nonrefundable).

A trick of a different nature can be performed if a good stock declines substantially in price. Suppose you had bought 100 shares of Whitney Corporation at $28 and the current market price is $18. Assuming that you consider this the bottom price for this stock, you buy 100 additional shares at $18. After 31 days you may sell the old stocks at a loss of $1,000 (assuming that the price is still $18) and use this loss for tax deduction purposes. In effect, you continue to hold 100 shares of Whitney but at the same time have a tax-deductible loss on your books. Of course, you will then not have a long-term position on the stock you bought at $18.

I must mention the volatility of "thin" situations and the way you may use them to your advantage. A "thin" stock is one in which relatively few shares (usually less than a million) are outstanding. In addition, in such issues a large portion of the available supply is closely held by management. A classic case of a "thin" situation is Cameo-Parkway Records, which moved from a little less than $2⅛ per share in early 1967 to $55 by September of the same year. Approximately 56 percent of Cameo's 620,000 shares is closely held, leaving a floating supply of 273,000 shares. It is widely believed that the limited numbers of shares outstanding was a major contributory factor for such a spectacular price increase.

I am sure you would like to know why "thin" stocks move faster than "thick" stocks. The reason is that the smaller the number of shares of a company outstanding, the smaller the number of stockholders sharing the total earnings of that company. For the same reason, any increments in earnings lead to faster increases in earnings per share, as compared to situations where large numbers of shares are outstanding. Since growth in earnings per share is one of the key indicators influencing demand for a stock, many people concentrate on buying thin-issue stocks only.

Like thin issues, stocks which are likely to be split also appreciate quite rapidly. The reason is more emotional than technical. For instance, if the stock of Whitney Corporation, currently selling at $75, is split 3 for 1, the price of the new stock will become $25, and each shareholder who now owns 1 share of Whitney will own 3 shares. In that event, the demand for Whitney is likely to increase substantially. The reason is that many people believe that lower-priced stocks advance (percentagewise) more rapidly than their higher-priced counterparts, and their belief is based upon the fact that people can buy a larger number of low-priced shares with a given amount of money. Experience shows that since enough people believe in this line of reasoning, many low-priced stocks do outperform their high-priced counterparts on a percentage basis. It may be worth your while to keep this fact in mind when you are looking for a stock to buy.

Let me now mention the possibility of short selling for arbitrage purposes. Short selling enables you to arbitrage (take advantage of price differences in different markets) in securities listed on more than one exchange. If the price of a stock on the New York Stock Exchange is lower than that on the Pacific Exchange, you may buy that stock on the NYSE and sell it on the Pacific Exchange, thereby making a profit. I should add that arbitrage manipulations are both tricky and difficult, and only professional investors can successfully engage in it.

In passing, I mention a shortcut of a very different nature. There exist in the market such institutions as American Research and Development which sponsor research in new products at leading universities. These institutions establish new corporations engaged in myriad research activities, issue stocks, and help them grow. In most instances the new stocks double, triple, or even quadruple in value in a short time. Therefore, watch for these corporations backed by American Research and Development and similar concerns and grab their shares as and when they are floated in the market.

In this chapter I have given you some ideas for making money which you can digest at your leisure. Let me reiterate that before you put any of your ideas into action, be sure to learn their applications well. Use the tools developed in this chapter, do not abuse them.

ACT V

BEHIND THE SCENES

The folklore of Wall Street is like any other. It consists of accumulated bits and pieces of knowledge. Many of these are imprecise or incomplete, and . . . contradictory.

—DAVID L. HOFFLAND

18

Folklore of Wall Street

THE LURE OF FOLKLORE

Stocks and bonds and the market in which they are traded are surrounded by stories that resemble folklore. David Hoffland, a bank investment officer, said not long ago:

Folklore represents attempts to explain and deal with the problems of human existence, and it mirrors the wisdom as well as the lack of wisdom of those among whom it is found. Folklore is distinguished from scientific knowledge by its lack of rigor. . . . Folklore . . . is imprecisely formulated and incapable of measurement. Much folklore consists simply of hypotheses too vague and unreliable to be called anything other than superstition.[64]

At first glance, you may find no resemblance between folklore and stock market stories or theories; for you would naturally assume that investment knowledge is *scientific*, that market theories are tested and incorporated into predictable and reliable theoretical models. If you believe this, you are only partially correct. Some stock market theories have never been tested scientifically; many such theories are about as unreliable and as unscientific as folklore.

In this chapter I plan to accomplish two objectives. First, I would like to point out that several of the market theories I discussed in previous chapters are really not "proven" theories. There are good reasons for their existence, but they have never been validated scientifically. However, since

201

these theories—which I would call *market legends*—seem to work most of the time, it will be interesting to learn more about them.

My second objective is to discuss briefly those beliefs which have developed from hunches and naïve generalizations. These beliefs, a permanent part of stock market folklore, if only because many people think that they "work," will be referred to as *market myths*.

THE MARKET LEGENDS

There are many legends in the stock market today. Two such legends are the theories that *resistance levels* and *support levels*, exist for both individual stocks and the whole market. In simple terms, resistance is a barrier to advancement, while support is a barrier to price decline. These theories attempt to explain why a certain stock is not apt to advance beyond a certain price level or why its price is not likely to decline below a given price zone.

Assume that a large number of shares of Scilk Corporation (engaged in pollution control) which had been trading between $18 and $20 experiences a rapid rise to $30 following President Nixon's announcement early in 1970 that his administration would give top priority to the air pollution problem. At $32 there is considerable selling by those who wish to cash in on their rapid gains; consequently, the price dips to $27. We now have two types of persons interested in that stock: those who believe the stock is getting ready for another major advance and those disenchanted stockholders who failed to sell their stock when it hit the high of $32. If the company continues to expect substantial increases in its earnings, the buying pressure for the stock will very likely increase, and a large number of shares will change hands between, say, $29 and $32. In technical language this is known as "churning" or "an area of consolidation." Since sellers become active in selling thin stock when the price reaches $32 and buyers come in as soon as the price dips to $29, we may say that for Scilk Corporation a resistance level (at $32) and a support level (at $29) have been established.

The logic behind the claims for the support and resistance levels is rather naïve. It is argued that if a person bought Scilk Corporation's shares at $32 and the price subsequently declines to $18, he is more than likely to "clean off the mess" just to "get even" when the price climbs back to $32. Similarly, if a stockholder was lucky enough to buy the stock when it was $30 and the price subsequently moved up to $47, he is likely to sell the stock should it decline to $29, "just to get back his money."

There is another aspect of this legend. You will recall that support level is a barrier to price decline and that resistance level is a barrier to price advancement. Though a barrier is an obstruction, it is by no means impassable; stock prices do break support and resistance barriers. Let us see how that might happen.

In our earlier example, if the outlook for Scilk Corporation is very bright, more and more people will buy the stock between $29 and $32 in the hope of a substantial price increase in the near future. A strong base will then be established around $32, and people will have to pay higher prices for that stock. Under these conditions, the stock will very likely break the resistance level. When that happens, the new high (say, $38–$40) will become the resistance level and the present ($32) level will constitute the support level. Incidentally, like individual stocks, the market also creates its own resistance and support levels. The market occasionally breaks them for roughly the same reasons which apply to individual stocks.

Two more legends of considerable interest to us involve the *odd-lot statistics* and *short interest* (an index of stocks sold which must be bought and delivered by sellers at a subsequent date). The odd-lotters are those small investors who, believing in the maxim "you can't go broke with a little profit," always appear to sell too quickly on a price rise. As a class, however, the odd-lotters always buy more than they sell. But more important, they buy when prices are high and sell when prices are low. This view is widely held in the market. As a matter of fact, based on the premise that odd-lotters are always wrong, and taking advantage of odd-lot figures regularly published in the *Wall Street Journal*, many astute and seasoned speculators gear their own activities to those of odd-lotters; they sell when odd-lot purchases increase and buy when odd-lotters sell.

The short-interest legend, which is just as interesting, is partially based upon the odd-lot theory. Essentially, short interest represents the volume of stocks which have been sold by those who did not have them in their possession. The sellers sold short because they expected prices to fall; they hope to buy the stocks more cheaply later and cover their short interest. Since the persons who sell short expect the price of the stock to fall, a large and rising short-interest position reflects the bearish outlook of the short sellers. However—and here is the twist—since according to the odd-lot theory the small investor is always wrong, this bearish outlook usually signals a strong market to the seasoned investor. Let me elaborate this point further.

According to the short-interest theory, a rising short interest is bullish for the market, whereas a falling short interest is bearish. The same logic holds good for individual securities. The reason is that short sellers eventually have to cover their positions; hence a rising short interest represents a growing volume of potential demand for the related stocks. Furthermore, the process feeds on itself: as the price of the stock goes up, short sellers are scared and begin to purchase stocks in order to cover their sales, thereby pushing the price still higher. These sales by short sellers scare other short sellers, who begin to make their purchases, and so on.

Two major flaws in the above explanation were spelled out by Barton Biggs.[65] First, the composition of the short interest is widely misunderstood. About two weeks after the Stock Exchange figures are published, the SEC releases numbers which break down the total short interest four ways, showing short sales by specialists and by each of three other groups. On the average, specialists account for about 55 percent of the total short sales. So it would be foolish to assume that the specialists behave like uninformed odd-lotters. Second, most statistical studies undertaken to test the hypotheses that increasing short interest in a stock is bullish for that stock have come to the following conclusion: A high and rising short interest does *not* have an upward price impact on stocks; nor does a declining short interest have any bearing on the price decline of that stock. For these two reasons Biggs concludes that "the only reason to read the short interest tables is to find out what the volatile stocks are. They don't prove anything else." Biggs's conclusion does fortify my own position: short interest is not a proven theory but a market legend. Often, nevertheless, it works.

In passing, I would like to mention a news item which appeared in the *WSJ* on June 17, 1970. The headlines read:

Wrong Again?
Small Investor Stays Bearish, So Analysts Foresee Market Upturn
Jump in Odd-Lot Short Sales Is Viewed as Sign Bottom Is Near in the Price Slide[66]

I think the above headlines are self-explanatory.

Another market legend, not so widely known, involves what might be termed the *stock-bond competition*. The theory holds that when bond prices are low (and bond yields are high), stocks will face heavy competition with bonds for investors' funds and, as a result, as long as bond yields remain high, the stock market will stay bearish. But when prices in the bond market firm up and bond yields decline, that is considered to be one of the best bullish indicators, and the expectation is that soon the stock market will begin to chart an upward course.

RANDOM WALK LORE: A NOVELTY

In an earlier chapter I talked about the celebrated Dow theory and its waning popularity. No matter how much confidence in the Dow theory declines, and no matter how small its effectiveness as a market predictor appears to be, proponents of the theory strongly assert that it provides at least some assistance in predicting future market trends. This assertion is undoubtedly based on the belief that successive changes in a stock's price level are dependent upon each other. Another group of investors, the proponents of the Random Walk theory, however, asserts that the position of the Dow theorists is untenable and that future price movements cannot be predicted by studying past price behavior.

In order to make a judgment about the validity of the Random Walk theory it is first necessary to understand the opposite views. In an interesting article, C. W. Granger has summarized these views in the following manner. According to him, the proponents of the theory deal with sequences of actual prices, either of individual stocks or of market indices. The question they pose is: Given such a sequence of prices, can one predict future price changes by using past prices? The answer is consistently "no." Granger says:

Two points about this work must be emphasized. Firstly, the type of question asked is similar to asking "What will the price of General Motors be next Friday?" Secondly, the prediction is to be made *only* using past prices of General Motors. Thus, prices are to be predicted in absolute terms and a limitation is placed on the kind of information that is to be used when making the prediction. The question of whether or not future prices can be predicted using *all* the world's available information, such as earnings, dividends, expectations, indices of business confidence or even prices of other stocks, is . . . [never raised].[67]

The opponents of the Random Walk theory reject it on several grounds. For one thing, they do not believe that ignoring all facts except past price behavior is a valid requirement. For another, they claim[68] that out of a given set of, say, 50 stocks, financial analysts can choose a group of 10 stocks which, on the average, will outperform the rest. These arguments by no means prove that the Random Walk theory is incorrect. They do, however, point out that the proponents and the opponents of the theory seem to make different sets of assumptions; consequently the twain shall never meet.

Therefore it is clear that the Random Walk theory has not so far been either proved or disproved. However, the results of an interesting study[69] conducted at the University of Michigan several years ago does provide some clue to the general belief of most investors that the theory usually works. This study covered the period January 15, 1950, to January 15, 1961, during which the Dow Jones Industrial Average increased by an impressive 218 percent. The list was composed of those 91 industrial stocks which reached a trading volume of more than 1 million shares during the calendar year of 1936.

In this study a hypothetical investor was assumed to invest $1,000 in each of the 91 issues on the 15th day of January in each of the 12 years, ending on January 15, 1961. It was further assumed that he reinvested all cash dividends, stock rights, and stock dividends. It was found that this investor's performance was as good as would be the case if he had invested in Dow Jones Industrial stocks. Also, it was found that the outcome would not have been very different had the hypothetical investor bought fewer than 91 stocks.

It is possible to conclude on the basis of the above study that if it doesn't make any difference which stocks are purchased by the long-term investor (or, in technical jargon, if the Random Walk theory of stock price movements is true), then all your efforts to understand the market and its theories have been misdirected. While I cannot quarrel with the findings of this or similar studies, I would repeat that at this time there are not sufficient reasons for accepting or rejecting the Random Walk theory. Consequently, I would be inclined to call this theory a Random Walk legend.

THE POPULAR MYTHS

Finally, let me describe some of the ubiquitous myths that are rampant in the stock market. It is important to reiterate that many investors are convinced that these theories work, and for this reason the myths are perpetuated.

One of the oldest myths in the market is: "Hold 'em forever." It is not uncommon for a person to say that he would never sell his HIF (Hold It Forever) stock because that was his father's favorite investment. This sentiment would be logical in some instances but totally illogical in others. For example, had a long-term investor put $1,000 in Xerox Corporation stock in 1957 when it was at its lowest and sold it on June 20, 1967, when it was at its highest, the value of his investment would have grown to $130,407. On the other hand, if the same investor had put $1,000 in Stutz Bearcat in 1957 and held it till today, he would have lost all his money.

The second myth is: "You can never go broke by taking a little profit." This is fallacious reasoning, for those who go in and out of the market collecting bits and pieces of money usually wind up generating large incomes only for their brokers. By attempting to outguess the market, they sometimes lose large sums of money. At other times they lose the opportunity to participate in the price appreciation of good stocks by bailing out too soon. Consider this classic case. If a person had bought 100 shares of IBM in 1914 for $2,750, he could have sold them in 1925 for $6,340. But if he exercised patience and held on to these shares, in 1961 the original 100 shares would have grown to 15,151, and the market value would have increased to $7,200,000.

The third myth is: "Always cut your losses quickly." This too is a short-term view of the world and is not always sustainable. Obviously, you do not wish to ride all the way downhill with a stock, but neither should you sell it hastily in the hope of picking up the stock when it reaches bottom. If you had bought 100 shares of Burroughs Corporation at 55 a share for $5,500 and had quickly taken a loss of $500 when it touched $50, you would have missed a price hike to the $240 level and would have lost a profit of $18,500.

Another myth of some validity is: "Don't sell on strike news." After all, you may argue, a prolonged labor strike might ruin a company's prospects for long-term growth. While this may be true in some cases, in others it is not. Ford Motor Company was hit by a long strike but quickly recuperated from its losses.

Here is the cutest myth of all: "A bull can make money. A bear can make money. But a hog never can." This has some validity as an admonition against always trying to buy at the low and sell at the high. It says that many people fail, due to greed, to make substantial profits because they hold on too long in the hope of making more. Again, this generalization is a part truth and is not a final guide to investment decisions.

There are several other beliefs so widely held that they have become an integral part of stock market folklore. One relates to low-priced stocks. Many believe that as a general rule the low-priced stocks move faster than their high-priced counterparts. Others prefer to buy low-priced stocks because they can buy more shares with the same amount of money.

Another widely held belief is that one should always sell on good news. It is argued that seasoned investors make their purchases before the good news comes out, since they always have advance information. Consequently, when the news becomes public knowledge and the small man begins to buy that stock in the hope of an appreciable price increase, astute investors are sellers of that stock, pirating away most of the price advance which has already occurred.

The faith in the traditional year-end rally should also be mentioned. Most losers, so it is said, wait until the very end of the year to take their tax losses. This creates an artificial selling pressure, thereby depressing the prices of many attractive stocks and providing excellent buying opportunities for those who have ready cash stacked in their vaults. In this situation one should make his purchases during the year-end sell-off period. I caution you not to put complete faith in this type of buying opportunity, since more and more investors are becoming sophisticated and are taking their losses earlier in the year.

I cannot close this chapter without referring to the myth of "Blue Monday." It is widely believed that the market tends to go down on Mondays, more so than on other days. There is no real truth to this belief, but if enough investors are convinced that it is true, perhaps they will bring their feelings to bear on the market and cause prices to decline.

In conclusion, I can do no better than to quote Professor James Lorie, who emphasizes the need for dispelling myths and strengthening the theoretical quality of market studies:

It is clear that much of the work done so far has had the effect of discrediting beliefs—and even some relatively sophisticated ones—about the behavior of security prices. Much of the work now in process centers on the careful testing of more such beliefs, and I feel safe in predicting that the majority of the findings will be of the same general sort.

If this were all that might be accomplished, and it is not, it would still be valuable work. For research workers, it is important to test the ground and clear it as a foundation for evolving theory. For the businessman and investor, it is also true that an awareness of ignorance is better than an erroneous belief, if only because it tends to eliminate buying the services of charlatans and attending to the insignificant.[70]

19

Unwalling Wall Street

One way of unwalling Wall Street is to suggest that Honoré de Balzac, who wrote *The Human Comedy*—the 19th-century epic which re-created French society of the time—might have found the Street a more exciting place to explore than Paris, had he known the mysteries surrounded by the Street's walls. Plagued by immensely complicated problems and drenched in the fragrance of success of the millionaires, Wall Street has always attracted—and continues to attract—people of all walks of life. In this chapter I plan to unfold some of the mysteries surrounding the stock market and talk about some of the reasons why Wall Street continues to be a place of major significance.

THE MYSTERIOUS WALL STREET

On November 13, 1970, Ralph Saul, president of the American Stock Exchange, mailed a very important letter to the ASE members. Using extraordinarily strong language, Saul stated that, in his opinion, the nation's stock exchanges and other securities industry components weren't effectively solving the industry's severe problems and that new organizations or arrangements for making and enforcing decisions might be necessary. In the words of David McClintick,[71] ". . . the letter amount[ed] to a fundamental indictment of the securities industry's existing structure and, by implication, a criticism of its principal internal and main external regu-

209

lators, the New York Stock Exchange and the Securities and Exchange Commission."

In this letter, Saul made a series of proposals to improve the securities industry's operations. He suggested that the industry should:

1. Develop organization and methods to coordinate industry operating systems, eliminate duplication, and make more efficient use of existing resources.
2. Reverse the continuing fragmentation of the central markets, often encouraged by regulatory policies that work to the disadvantage of the public and the industry.
3. Develop better methods for bringing the views of the major elements involved in our markets into the decision-making processes.
4. Develop, in cooperation with government, agreement on major public policy objectives so that the securities industry can plan with greater certainty and the self-regulators can exercise their responsibilities more effectively.

Saul's criticisms and proposals take on special meaning when viewed against the background of an ailing Wall Street: Three years of crisis had rudely shaken investor confidence in Wall Street. An analysis in depth of the nature of this crisis was prepared by *Business Week*.[72] Let me summarize from this article some of the important aspects of the crisis.

One of the major problems facing Wall Street is that it permits the professionals and the nonprofessionals to share the same market, even though their objectives and methods of operation are very different. It is interesting to note that Wall Street is planning a 50 percent raise in commissions for small investors on the ground that brokers lose money in their business. At the same time, it proposes that banks, mutual funds, insurance companies, and other institutional investors receive "volume discounts" of up to 25 percent.

Big investors have various advantages over their small brothers. They have more information about the market and individual stocks than the small investors. Also, a great many big investors often avoid the public auction market and negotiate prices among themselves. This diverts enough trading from the New York exchanges to threaten the key role that these exchanges play, and it establishes a double trading standard—one for big investors and one for small ones.

A different sort of problem is created on Wall Street by the advent of large-scale computers and the associated plans to use them for automatic trading of stocks. In 1971, nonmember brokers and dealers are likely to begin trading the NYSE and the AMEX stocks over a nationwide computerized network. When that happens, the brokerage business may suffer a heavy loss.

During the 1967–68 boom, the 15-million to 20-million-share days caused an unprecedented paper mess which still haunts Wall Street. Many brokerage firms credited investors with stocks which they never bought, while others failed to deliver securities to their purchasers. At one point, certificates for some $4.1 billion worth of stock were overdue. During the 1969–70 slack, the problem was eased but not solved. All parties concerned recognize that steps must be taken to ameliorate the situation, but no one is quite sure what must be done.

Of all the problems mentioned, none is more acute than the liquidity problem facing the entire securities industry. During the heyday of 1967–69, many brokerage firms treated the market like a king-size gambling casino, trading in highly volatile stocks and spreading themselves very thin. Then, when the market slump occurred, their finances crumbled. Today one hears of one brokerage firm after another closing its doors or merging with another firm because of its inability to meet the Street's capital rule. Worse, the trust funds set up to help the troubled firms are too small to cope with the situation.

I have mentioned only some of the problems facing Wall Street. There are others which also need to be solved. But instead of describing the other problems, I would prefer to undertake an in-depth discussion of some of the major problems.

Paper Blizzard and a Think Tank

One of the mysteries of Wall Street is the way in which it braves the paper blizzard which blows over it. Let me describe the nature of this blizzard and what is being done to save the Street from it.

On January 2, 1970, the city of New York was hit by two blizzards. Outdoors on Wall Street the white stuff piled up, halting traffic and creating road hazards. Inside, Wall Street was hit by a paper blizzard that created worse hazards. At 3 P.M., a delivery clerk pushed through messengers and griped: "How long do they think we can keep going like this?"

Unfortunately, the securities industry is going to go on choking on its paper work for a long time to come. The governors of the New York and the American Stock Exchanges have been searching frantically for ways to break the paper work glut. Yet all indicators point to the fact that, unless proper steps are taken, Wall Street will be ill equipped to handle the 30-million to 40-million-share trading days which are expected by the late 1970's. In fact, a 25 million–28 million share day during the latter part of 1971 appears to be a distinct possibility.

That is frightening. Wall Street currently cannot cope with a daily volume of 15 million shares for any length of time. Despite stiffer regulations, short weeks, and trading limits on some brokerage houses, the paper blizzard is still not efficiently controlled.

All along, the exchanges have attemped to do something about this chaos. As early as the fall of 1968, a system was devised by which the New York and the American Stock Exchanges could feed all trades into computer systems that were doing an efficient job of keeping the tape abreast of current prices. The same systems could analyze trading patterns to detect unusual situations that would have required immediate action. The NYSE also used computers installed below the main trading floor to keep tabs on odd-lot transactions.

That is not all. Computers in clearinghouses for both exchanges and for some over-the-counter stocks yielded faster and better clearing information for brokers. Plans called for eventually making stock transfers through the clearinghouse computers without handling stock certificates.

As is always the case with the Street bosses, they were dissatisfied with the progress. So in February, 1969, the two big exchanges announced that, for an estimated cost of $1.1 million, they had taken the paper work mess to a "think tank." The RAND Corporation of Santa Monica, California, was hired to bring fresh ideas, or what is known as a systems approach, to the paper work crisis. RAND was asked to solve, among others, two major problems. One problem related to the way in which a transaction passed through 50 different steps. RAND was asked to devise a means by which the computerized clearing function could be integrated with the CCS, which kept stock certificates on deposit and simply recorded transactions among brokers' accounts without the certificates physically moving from place to place.

The other problem was to straighten out the mess which had accumulated in the amorphous over-the-counter market, where many little dealers operated with no central marketplace and where most of the Street's errors and failures to deliver stocks originated. As possible solutions to these problems, RAND hoped to create a nationwide system of regional clearinghouses interconnected by computers. This network could also be incorporated into CCS.

After a year and a half of intensive study, RAND Corporation produced a voluminous report in the fall of 1970 in which it asserted that substantial cost savings could be attained without altering the industry's overall structure. The Corporation also pointed out that the most effective steps would include a combined effort by major banks in New York to automate their transfer facilities and to enforce existing stock market rules requiring brokers to accept partial deliveries of securities from one another. However, the report did not recommend the establishment of a central depository to reduce the physical handling of stock certificates.

The RAND report was received enthusiastically by industry leaders. But how many of the recommendations will be finally put into action—and when—still remains to be seen.

During the recession of 1969–70, when RAND was still working on the paper problem, the average daily volume on Wall Street appeared to recede as the market suffered a major setback and investors lost millions of dollars. However, the governors considered this easing of the problem as purely temporary and therefore did not give up their efforts toward taking permanent steps for handling the paper work. For instance, during the summer of 1970, the NYSE sent out a memorandum of security analysts to its members urging the greater use of large-denomination certificates. This, according to the exchange, was expected to reduce "unnecessary handling, record keeping and expense to companies, transfer agents, as well as to all those who receive, deliver or hold the certificates." Another effort to reduce paper work was made when the exchange expressed its interests in a modified-fees plan. According to this plan, the brokerage fees for small transactions would be raised which, it was hoped, would discourage small investors from entering into numerous small transactions and generating "useless" paper work.

In this connection, I would like to mention that during the latter part of 1970 the securities industry took a number of steps that laid the groundwork for the elimination of the stock certificate. Thus, said Eli Weinberg:

. . . we are faced with the paradox of the securities community's developing much-needed programs for central automated clearing facilities, insurance for investors against losses due to brokerage house failures, automated handling of odd lots, use of CUSIP (Committee on Uniform Security Identification Procedures) number systems, but stopping short of working directly toward the goal to which these steps can lead—the elimination of the stock certificate and with it the myriad of problems that this paper generates.[73]

The securities industry finds the back-office problem as damaging on an 8-million-share day as on a 16-million-share day. Firms are unable to cope with the massive paper work, partly because of the high cost of handling. The elimination of the stock certificate might solve—or at least reduce—the problem. However, so far the securities industry has refused to support such a move.

Wall Street continues to be plagued by the paper work mess, and no one expects that the problem will go away. However, if RAND Corporation's suggestions are implemented, paper work can at least be brought under control.

When Brokers Go Broke

The paper work mess is only one type of problem which Wall Street faces today. The problem really gets sticky when brokers begin to go broke.

In a very real sense the brokers are the cornerstone of investor confidence. They play a very important role in making an orderly market, as well as in shifting stocks from sellers to buyers. All this is done fairly smoothly when the market is good, but what happens when the market turns sour is a very different matter.

The 1969–70 market crash provided the testing ground for the viability of brokerage firms. During this period, some 150 U.S. brokerage houses went into liquidation, including half a dozen major member firms of the NYSE. Hundreds of other brokers were forced to merge or drastically cut back their operations. True, the New York and American Stock Exchanges maintained trust accounts to bail out the ailing but deserving brokerage firms; but because of the magnitude of losses, the trust funds proved too small to provide any real assistance. At the latest count, in November, 1970, at least 25,000 investors had assets in brokerage accounts frozen pending disposition in the bankruptcy courts.

What had gone wrong in the brokerage business to bring about this catastrophe? It appears that the combination of too much spending to solve the paper mess, too little income during the market crash, and too much commitment in go-go stocks had all contributed to a collapse of the brokerage business. Besides, during the 1967–69 market boom, many firms let their standards slip to the point where they lacked the necessary financial strength and managerial skills to serve the public market.

One of the giant brokerage firms which did not survive the crisis was Hayden, Stone, Inc., founded as long ago as 1892. It had survived two world wars, the Great Depression, and several later recessions. But it could not bear the intolerable burden of the 1969–70 market crash. In desperation, in the summer of 1970 it merged with Cogan, Berlind, Weill & Levitt, Inc.

Another legendary Wall Street firm—Goodbody & Company—could not endure the stresses that the last few years have generated: first, the incredible prosperity of the late 1960's when everybody wanted common stocks, followed by the recession of 1969–70 when everybody seemed to lose interest in them. Early in the fall of 1970, the company was informed by the Street bosses that it was in violation of the exchange's capital regulation. Goodbody first disclosed its plan to raise $30 million in order to comply with the law. After a careful study of the company's plans, the Big Board pointed out to Goodbody that, of the new financing of $30 million, $10 million would not count toward fulfilling the firm's capital needs, since this amount represented a planned conversion by the families of Goodbody partners of the already existing subordinated loans to limited partnership interests in the firm. Almost simultaneously, Goodbody's previously announced acquisition by Shareholders Capital Corporation fell through when the Los Angeles–based mutual fund manager pulled out of the deal.

Left with no other alternative, in October, 1970 Goodbody approached Merrill Lynch, Pierce, Fenner & Smith, Inc.—the largest brokerage firm—with the hope that they would acquire the financially straitened firm.

Merrill Lynch, backed by a planned $30 million guarantee from the NYSE member-firm community, carefully considered the proposal and finally agreed to acquire Goodbody. The news made quite a splash on the financial scene and raised some questions about a possible antitrust action. Merrill Lynch had some 1.3 million customers, 200 branch offices, and $288 million capital. Goodbody, with about 350,000 customers, 90 branches, and $35 million capital, ranked among the five largest. The merger could produce a giant much too powerful for a competitive industry. However, considering the singular situation, it seemed unlikely that any antitrust action would be taken to block a merger.

On November 5 Merrill Lynch finally came to the rescue of Goodbody: it signed a series of agreements with Goodbody that implemented previously announced terms of acquisition and at the same time the Board of Governors of the NYSE endorsed a proposed constitutional amendment that would assess Big Board members up to $30 million to indemnify Merrill Lynch for certain losses in the proposed acquisition. The merger was finally completed on December 10, 1970.

Like the stories of Hayden, Stone, Inc., and Goodbody & Co., there are other distressing stories of mergers and liquidations which have recently been written on the walls of Wall Street. Although the plot of each story is unique, each has a common theme: each firm violated the Big Board's capital rules which specify that a member firm's liabilities may not exceed 20 times its liquid capital. This raises some serious questions: Why are all these firms short of capital, and what prevents them from raising the required capital on the market? These questions cannot be answered without an understanding of the complicated capital requirements which each firm must fulfill.

The Wall Street capital requirements are simplified by Carol Loomis. The basic capital requirement is that every exchange member firm doing business with the public must have at least $1 of net capital for every $20 of aggregate indebtedness. Roughly the same requirement extends to all broker-dealers who are not members of the exchange but who do business with the public. Aggregate indebtedness includes credit balances owed to customers and money owed to other brokers and to banks. Net capital includes a firm's total equity and debt capital after certain deductions are made in the interest of safety. For example, a firm must deduct its investment in furniture, since this is not a readily marketable asset. Similarly, at least 30 percent of the value of any common stocks owned within the firm must be deducted—in a process known as "the haircut"—to arrive at net capital. Finally, there are "penalty" haircuts, which are intended to discourage certain kinds of business (mainly commodities) or to discipline the broker whose substandard operations leave something to be desired.

After all deductions are made, the residue—called the net capital—may not be sufficient to pay off the creditors in case of liquidation. The reasons are explained by Loomis:

One of these is that net capital, even after all of those deductions, may still have some rather strange components. For the brokerage industry, unlike more normal businesses, does not raise all of its capital in the form of cash. Instead, many firms get part of their capital in the form of securities, which in effect, they borrow and treat as debt. The lenders are normally customers of the borrowing firm or sometimes outside investors, and their loans usually become identified on the firm's balance sheet as "subordinated accounts" or "secured demand notes." These lenders continue to own their securities, and to benefit from their dividends, interest, and appreciation (or, as the case may be, suffer from their depreciation). Then, as payment, they receive interest from the borrowing firm—the normal rate has been 4 percent—or some other form of compensation. In good times, it is a very nice deal for the lender. What investor would not like to earn an extra 4 percent interest on his securities while holding them? But in bad times, the deal turns sour, for another part of the arrangement is that the lender must subordinate his claims against the firm— i.e., his right to recover his securities—to the claims of all other creditors. Thus, if a borrowing firm runs into real trouble, lenders of this variety are likely to end up losing their shirts.

The firms that borrow these securities do so in order to build their net capital and stretch their capacity to do business. But in a bear market, these stocks (on which a haircut would apply) are apt to decline in value, with the result that the firm's capital also shrinks.[74]

What, then, are the steps which must be taken to avoid the capital mess on Wall Street? There are several steps which would improve the situation. Among these, the following rank as the most important: (1) a crackdown on brokerage firms; (2) improvement in the brokerage fees structure; (3) customers' insurance; and (4) public ownership of brokerage firms.

A Crackdown on Brokerage Firms

The present crisis in brokerage firms has demonstrated beyond a doubt that many of these firms have neither the financial nor the technical power to serve the public. Worse, it has shown that all too often brokers have excited their customers' speculative fervor and have committed themselves heavily in speculative stocks, often with disastrous results. For example, in March, 1970 Hayden, Stone, Inc., acquired blocks of five stocks worth nearly $18 million from lenders who, as compensation, received long-term options to buy Hayden stocks. Of this $18 million, $3.3 million was represented by shares of Four Seasons Nursing Centers, which in May, 1970 were suspended from trading by the SEC. Hayden suffered losses because of precipitous declines in the prices of CMI Corporation, Carousel Fashions, LSB Industries, and Woods Corporation. Another major brokerage firm, Kleiner & Bell, was pushed into liquidation when the conglomerate company called Commonwealth United collapsed in the bear market. Similar stories can be told about Gregory & Sons and Dempsey-Tegeler.

The shakeout of brokerage firms has raised doubts about the quality of their management and has underscored the need for the New York Stock Exchange to become involved in the management of these firms. The first such involvement of the exchange in the affairs of member firms was in 1968 when it began to put firms on "restriction," limiting their freedom to seek new business or to expand until they could show competence in handling their back-office problems. No less than 105 of the exchange's some 600 member firms were put on restriction at one time or another.

In 1969, the exchange began to interfere more directly with the management of member firms. It ordered certain firms to liquidate, close down some of their branch offices, merge with other firms, and improve their quality of management. In addition, the exchange began to impose its capital rules much more strictly than before.

The NYSE took another major step in this direction by sending a confidential circular to top management of member firms. The circular disallowed for capital purposes so-called control securities—those owned by a person or group effectively controlling the affairs of the corporation that issued the securities. The exchange also placed certain restrictions on the treatment of control stock pledged as collateral in customers' margin (credit) accounts. All this has had an impact on the brokerage business, although it is too early to tell just how much improvement will result from these interferences.

Improvement in the Brokerage Fees Structure

Ever since the market upsurge began to taper off in 1968, one of the major gripes of the brokerage firms has been that the commissions permitted under SEC rules were much too low relative to their high operating costs. After mulling over the question for more than two years, in February, 1970 the exchange disclosed a plan for the new schedule of commissions (see Table 19–1).

TABLE 19–1

PROPOSED BROKERAGE FEES STRUCTURE

Shares	Commissions on $40 Stock		Percent Change
	Present	Proposed	
30	$ 17	$ 26.20	+54¾
100	39	65.56	+68
200	78	86.43	+11
300	117	106.03	− 9
1,000	390	243.74	−38
100,000	23,160	16,790.37	−28

Source: Business Week, February 21, 1970.

The new commissions would provide member firms with a 10 percent increase in revenues. Small investors would pay for the increase, while the institutional and other large investors would get a break in commission rates. The most important change to be brought about by the new schedule would be that commissions would be based upon the actual cost per transaction rather than upon dollar volume.

As might be expected, the new commission plan touched off a furor among small investors. Quite legitimately, they began to complain about the increase in commissions on small transactions—sometimes as much as 115 percent—when charges on big trades were scaled downward. But their major gripe was that they were being tapped for more money at a time when the securities industry's customer service was being plagued by mistakes, late stock deliveries, and, in some cases, no stock deliveries at all. While recognizing these as legitimate complaints, the NYSE supported its plan on the grounds that its members had not had a rate hike since 1958 and that larger commissions would pave the way for better service performances by the firms.

FIGURE 19–1
CAPITAL RATIOS OF NEW YORK STOCK EXCHANGE MEMBER FIRMS
(May 31, 1970)

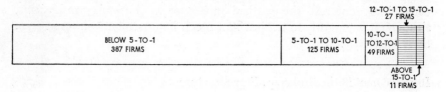

Source: Fortune, July, 1970, p. 141.

As the weeks passed, the stock fees controversy worsened. On April 22, Robert W. Haack, president of the NYSE, felt obliged to present in full-page newspaper advertisements "eleven facts to help . . . understand the changes in stock fees." Two months later, on June 11, John Schreiner, assistant professor of finance at the University of Minnesota, published in the WSJ a full-length article, "Stock Fees: Debating the Big Board," evaluating the various aspects of the proposed plan and recommending readjustment of the plan in favor of the small investor.

Early in October, the WSJ carried an article showing (see Table 19–2) that during 1969 only 12 of the top Big Board firms were in the black on commission business; the rest incurred losses, in some instances as much as $50 million each. The news of the poor showing by brokerage firms influenced the SEC, and during the third week of October the commission finally reacted to the exchange's new fees plan. While the SEC cleared major portions of the plan, it demanded modification of some of its key parts. The SEC asked that rate increases in the 100-share to 400-share range of orders be rolled back as much as 25 percent from the rises originally proposed by the Big Board. In a challenge to the Big Board's traditional concept of fixed minimum commissions, the SEC asserted that fixed

TABLE 19–2

PERFORMANCE OF TWELVE BIG BOARD FIRMS

Firm (1968 Ranking)	Ratio Securities Income to all Income	Registered Reps. Salaries	Total Operating Expenses (a)	Partners Comp.	Profit Before Fed. Taxes	1969 Net Profit	1968 Net Profit
1. Salomon Bros. (1)	31.2	9.9	34.7	4.3	61.0	28.8	21.2
2. Goldman, Sachs (2)	46.6	12.3	58.0	2.8	39.2	18.5	16.2
3. Donaldson, Lufkin (3) . .	81.1	. . . .	37.6	24.3	38.1	18.0	15.6
4. White, Weld (4)	46.0	24.1	78.8	3.3	17.9	8.5	12.8
5. A.G. Becker (6)	55.5	7.4	69.1	15.0	15.9	7.5	11.5
6. Shields (9)	63.4	15.0	73.8	10.4	15.8	7.5	8.5
7. Smith, Barney (8)	50.0	17.1	83.1	3.1	13.8	6.6	9.7
8. Oppenheimer (5)	80.8	16.2	85.9	2.5	11.6	5.5	12.4
9. Kidder, Peabody (13)	46.4	19.0	84.3	5.6	10.1	4.8	6.4
10. Eastman Dillon (27) . . .	46.8	22.9	90.9	1.7	7.4	3.5	1.4
11. Burnham (18)	66.7	12.7	88.6	5.7	5.7	2.7	4.2
12. Bear, Stearns (12)	61.8	14.6	76.5	18.8	4.7	2.2	6.7
13. Reynolds (19)	58.1	25.1	95.7	5.0	d0.7	d0.3	4.0
14. Clark, Dodge (14)	63.2	12.3	93.9	7.5	d1.4	d0.7	6.2
15. Loeb, Rhoades (17)	66.6	11.7	99.4	3.2	d2.6	d1.2	4.8
16. Dean Witter (16)	53.8	17.4	97.8	7.9	d5.7	d2.7	5.3
17. Dominick & Dom. (24) . .	72.5	13.7	100.5	5.2	d5.7	d2.7	2.5
18. Merrill Lynch (15)	48.7	25.7	101.7	4.7	d6.4	d3.0	6.0
19. Lehman Bros. (11)	29.2	14.5	105.7	2.3	d8.0	d3.8	7.1
20. Hentz (21)	58.7	25.5	107.0	4.0	d11.0	d5.2	3.5
21. Harris, Upham (22)	73.0	35.0	107.1	4.7	d11.8	d5.6	2.8
22. E.F. Hutton (28)	59.1	27.8	108.5	4.9	d13.4	d6.3	1.4
23. Paine, Webber (34)	56.7	29.6	109.5	5.6	d15.1	d7.2	d2.0
24. Weis, Voisin (31)	67.4	15.3	108.7	7.8	d16.5	d7.8	0.4
25. Hornblower (29)	44.7	25.5	114.0	2.9	d16.9	d8.0	1.0
26. Walston (25)	58.7	29.9	109.6	8.5	d18.1	d8.5	2.0
27. Goodbody (37)	59.2	26.6	114.6	3.6	d18.2	d8.6	d4.8
28. W.E. Hutton (26)	62.3	22.9	113.1	5.2	d18.3	d8.7	1.4
29. Shearson, Hammill (30) .	57.5	30.5	115.5	7.0	d22.5	d10.6	0.9
30. Bache (32)	59.4	28.9	122.4	4.6	d27.0	d12.7	d0.1
31. F.I. duPont (33)	52.5	29.1	133.2	7.5	d40.7	d19.2	d1.3
32. Hayden, Stone (38)	50.2	28.2	142.6	7.8	d50.4	d23.8	d9.8
AVERAGES OF 32 FIRMS	53.8	22.2	99.6	5.8	d5.4	d2.6	z3.7

a Besides registered representatives (salesmen's) compensation, includes clerical, administration, communications, occupancy, equipment, promotional and other operating costs.

d Loss.

z Average of 38 firms in 1968.

Note: Above are the 1969 operating ratios, in percentages figures, of the 32 largest New York Stock Exchange member firms surveyed in the report. They are clearing firms that had commission revenue of $20 million or more from 1969 securities transactions. Also included are the firms' 1968 profit margins and their relative standings in 1968, when there were 38 firms grossing at least $20 million commission revenue.

Source: Wall Street Journal, October 9, 1970, p. 3.

rates for portions of stock orders over 100,000 were neither "necessary nor appropriate," and suggested that the plan be modified.

In closing the discussion of this topic, I would like to point out that even with the acceptance by the SEC of the modified fees plan, the stock fee debate was not ended. On November 11, 1970 the *WSJ* carried the following news item, which strongly suggests that this debate would likely continue for some time to come:

Leaders representing practically all segments of the securities industry are to meet this afternoon with the ultimate purpose of developing a united position from which to negotiate with the Securities and Exchange Commission on a new brokerage-fee schedule, industry sources disclosed.[75]

Customer's Insurance

When Francis I. du Pont & Company closed its brokerage branch in Kuwait early in 1970 as part of a general retrenchment program, the resident sheikh temporarily held as hostages some of the company's key personnel, pending a settlement of accounts. Since most investors are not fortunate enough to be able to take the action that the sheikh took, and since many investors have been—and continue to be—hurt by widespread brokerage firm failures, it is apropos to talk about some type of investor protection.

Recent actions by uneasy investors have been geared to shielding themselves from the danger of broker failures. Some have gone to unusual lengths. One investor tried unsuccessfully to find an insurance company that would sell him a policy to protect him against the possible insolvency of his broker, perhaps on a group basis with other investors. Other investors have removed—and continue to remove—their securities from control of their brokers as quickly as possible after transactions are made in their behalf. The lack of confidence in the market is rather frightening, since the whole system of trading stocks is based on a "self-regulating" monopoly of member brokers, and the success of this system is assured only if investors are happy with it. It is doubtful, however, if investors as individuals can solve this problem. They need help, and need it urgently.

A key agency which is empowered to take important measures in this area is the National Association of Securities Dealers (NASD). In early 1970, the NASD began its efforts to determine the potential risk to public investors of any insolvency that might occur among NASD nonmembers. There were approximately 3,800 NASD members who did not belong to stock exchanges and thus were not protected by the trust funds that most stock exchanges maintained. About 700 other members of the NASD, the self-regulatory group which policed the over-the-counter securities market, did have overlapping stock exchange membership and were therefore partially protected. Unfortunately, the NASD was unable to gather sufficient information to enable it to suggest any firm actions. One major unanswered question for the NASD was how much customers' cash and securities were normally left on deposit with its nonexchange members. Such deposits were common among firms that performed stock brokerage business for public investors, and it was these deposits the customers lost when the firms closed their doors.

While the NASD does not yet have all the information it seeks, it has by no means given up. It is currently engaged in the task of getting some data on its nonexchange members, so that some action can be taken to protect the public if a nonexchange broker collapses.

Let us move on to the question of protection for those investors who are served by firms operating on the major exchanges. The law does provide for compensation of investors out of special trust funds for the losses incurred by them as a result of failures of brokerage firms. The New York and the American Stock Exchanges have access to such trust funds, but these funds have long since been depleted because too many firms had to be bailed out with these funds. At the present time there is nothing comparable in the vast over-the-counter market which may be used to protect investors trading in that market.

The issue of enlarging the existing trust funds received considerable national attention in the summer of 1970, when widespread brokerage house failures pointed to the inadequacy of the existing trust funds. The first major step was taken in July, when the SEC and the Treasury developed a plan to fulfill the need for a large trust fund. Under this plan, an initial $75 million fund which would grow to $150 million within five years, would be backed by a $1 billion credit line with the Treasury. Brokers would pay one eighth of 1 percent of their 1969 revenues (or $7 million) to initiate the fund. To that $7 million, plus $3 million from stock exchange funds, would be added a $65 million bank credit line. Future assessments of up to one half of 1 percent a year would bring the pool to the $150 million total.

The plan was received by the industry with mixed emotions. To some it was too ambitious; to others it wasn't ambitious enough. Among those in the latter group was Senator Edmund Muskie (D-Me.), who introduced in the fall of 1970 a House bill that would create a $1.15 billion pool to protect investors against loss when brokerage houses fail. The pool would be controlled by the Securities Investor Protection Corporation, a quasi-governmental body to be set up for this purpose.

Interestingly, the Senate Banking Committee accepted neither the SEC nor the Muskie plan, but approved a compromise plan instead. The Senate version would create a $75 million pool at the start—$10 million from brokerage houses and stock exchanges, plus a $65 million bank credit line, backed by a $1 billion credit line with the U.S. Treasury. Another version of this bill was being considered by a House Commerce Subcommittee at the turn of the year, and it did not appear that Congress could complete action on this bill much before the fall of 1971.

While the case for establishing a king-sized trust fund was bogged down in the House, the problem of shaky brokerage houses continued to haunt the securities industry. Left with no alternative, and in order to supplement the already depleted trust fund, in October, 1970 the exchange sought to add between $50–$80 million to its fully committed $55 million special trust fund. Meanwhile, a monkey wrench was thrown by an investor into the trust fund battle. A client of Robinson & Company, a former NYSE member in bankruptcy, filed a class action motion to halt further disbursement of trust fund money until the rights of Robinson's customers to fund assets were determined. The Robinson dispute focused on the fact that having access to a large trust fund wasn't sufficient to solve all problems; steps would have to be taken by the authorities to *prevent* widespread firm failures if law and order were to be restored in the securities worlds.

In January, 1971, the 91st Congress passed legislation setting up the Securities Investor Corporation. The Corporation protects investors up to $50,000 for securities and $20,000 for cash from the loss caused by the failure of a brokerage house.

Public Ownership of Brokerage Firms

On November 1, 1970, James Davant, managing partner of Paine, Webber, Jackson & Curtis, mailed the following letter to all the firm's customers:

We are pleased to announce that our firm, which has operated in the partnership form since 1879, has decided to incorporate. A corporation with the name Paine, Webber, Jackson & Curtis Incorporated has already been formed and we presently anticipate that the transfer of assets from the partnership to Paine, Webber, Jackson & Curtis Incorporated will take place prior to the opening of business on December 1, 1970.

Addition of the word "Incorporated" to our name will in no way alter our basic policies or fundamental operating procedures.[76]

The letter was indicative of the prevailing trend in the securities industry toward public ownership of brokerage firms.

Given the soaring volume of paper work and the need for more capital to finance the myriad services performed by brokers, it does not seem surprising that firms have definitely begun toying with the idea of going public. After all, the size of the investment community has clearly outstripped the facilities available to handle the necessary transactions, and the unilateral efforts of brokerage houses are at best likely to provide only a stopgap solution.

While some firms have already expressed their desires to transform themselves into publicly owned corporations and several others are contemplating a similar move, not everyone concerned with this problem is willing to accept this as a better alternative. As Carol Loomis points out, there are four reasons for such an opposition to the idea:

One, the Exchange's constitution at present effectively prohibits public owner-ship. Two, the Exchange community has for years hotly debated the advisa-bility of changing the constitution to permit public ownership. Three, the main reason it has not done so is that many of the Street's leaders fear that public ownership will lead to institutional membership—i.e., to a situation in which such big customers as the mutual funds and insurance companies will become members of the Exchange, a development that might well destroy the brokerage industry as it is now constituted. Four, while the industry has ample grounds for worry about this threat, public ownership could over the near term bring the current owners of Wall Street some extraordinary wealth—just how extraordinary most people have not realized.[77]

Partly for these reasons and partly for the exchange's traditional reluc-tance to make any change in Wall Street's rules, no one believed that the Street bosses would ever entertain the idea of public ownership of the exchange firms. However, on May 21, 1969, Donaldson, Lufkin & Jenrette, Inc. (DLJ), shook Wall Street's age-old tradition by announcing that it would sell its shares publicly.

Much water has flowed since that historic announcement. At first, the chairman and some senior officers of the exchange attempted to persuade DLJ to give up the idea to go public, but the firm decided to go ahead with its original plans. This raised the basic issue of public ownership of other firms, forcing the New York and the American Stock Exchanges to take positive steps toward finding a permanent solution to this sticky problem. RAND Corporation was entrusted with the task of determining the causes of "fails"—that is, the failures to deliver that result when one broker does not promptly come through with the securities he owes another—and of determining a methodology to reduce them. In September the NYSE's Board of Governors approved 15 amendments to a constitution that for 177 years had forbidden member firms to go public. These amendments specified that for at least the next three years, outsiders will not be able to own more than 49 percent of a firm and member firms will not be per-mitted to trade for any nonmember customer who owns a participation of 5 percent or more in the profits of the firm. Furthermore, it was required of all outside shareholders with more than 5 percent of the capital of a firm to obtain approval of the Board of Governors. In March, 1970, the SEC decided to back the New York Stock Exchange's plan to allow member firms to sell their stock publicly. In the following month (April, 1970), DLJ capped the decade by becoming the first member firm to go public, offering 800,000 shares of its common stock at $15 a share. And with that, a new tradition of public ownership of brokerage houses was firmly established.

BYPASS THE BROKER

So far I have been talking about various problems with brokerage firms which have developed in the recent past. A natural question is: "Can the broker be bypassed?" The answer is a qualified yes. Let me elaborate this point.

An article in *Business Week*[78] pointed out that one company had completed a master plan for bypassing the broker. Early in 1969 the Institutional Networks Corporation (INC), a tiny company by any standards, unveiled a system which by electronic means would permit large institutional investors to trade big blocks of stock instantly and anonymously. There would be no paper work and no errors. Banks, insurance companies, mutual funds, pension and endowment funds, and so on, would be able to trade, regardless of geographical location, without brokers and without commissions. To grasp the implications, all you need do is remember that institutional trading in the stock market accounted for roughly 50 percent of brokers' business in 1969. What's more, a large number of brokerage houses subsist entirely on institutional business.

Some of the details of the system suggested by INC are intriguing. To begin with, the minimum trade is 500 shares with a value of $25,000, so a subscriber can break up his blocks and work several deals at once. The subscriber can withdraw an entry at any time; he can also feint and parry in the marketplace at will. He can accumulate or distribute shares in complete secrecy. While negotiating a deal, he can put his "book entry" on "hold," so that the computer doesn't sell his position out from under him. Finally, because the system is separate from the exchanges, deals will not affect prices on the stock market. That means that heavy institutional selling will not send the public price plunging nor can a fund drive up a thinly capitalized issue with its own buying.

Obviously, the INC system faced rough going. For one thing, many institutions would want to maintain ties with brokers who also underwrote new issues or set up private placements. For another, launching this system would put numerous firms out of business. In any case, many institutions appeared to be interested in the concept, and someday it might get off the ground.

The suggested INC plan was just the beginning of a new trend toward automated trading. It was followed by the development of three major block trading systems—Big Board, Autex, and Instinet—all designed to make trading by computers a reality. The three systems differed substantially, but each was meant to give large stock buyers and sellers, such as mutual funds, banks, and insurance companies, something that ordinary investors took for granted, namely the ability to find a ready trade.

The Big Board system was designed to handle issues listed on the Big

Board with a minimum entry of 5,000 shares or a block value of $200,000 or more. Entries must specify block size, but not price. Use of the system implies willingness to trade at or near the price on the trading floor. When a subscriber wishes to trade, say, 5,000 shares of XYZ, the consoles display the symbol XYZ, indicating that an entry had been made. In making an entry, the subscriber picks a broker to handle the transaction. If there is a match, both buyers and sellers are notified, with the request that they contact each other directly.

The Instinet system accepts entries of at least 500 shares with a block value of at least $25,000. Mechanically, this system permits institutions to completely execute a trade, bypassing both brokers and exchanges. Each transaction is kept secret by the use of special serial numbers.

The third system, Autex, was designed to act like a magazine publisher. The brokers would be like the advertisers and would pay to advertise their merchandise, whereas Autex would be like the magazine that accepted the advertisements in order to enhance prospects of sales. Functionally, only brokers would be able to make buy-sell entries, and only institutional consoles would display them. Whenever a subscriber wished to flash a block (at least 1,000 shares) he could have it done on the console. The broker's name would be listed with each entry, and institutions would be permitted to contact any broker directly or through another broker.

I should now like to mention the National Association of Security Dealers Automatic Quotation (NASDAQ) system. This is the automated quotation system of the National Association of Security Dealers, a nationwide network for supplying quotes on 2,500 over-the-counter stocks and permitting OTC dealers to enter their bid and asked prices. The system was put into action early in 1971. Now that the NASDAQ is working on a full-scale basis, it has established an automated market system permitting dealers to buy and sell by pushing buttons on their desk-top consoles.

In passing, I should mention that, even if these sophisticated block trading systems and other types of automated trading systems function efficiently, given the present thinking of both investors and brokers, it appears that the broker will remain the kingpins of the securities market. Furthermore, it is not at all clear whether they can ever be entirely replaced by the computer.

Not-for-Profit Stock Exchanges

An article of considerable interest to us which recently appeared in the WSJ[79] concerned the decision of some of the nation's major stock exchanges to become nonprofit corporations. Herbert Lawson, author of the article, pointed out that the Pacific Coast Stock Exchange—the nation's third largest securities exchange—had already submitted to the SEC its plans for incorporation. In addition, the Philadelphia-Baltimore-Washington Exchange had advised the SEC that it wanted to incorporate. Even the NYSE was considering the possibility of incorporating as a nonprofit corporation.

The reason for this sudden interest in incorporation is simple. An increasing fear has been felt among member firms that they do not have enough legal protection against huge losses. They feel that their foundation has been shaken by the recent liquidation of many brokerage firms. Brokers and exchange officials worry that a court may find an exchange guilty of negligence in the collapse of a member firm and then decide that its customers may sue the surviving members to recoup any losses. Limiting their liabilities would therefore appear to be a major reason for the interest in incorporation.

While the philosophy of the stock exchanges becoming nonprofit corporations is not a bad one, it has side effects. As Lawson puts it:

The move could set off a sharp controversy among investors and within the Securities and Exchange Commission. From their beginnings, most exchanges have been voluntary associations of member firms, each of which stood behind the others to guarantee the financial integrity of the exchange. The incorporation concept, aimed at limiting the liability of member firms and exchange officials, could well suggest to jittery investors that the exchanges are shrinking from their responsibility. . . .[80]

What the outcome will be is not yet clear; however, it appears certain that some structural changes will come about in the exchange business as a result of the developing interest in nonprofit stock exchanges.

THE FINANCIAL PR

In recent years investors have begun to face a problem which is in some ways similar to the Street's paper blizzard problem. Investors are deluged with so much information that a systematic appraisal is beyond their abilities. What can they do to survive in the Wall Street world?

Actually, Wall Street does not have any business of its own. It exists because investors are interested in dealing in company stocks which are publicly held and traded on Wall Street. And therein lies a complicated problem. In order for an investor to be interested in a stock, he must first be exposed to the "company story." But who can tell the story not only to him but to the analysts and the press as well? In these days of specialization, the job can be handled only by a professional man conversant with all the angles. That man is the company financial PR, or public relations man.

Corporate and financial public relations have come a long way since Ivy Ledbetter early in this century advised John D. Rockefeller, Jr., to don overalls and hop on a donkey at a Colorado mine as a device for dispelling the image of "Mr. Jr." as a ruthless capitalist. Nowadays the financial PR man is more concerned with public acceptance of the corporation and its managers in the marketplace. And his role there is changing fast, too. Financial PR men used to earn their bread and butter mainly by writing a few stories for clients in the financial press, arranging analysts' meetings, and mailing quarterly statements and annual reports to shareholders. In recent years, the role of the PR men has dramatically changed. Today they interpret laws governing securities so executives may take the right steps on disclosure. They are helping companies fight off takeover attempts. They talk to security analysts. And they analyze the effect of the economy on their clients and on the industries in which their clients operate.

The demand for financial PR men has arisen for several reasons. The boom in new issues has put analysts' time at a premium, corporation disclosure rules have become tougher, and takeover moves are more frequent than ever. Besides, more men and women are concerned with Wall Street's activities and are demanding more information about the companies before they risk their dollars.

WORLD'S SMALLEST STOCK MARKET

In Pittsburgh there is a tiny stock market in which only a very select group of traders can operate. Hardly known to investors in this country, this market is part of a business game course at Carnegie-Mellon University. The trading manual for the game states the following:

The GSIA Management Game Stock Market is controlled by a program on the PNB time-sharing service. The market includes the eight following securities:

Security Number	Name
1	Firm 1–1
2	Firm 1–2
3	Firm 1–3
4	Firm 2–1
5	Firm 2–2
6	Firm 2–3
7	Government bonds
8	Market portfolio

The market lists the shares of six mythical detergent makers. The concerns are managed by six-man teams of students who play the roles of corporate presidents and vice presidents in charge of production, finance, marketing, and other areas. Like executives in real life, the students run their companies by making basic business decisions—setting production levels, budgeting, advertising, spending, developing new products, and setting selling prices.

In this game, which is completely automated, there are three types of orders. First, there is the market order to buy or sell at the highest current bid or the lowest currently offered price. Then there is the limit order, which is an order to buy or sell at a specified price. Finally, "delete" is an order to cancel an unexecuted limit order previously entered.

Although this stock market is to be played only as a game, the university has taken great pains to bring it to life. In an effort to add reality, the school has recruited business executives from such firms as Gulf Oil, Westinghouse, and Koppers to sit on the board of directors' meetings. As a result, players in this stock market have been able to acquire valuable market experience which would otherwise not have been possible.

THE MARKET KNOWS NO BOUNDARIES

An important characteristic of the stock market is that it does not discriminate against anyone, not even convicts. In the past, brokerage firms such as Bache & Company have designed investment courses as part of San Quentin prison's program of general education.

During January, 1969 Victor Rosasco, vice president of Bache & Company, appeared before 68 inmates of the San Quentin prison, all of whom were participants in a rehabilitation program of general education that enrolled 1,800 of the prison's 3,800 occupants. San Quentin was selected for this course because education ranked high in the prison's approach to penology. Rosasco tried to clarify—and was partly successful—the mysteries that surround puts and calls, shorts and longs, and P/E ratios.

Bache & Company is not the only brokerage firm with an eye on prisoners. About the same time that Rosasco was talking to the San Quentin inmates, J. Patrick Kelly, a securities salesman at Paine, Webber, Jackson & Curtis in Washington, D.C., was discussing investment principles with the District of Columbia Youth Center inmates. His hope was that if these men learned "how the fat cats make it legally," they would be able to break the grim cycle of jail to street and back to jail.

Initially, Kelly did not succeed in exciting these youths. Many of them thought the stock market had something to do with animals. However, Kelly did not give up. He introduced them to an investment game to teach them about blue chips, growth stocks, speculative ventures, and balanced portfolios. In the following months, the inmates followed the financial pages diligently and "played the market" with religious fervor.

Teaching stock market theory to prisoners is in itself an interesting story, but the implications are deeper. Stories like these seem to suggest that the investment world is for all people, regardless of status.

A BILLION-DOLLAR RUMOR FACTORY

The most interesting thing about Wall Street is that nothing beats its rumor factory. The heart of the financial community is its telephone lines;

the men in the market have succeeded in developing a relaying information system which moves faster than sound. Not only are brokers' branch
networks connected by teletype systems, but hundreds of brokerage-house
floor personnel and trading clerks, as well as institutional traders, are connected to each other by direct lines that eliminate the need to dial a
telephone or punch a keyboard. It is little wonder that in that billion-dollar
rumor factory a million people can become aware of a rumor in a matter of
seconds.

The way a rumor spreads is very interesting.[81] It may begin when someone casually mentions some news he picked up at breakfast. Barely half an
hour later, brokers have heard it from fund managers, who heard it from
other brokers who were told by friends at investment banking houses, who
heard it from traders who had just been called by institutional clients, who
in turn had heard it from. . . . What's more interesting is that when the
rumors are false they seem to spread faster. For instance, one broker a few
years ago inadvertently started a rumor while lunching with a friend.
"How's this for the perfect merger—Sears and Chrysler," he said, and then
proceeded to explain why the two companies must eventually merge. At a
business meeting a few weeks later, someone took him aside and said: "I
have it from a very good source that Sears is preparing a tender offer for
Chrysler."

Here is another example of how rumors spread. Once, not so long ago,
Samuel Sloan III, who was Hayden, Stone's senior floor partner, said:
"Someone walked by me on the floor and yelled, 'Hey, I hear there's a
rumor that Morgan [Guaranty & Trust Company] will lower the prime
[the rate of interest charged on loans to the best customers].' It spread like
wildfire." Before that rumor started, the Dow Jones Industrial Average had
lost 170 points and was still going down. When the rumor spread, volume
increased and the long-awaited rally began. Suspecting foul play, Reuters
immediately contacted Morgan, as did Dow Jones, Inc. Ellmore C. Patter-
son, Morgan's president, did not hear the rumor until he returned from
lunch shortly after 2 P.M. He immediately instructed the public relations
man on duty to deny the rumor to the wire services and to other news
media that had called for a statement. As soon as Morgan's denial was
made public, the rally eased, only to reappear two days later, pushing the
DJIA up by 23 points.

False rumors do not make up the full story. "This is a gossipy business,"
said a Boston mutual fund manager. "It's something like a ladies' bridge
club—everybody likes to talk." I recall that on June 9, 1965, near the end
of the market correction that year, word got around that President Johnson
had suffered a heart attack. That day the DJIA fell more than 7 points,
and investors lost $5 billion in paper profits in a matter of hours.

Most rumors, either totally or partially false, originate by accident.
What is ultimately so sad about the product of the rumor factory, however, is that contradictions begin to develop by the time the rumor has

gone full circle, and the little man is always trapped between contradictions. Of course, you should not lose sight of the fact that, although the rapid information system permits the quick spread of rumors, it performs a useful and important function by speeding the dissemination of valuable information.

While rumors have generally been part of the stock market "life," Wall Street may be on its way to buttoning its lips. Anyone who acts on stock tips by insiders or others who have a special relationship with a company may now run afoul of the law. What spurted this interest of Street bosses in controlling actions on the basis of rumors is, among other items, the sale of Douglas Aircraft stocks in 1966.

Richard Donnelly[82] tells the Douglas story in the following manner. Sometime after 2 P.M. on June 21, 1966, Roland Wilhelm, an aerospace specialist and a vice president of Madison Fund, the big closed-end investment company, received a phone call from Merrill Lynch's institutional salesman regarding some disappointing news concerning Douglas Aircraft. Within an hour, Wilhelm sold all his holdings of Douglas (6,000 shares). Furthermore, between June 21, 1966, and June 23, 1966, prior to the disclosure of the bad earnings report by Douglas, the privileged institutional clients of Merrill Lynch sold 198,000 shares of Douglas.

There have been other cases of an "irregular flow of knowledge." For instance, it was brought to the attention of the SEC that the Glen Alden Corporation supplied "material" information about itself to some mutual funds without making the same information available to the public. The SEC had also been informed that Texas Gulf Sulphur Company's insiders profited by advance information about a valuable ore strike.

Disclosures such as these have rocked Wall Street since 1966, but it was not until the summer of 1970 that a decision was taken to deal with such malpractices. In his initial decision, published June 29, 1970, Hearing Examiner Warren Blair pointed out that:

. . . the special obligation of affirmative disclosure of material information imposed upon insiders under the anti-fraud provisions is not limited to those holding positions as corporate officers, directors, and controlling stockholders, but falls upon all persons who "are in a special relationship with a company and privy to its internal affairs, and thereby suffer correlative duties in trading in its securities."[83]

Thus, argued Blair, the tippers fall within the description of persons with a special relationship when, through an insider, they become aware of information which should be used "only for a corporate purpose and not for personal benefit of anyone." On the basis of these arguments, Blair concluded that tippers incur the same disclosure obligations as corporate insiders. The only difference is that "disclosure to the world is not required of tippees, only that there be equality of information with those with whom they trade."

It will be some time before Blair's decision can be transformed into operational rules. If and when such rules are developed and implemented, the insiders, or tippees, will be compelled to keep quiet. But the prospects do not appear to be very bright at the present time.

War and Peace on Wall Street

In this concluding section I reproduce a news item which recently appeared in *Business Week*. Certainly, after reading it no one can accuse Wall Street of noninvolvement in the country's political, social, and economic problems.

FIGURE 19–2

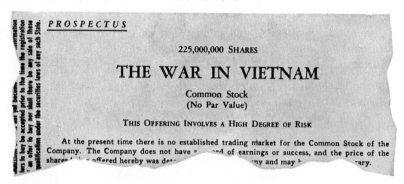

An offer to sell the Vietnam war

In format, it is the typical legalese required when a company wants to sell securities. In content, it is one Wall Street lawyer's way of expressing frustration over the war. Burton R. Tauber, 35, wrote a prospectus for 225-million shares in the War in Vietnam ("hereinafter referred to as 'the Company'") and this week it goes on the newsstands. Tauber plans to turn over his royalties to the peace movement.

"The business of the Company," says the 14-page document, "consists primarily of acquiring and destroying real estate." Standard prospectus headings are followed by macabre humor. Under Application of Proceeds: "Salaries and fringe benefits, including burial expenses and prostheses for employees." Under Management: "Mr. Nixon [is] chief executive officer. Spiro T. Agnew [is] in charge of public relations. . . . Prior to joining the Company Mr. Agnew did not exist."

Authorized long-term debt is listed as "none," debt outstanding, "unfathomable." In acquiring a "Cambodian subsidiary," the Company "only lost 360 employees, but captured 6,880 tons of rice. . . ."

Source: *Business Week*, September 5, 1970, p. 20.

ACT VI

THE HORIZON

> *"I hope someday we'll be affluent."*
> *"We are affluent, dear; you mean someday we may even have some money?"*
> —AN INDIAN PROVERB

20

Affluence at Any Speed

ON "RAGS-TO-RICHES" STORIES

In a book published in 1962 by the editors of the *Wall Street Journal*, Warren Phillips, managing editor of the *WSJ* wrote:

Americans have always been fascinated by the mechanics of business success. Seventy-six years ago, students at Pittsburgh's Curry Commercial College pressed Andrew Carnegie for advice on how they might follow in his footsteps. Mr. Carnegie, who moved up from a $1.20-a-week job in a cotton mill to become an organizer of the United States steel industry, told them to "aim for the highest. . . . Put all your eggs in one basket, and watch that basket." And "never enter a barroom." Today, the mass sales of books describing how individuals made millions in real estate and the stock market indicate that the public has lost none of its curiosity about how fortunes are built.[84]

The book had a wide sale, testifying to the interest on the part of the public in making a fortune on the stock market. The success stories of tough, daring, and imaginative men and women like Clement Stone, Sydney Baron, Thomas Bolack, J. Walter, and Catherine Clark who began from scratch and attained what they wanted in their golden venture, often create fantasies in the minds of inexperienced investors and encourage them to dream of doubling their money overnight. However, such optimism has dangers that must be brought to light. In this chapter I propose to deal with this issue and show that affluence should be secured at a *reasonable* speed if it is to be sustained over a relatively long period of time.

235

A Balanced Portfolio? Who's Got It?

Books which eloquently demonstrate that "rags-to-riches" success stories are anything but myths make interesting reading. However, they rarely provide practical guidelines for those who would like to approach the stock market *systematically* and who hope for a *reasonable return* for their money. Consequently, these people must develop their own methods of operation and decide upon their own range of expectations.

Let me begin by saying that, in my opinion, the only way to approach the market systematically is first to build a balanced portfolio. I am sure many investors would argue against this on the grounds that anyone who has only a few thousand dollars to invest in the stock market cannot build even a *portfolio*, let alone a balanced one. If you feel this way, you are wrong in your thinking. You can no more afford to throw your money into the stock market haphazardly without building a balanced portfolio than you can afford to bury your hard-earned money in the backyard. No matter how little money you have to invest in the stock market, you must carefully develop a *portfolio* and make every attempt to maintain a balanced portfolio at all times.

You might like to know why you should *have* to bother about a balanced portfolio when other people are making millions in the market without owning such a portfolio. My response to your question is: Most people who make a killing in the market tend to boast about their luck and seldom attribute their success to good management. The fact is that the odds against making big fortunes in the market by good luck are far greater than those against winning the Kentucky Derby. Besides, even though Samuel Mitchell might not like to admit that it was his good judgment which induced him to buy and hold 100 shares of Haloid at $30 a share and watch it grow into several million (as Haloid was transformed into Xerox), the fact remains that Mitchell's success was for the most part due to good management rather than to good luck.

The Concept of a Balanced Portfolio

In explaining the concept of a balanced portfolio I am reminded of the plight of the person who tried to describe a giraffe to a boy who had never seen one. The man threw up his arms in despair, saying, "It is hard to describe a giraffe, but you will instantly recognize it when you see one." Instead of defining balanced portfolio, then, let me describe an incident which I feel will do the job.

During the course of a conversation with my friend Sam a couple of years ago, I discovered that to him the word *portfolio* implied stocks worth millions of dollars. Sam was an auto executive and had earned close to $28,000 the previous year. I was greatly amused by his thinking on this subject and decided to explore the matter further with him. I soon discovered that he had a *portfolio* (he did not know it) worth $15,000, consisting of the following stocks: Fuqua Industries, Abbott Labs, General Portland, Bendix Corporation, Motorola, Inc., Raytheon Company, Sperry Rand, and Avco Corporation. I recognized instantly that my friend's portfolio was a "high-risk mess," that none of the items were what I called *investment-grade* stocks, *capital gains, good-quality* stocks, or *special-situation* stocks. All of them appeared to be *businessman's risk* types of stocks. I defined investment-grade stocks as those of prime-quality companies whose earnings records had shown an ability to weather periods of adversity and which were growing as fast as or faster than the national economy. The category which I called capital gains, good-quality consisted of stocks which were meant for investors seeking capital appreciation in well-established companies with demonstrated earning power. Stocks falling into the classification of special situations had above average potential for capital appreciation but also carried above average risks with them. Finally, businessman's risk stocks were defined to include those securities which were suitable for capital appreciation but which were cyclical or highly speculative stocks and as such carried considerably greater risks than those in the other categories.

At this point I decided on the following approach. First, I explained to Sam that every investor, no matter how small, must carefully plan and manage a group of stocks (portfolio) that would serve his basic objectives. Next, I laid out a set of objectives which an average investor would want to achieve. At the top of this list I put down the need for holding some cash. I explained that it is bad policy to put into stocks the money he knew he would soon need for his children's education, home improvement, impending vacation, and emergencies. I then pointed out to Sam that since he was dealing with probabilities and uncertainties, it would be good practice for him to put a portion of his funds into a savings account, so that he would have on hand sufficient cash to buy stocks whenever they appeared cheap or it seemed that they would appreciate in value because of special situations. Finally, I estimated the balance of money which Sam could *safely* put in stocks. I explained that, first of all, he needed some protection against inflation for his money and that buying investment-grade stocks was ideal for this purpose. Next, I suggested that a portion of the money be put in capital gains, good-quality stocks, so that he would have some income, a reasonable safety of principal, and participation in growth. Finally, I asked Sam to put the remainder into special situations and/or businessman's risk stocks to satisfy his speculative desires.

After my friend and I had gone through this little exercise in developing a balanced portfolio for him, I discovered that he was not the "swinger" type at all. He had always wanted a balanced portfolio and, taking the long view, could not be happy in any other way. So, with a little help, he was able to switch from "just a few stocks" to a "balanced portfolio" without putting any more money into the market than he had originally invested.

GETTING RICH SAFELY

If you ask an investor the simple question, "What is your objective?" you will more than likely get the answer, "To make money, what else?" If you go a step further and ask just how much return on his money would satisfy him, you are unlikely to get a consistent answer. The aggressive investors might want to become millionaires in a couple of years, while the more conservative ones might say, "We're told that during our lifetime an annual return of 25 percent on the money invested is clearly attainable, and we would not be satisfied with anything less."

Such unrealistic expectations have arisen because of the publicity given to the new millionaires and how they made their fortunes. A wise investor who is anxious to succeed in reaching his investment objectives must first develop a firm basis for establishing his long-term objectives, and then periodically determine whether or not he is reaching them. However, this is easier said than done. Let me explain.

Setting up a realistic goal and measuring one's achievements raise two questions, namely, what constitutes a reasonable goal and what is a valid yardstick for measuring performance on the stock market. In the short run, the most important criterion is not how much one's holdings go up or down but how they do relative to the market "average" (that is, the Dow Jones Industrial Average or the Standard & Poor Indexes). But in the long run the growth of investment values has to be related to something more basic. An expectation of an annual rate of return of 25 percent is not only unrealistic but dangerous.

I mentioned that either of two market averages, Dow Jones or Standard and Poor's, can act as the yardstick for measuring portfolio results. Since the former is the more popular, I will use it in future discussion.

Let us now turn to the more difficult question: How much should an investor's portfolio grow each year? To answer this question one should begin by recognizing that in the long run the annual rate of return from a typical list of stocks must reflect—in fact, closely correspond to—the combined rate of growth in the gross national product (GNP) and the distribution of dividends by corporations. The reason for this thinking is as follows: An investment return represents a return for capital appreciation (of which growth in GNP is the best estimate) as well as a return for profits of corporations (of which dividend distribution is the best estimate). If we could show that the historic increase in the GNP has been 15 percent and the long-term average annual dividend distribution has been 10 percent, then we would be justified in expecting an annual investment return of 25 percent.

Unfortunately, stock market history does not warrant an expectation of such a high rate of return. An important study conducted by the Cowles Commission several years ago found that, from 1871 to 1938, all industrial stocks listed on the New York Stock Exchange provided an average annual rate of return (or both capital growth and dividend) of 9 percent. In another study, "Rates of Return on Investments in Common Stock: The Year-by-Year Record, 1926–65," Lawrence Fisher and James Lorie discovered that during this period (1926–65) the average annual rate of return on investment was 9.3 percent.[85]

A closer look into the 9-percent rate-of-return figure reveals an interesting fact. During the last 50 years or so, at current prices the GNP has grown at an average annual rate of about 5 percent, whereas the rate of growth in dividends over the same period appears to have been around 4 percent. It would therefore appear reasonable for an investor to expect in the long run an annual rate of return of around 9 percent.

I wish I could say this was the end of the story, but unfortunately it is not. In a staff letter published during 1969 by David L. Babson & Company, Inc., the complications of measuring short-term investment performance are clearly spelled out.[86] According to this letter, during shorter periods the measurement of the annual return on common stocks is immensely complicated by the continual changes in the valuations which investors have been making about the "worth" of individual stocks. This is evident from Table 20–1.

TABLE 20–1
MEAN PRICE-EARNINGS RATIOS, DOW JONES INDUSTRIAL AVERAGES

1970	14	1961	21	1952	11
1969	14	1960	20	1951	10
1968	16	1959	18	1950	7
1967	16	1958	18	1949	8
1966	15	1957	13	1948	8
1965	17	1956	15	1947	9
1964	18	1955	12	1946	14
1963	17	1954	12		
1962	17	1953	10		

The table shows that during 1946–70 the mean P/E ratio has ranged from a low of 7 (1950) to a high of 21 (1961). This implies that if a company had exactly the same earnings—say, $10 per share—in each of these years, its price would have risen from $80 in 1950 to $210 (162 percent) in 1961 and would be down to $140 in 1970, for no other reason than the change in investors' attitude toward that stock. In a world of widely changing P/E ratios, how can one develop a reasonably accurate measure of investment expectations? The answer is that over a short period of time he cannot. The decline in P/E ratios between 1961 and 1970 (from 21 to 14) amounted to 33 percent, which substantially offset the gains in the value of investment one would expect in nine years based on the historic 9 percent annual growth of earnings. The staff letter points out:

For this reason, when measuring their results against the long-term yardstick, investors should be careful that conditions at the beginning point were similar to those at the end period, i.e., comparisons should be made for a full cycle—from peak to peak or trough to trough. Otherwise, there will be too much distortion to give a valid rate of investment return.[87]

Over the long run, P/E ratios tend to hover around 14 or 16. Because the 1970 P/E ratio falls within this range, it is safe to assume that the future expected average annual rate of return from all stocks (dividends and capital growth combined) will approximate the historic average of around 9 percent.

A Bright Star

You may have been disappointed to learn that your money is not likely to grow more than 9 percent a year. While nothing can be done to alter that situation, here is a piece of information that may cheer you a little. Data suggest (see Table 20–2) that, during the period 1958–68, many professional managers have been able to secure average investment return (capital appreciation and dividends paid) of more than 9 percent per year.

TABLE 20–2
Average Annual Change in Net Assets per Share
Plus Dividends

Average Annual Return	1958–1968
18 large growth funds	13.0%
22 smaller growth funds	13.7
30 growth and income funds	9.2
25 balanced funds	8.0
17 income funds	8.3

Source: Arthur Wiesenberger Services, Investment Companies, New York, 1969.

However, do not overlook the fact that this 11-year period does not include 1969–70, the years of severe market decline. If you examine the scoreboard of these fund managers during the period 1958–70, much of the impressiveness of their performance would disappear.

What About a 25 Percent Return?

Now that I have told you that during 1958–68 a group of funds obtained 13.7 percent return on their investment, you may want to shoot for an annual return of 25 percent yourself. I won't say it's absolutely impossible. But I will have to say that in order to get a 25 percent annual rate of return over a reasonably long period you must possess plenty of skills, have lots of luck, and be prepared to do a little dreaming every now and then.

Let me show you the unreasonableness of such a bizarre expectation. Table 20–3 and the Figure 20–1 show how $100,000 portfolio increases over varying periods at different rates.

FIGURE 20–1
How Money Grows, and Grows, and Grows

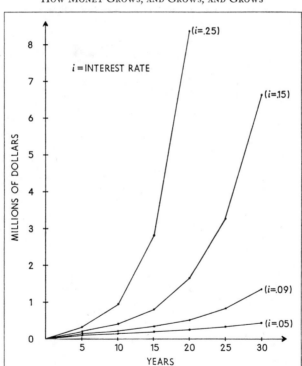

You can see for yourself the absurdity of expecting a 25 percent annual return. At that rate, over a period of 30 years $100,000 would grow to $80.8 million.

TABLE 20–3
GROWTH OF $100,000 INVESTMENT IN THE LONG RUN

Compound Rate (Percent)	10 Years	20 Years	30 Years
5	$ 163,000	$ 265,000	$ 432,000
7	197,000	387,000	761,000
8	216,000	466,000	1,006,000
9	237,000	560,000	1,327,000
10	259,000	673,000	1,745,000
15	405,000	1,673,000	6,621,000
20	619,000	3,834,000	23,738,000
25	931,000	8,674,000	80,780,000
40	2,893,000	83,668,000	2,420,130,000

So What's the Verdict?

I hope I have convinced you that the only way for you to go about making money in the stock market is to operate on a balanced-portfolio plan. Furthermore, you should not pin long-term hopes on superhigh growth rates that are only attainable in some years and at considerable risk. Experience suggests that an overall annual return of about 9 percent from both capital appreciation and dividends is a reasonable expectation, and you may fix your horizon on that basis.

> While I am certain of nothing, I am not even
> certain of that.
>
> —SIDNEY HOMER

An Economic Profile
of the Seventies

HAPPY NEW YEAR

On December 14, 1970, precisely at 3:48 P.M., the Gross National Product of the United States passed the trillion-dollar mark. In typical Wall Street style, the market celebrated the New Year two weeks in advance by registering a sharp advance. Measured in constant 1957 dollars to eliminate the effect of inflation, of course, there was little cause for a big celebration.

Some people will remember the year 1970 with pleasure—traders who shorted their stocks, couples who got married, and scientists who made significant discoveries. But there are others—those who made false starts and unsatisfactory finishes—who will remember 1970 with pleasure only because it is over.

Now that the present has become the past, and the future is here, it should be fun to take a fresh look at the new past, the present, and the future. After all, in the general scene of human action, events must be grouped under the heading of time. The present is in a sense the whole of life, embracing all that is. "Within this present," says G. L. S. Shackle, "the solitary moment of actuality, we call up mental pictures of 'the past' and we imagine possible experiences and actions which compose some one out of a limitless number of conceivable 'futures.' "[88] It is in this spirit that I undertake to review the past, the present, and the future of the "trillion-dollar" economy. Let us hope that out of this exposé will come some insights into the future for you, the investor.

The Glorious Past

In the year of Our Lord 1970, the United States became a "trillion-dollar" economy, or what Norman Macrae has called the neurotic trillion-aire. This rise has not been even: the United States became a billion-dollar economy in the early 1830's; it reached the $10 billion mark in 1880; and the $100 billion mark was reached in 1929 and again in 1941 (see Figure 21–1).

In contrast to the pre–World War II growth, since the end of World War II the U.S. economy, measured in current dollars, has grown by leaps and bounds: $250 billion in 1948, $500 billion in 1960, and $1,000 billion in 1970. This means that in the 10 years between 1960 and 1970 the GNP has doubled (by the standard of dollars); by contrast, it took 25 years, on the average, for the GNP to double in the prewar years.

The varying rates of growth in the GNP do not emphasize one important point. In this century every decade has experienced certain unique problems that have taxed the brains of public policy makers in the subsequent decade. At the beginning of this century the country was beset with financial problems. During the 1910's the problem was that of waging World War I. The roaring 1920's are remembered as an era during which major adjustments had to be made in order to transform the wartime economy into a peacetime economy. The Great Depression occurred during the 1930's, while the 1940's were taken up with World War II and the postwar reconstruction of the war-shattered economies of the world.

During the 1950's the fear of depression was displaced by the fear of persistent inflation, and for the first time deficits in the balance of payments were recognized as a major economic problem. In addition, toward the end of the decade unemployment reemerged as a vexing problem, and there seemed to be no consensus as to what combination of economic policies would reduce unemployment to an acceptable level.

During the 1960's the country's many problems seemed to intensify. While unemployment continued to plague the economy, the acceleration of the rate of inflation became a major source of concern for policy makers. There were recurrent deficits in the government's annual budgets, primarily due to the Vietnam War, and toward the latter part of the decade the economy stagnated.

Of all the economic problems affecting the U.S. economy during the decade, none were more acute than the simultaneous progression of a high rate of inflation and a low rate of real economic growth (measured in

FIGURE 21–1

PROFILE OF A TRILLION-DOLLAR ECONOMY

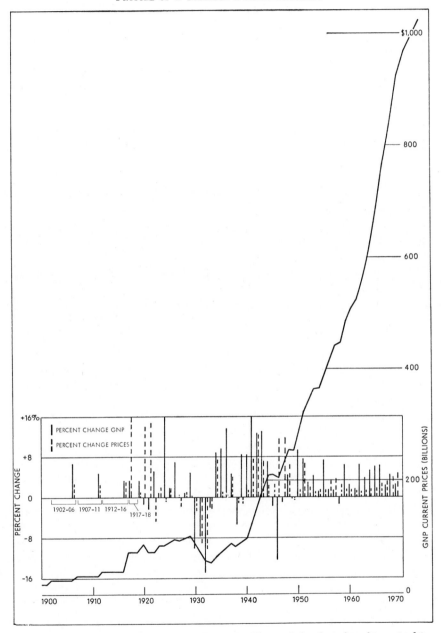

Source: *Business Week*, October 17, 1970, p. 75. The graph has been brought up to date.

constant prices). The acceleration of price inflation since 1965 was far greater than any experienced since the Korean War. At first inflation was moderate, but prices gradually climbed until in 1969 overall prices rose more than 5 percent and economic growth came to a halt.

From 1964 onward the economy received many expansive shocks which were responsible for its poor performance. Expenditures of the federal government increased faster than receipts until mid-1968. Income tax rates were reduced in early 1964 in order to boost the sagging economy. As a result of the intensification of the Vietnam War, the defense expenditures of the government, which had risen at a 1.3 percent annual rate from 1957 to 1964, increased at the rate of 14 percent from 1964 to mid-1968. Growth in nondefense outlays was also accelerated from the 9.6 percent rate from 1957 to 1964 to a 12 percent rate from 1964 to mid-1968.

The monetary policy of the Federal Reserve was also expansionary during this period. From late 1964 to early 1969, money supply increased at a 5.3 percent average rate, up from a 3 percent rate earlier in the decade and a 2 percent rate in the 1950's. Except for the nine-month period of restraint from the spring of 1966 to early 1967, monetary expansion was at a very rapid 7 percent average rate. Overall percentage changes in the GNP, the price level, and the money supply during 1951–70 are given in Table 21–1.

It must be obvious that developments such as those outlined above would bring about deep-rooted structural changes in the American capital market in general and in the stock market in particular. That is exactly what happened. Sidney Homer has emphasized the four changes which occurred in the U.S. capital market, especially since 1965.[89] According to Homer, the most obvious change had been the rise in interest rates. Treasury bill rates increased from the low of 4 percent in early 1965 to the 1970 high of over 8 percent. Similarly, prime new corporate bond yields rose from 4½ percent in early 1965 to over 9 percent in 1970. The second important structural change was a sudden rise in the volume of equity financing by corporations, both in the form of convertible securities and in straight equities and warrants. In late 1969, net equity financing suddenly rose to an all-time record, and in 1970 the volume doubled.

The third structural change resulted from the massive intervention of the federal government in an effort to rescue the market for home mortgages. In the past the mortgage market had normally been an institutional affair, and the government had not attempted to increase the flow of funds into the real estate sector whenever there was a need for such assistance. However, after housing was accorded a high social priority several years ago, the federal government had been making a large amount of mortgage purchases by selling an enormous volume of federal agency securities into the market as high yields.

The fourth structural change was brought about by a public demand for

TABLE 21–1
CHANGES IN GNP, PRICE LEVEL, AND MONEY SUPPLY

| Year | Year to Year GNP | | % Change in | |
	Current $	On 1957 Prices	Money Supply	Price Level
1951	15.3	7.9	5.5	6.7
1952	5.2	3.1	4.0	2.2
1953	5.5	4.5	1.0	0.9
1954	0.1	−1.4	2.6	1.5
1955	9.1	7.6	2.2	1.5
1956	5.3	1.8	1.2	3.4
1957	5.2	1.4	−0.7	3.7
1958	1.4	−1.1	3.9	2.6
1959	8.1	6.4	0.6	1.6
1960	4.1	2.5	−0.6	1.7
1961	3.3	1.9	3.2	1.3
1962	7.7	6.6	1.5	1.1
1963	5.4	4.0	3.8	1.3
1964	7.1	5.5	4.3	1.5
1965	8.3	6.3	4.9	1.9
1966	9.5	6.5	2.2	2.7
1967	5.8	2.5	6.7	3.2
1968	9.1	4.9	7.2	4.0
1969	7.7	2.8	2.5	4.7
1970	7.2	0.0	5.4	7.2

Source: Adapted from Stephen Packer, "New Era for the Capital Markets in the 1970's?" *Financial Analysts Journal,* July–August, 1970, p. 11. The table has been brought up to date.

very high performance standards among institutional portfolio managers. Investors no longer appeared to be satisfied with just the rising incomes of pension funds, endowment funds, and even personal trusts which their managers had generated; they were also interested in the changes in market values of the portfolios of the funds in which they participated.

In addition to the structural changes in the American capital market, the stock market has undergone rapid transformation. After the widespread bloodbath of 1969 and 1970, during which dozens of brokerage firms, hundreds of institutions, and thousands of investors were wiped out, Wall Street no longer remained the place everyone optimistically entered just to make a fast buck. Currently, the capital rules are being changed to provide brokerage firms with a sounder operational base. Investors' insurance against losses is no longer a dream but a reality. Many go-go funds are gone-gone, and room for the casual investor has greatly shrunk. There still exists a group of investors who indulge in an immature interpretation of performance, concentrating on the success of near-term stock market speculations, but their number has substantially lessened. There is a new species of investors who are tempted to follow the example of the Scottish Presbyterian minister who said to his congregation, "We come, noo, brethren, to a verra considerable deeficulty. Let us look it squarely in the face and pass on." Finally, and fortunately, the individual and the institutional investors who aim primarily at enrichment over the long term are still there.

THE AMBIVALENT PRESENT

This is the background against which the immediate past—the year 1970—should be evaluated. It is, of course, possible to describe the day-to-day and week-to-week events that took place during the year. However, a more meaningful survey would transcend such details and highlight the underlying trends on which a successful approach must be based.

The year 1970 was eventful in many respects. In terms of the market performance it was unequivocally a chaotic year. Viewed from another angle, it highlighted the unprecedented social, political, and psychological uncertainties which affected and will continue to affect growth prospects for the 1970's. It was also a year in which the gap between aspiration and achievement widened disconcertingly for the nation and for individuals. During 1970 everyone felt strongly that the nation must lose no time in coming to grips with its problems and in narrowing the gap between what it is and what it wants to be.

At the turn of the year the economy continued to be plagued by two ills: war and inflation. The policy makers—the administration and the Federal Reserve system—frantically tried to reduce these two problems to manageable levels, but the results were none too happy. Defense cutbacks set the unemployment rate on a steep rise, and the anti-inflationary credit restrictions further aggravated unemployment. By spring the country seemed to be winning the war against inflation, partly at the cost of a high rate of unemployment.

Before the nation could celebrate its partial victory, however, a series of national crises occurred: the invasion of Cambodia by the United States, the shootings at Kent State, the bankruptcy of Penn Central, and the much-publicized "liquidity crisis" on Wall Street. The effect on the stock market of these and lesser crises was disastrous. The market suffered its most violent plunge in 40 years, and investors' confidence was profoundly shaken.

This traumatic experience, which the economists labeled a "mini recession," induced the Federal Reserve to adopt an expansionary monetary policy. The Administration also openly committed itself to economic recovery.

The effects of these policy shifts were encouraging. The prices of high-grade bonds and stocks started a strong rally that by year-end had erased all of their earlier 1970 losses. The rate of price inflation slowed, although the problem was by no means solved. Interest rates and long-term bond yields declined sharply from the all-time peaks reached at midyear, but they were still at historically high levels.

Of all the events occurring in 1970 none was more dramatic than the fact that, before the year's end, the United States became the first trillion-dollar economy in the world. This figure, even though subject to correction if inflation were accounted for, dramatized the most important aspect of contemporary U.S. economy: its sheer size, with all the attendant problems. As *Business Week* put it:

Most of the great opportunities that offer themselves today, and most of the serious problems that demand solution, are associated with bigness. For much more is involved in the growth of the U.S. than just a change of scale. The $1-trillion economy is not just a scaled-up version of the $100-billion economy of 1941 any more than a tiger is an outsize house cat. There are major structural differences, not just in patterns of production and consumption but in the basic processes of decision-making and governance. These differences are the source of both new problems and new satisfactions for all Americans.[90]

So here it is, the U.S. trillion-dollar economy—big, powerful, neurotic, and optimistic—ready for a journey into the future in an age of uncertainty.

The Future: Super but Seething

We have noted the conditions in which the United States finds itself at the beginning of the present decade. In this decade, 231 million Americans will work hard and play hard. Also, they will worry more about the jobless, the destitute, the sick, pollution, and big-city problems. Inevitably all this will change the nation to the extent that it will emerge as a different nation. Our immediate interest, therefore, is to develop some framework within which investors can play the market game in the "changed" nation.

President Nixon told Congress in his 1970 State of the Union message:

As we move into the decade of the seventies, we have the greatest opportunity for progress at home of any people in world history. Our gross national product will increase by 500 billion dollars in the next ten years. This increase alone is greater than the entire growth of the American economy from 1790 to 1950. The critical question is not whether we will grow, but how we will use that growth.

Notice that in his message the President took the rate of economic growth for granted and that he underscored "other" structural problems which would most likely plague the economy in the years to come. These structural problems were summarized by Charles Silberman of *Fortune*:

What is the significance, for example, of the apparent weakening of "the Protestant ethic," with its emphasis on hard work, self-reliance, and self-denial, and the growth of new attitudes toward work and life? The attitudes have shown up in several different ways. There is the revolution in sex mores, or at the least, in attitudes toward sex—witness the transformation of the movies and of the legitimate theatre. There is the growing emphasis on immediate rather than deferred gratification—both cause and effect of the "credit-card economy." Even the banks now advertise "Why wait?" There is the general questioning of authority, tradition, and custom, exemplified not just in the pervasiveness of protest and rebellion, but in increasingly casual (and usually more comfortable) modes of dress. Most important, perhaps, there is the growing search for meaning and purpose in our lives, the attempt to find some justification for activity in social and moral terms . . . corporate presidents and chairmen increasingly seem to feel the need to justify business operations not in traditional profit terms but by referring to their corporate contribution to solving urban, racial, or environmental problems.[91]

Although what I have said so far is important, it does not tell the whole story. Other major changes of great significance must be taken into account.

The New Fashions in Financing

The fastest-growing "minority group" in the United States is the people who own common stocks. The number of shareholders has soared from 6 million in 1952 to 12 million in 1959 to 20 million in 1965 and to over 30 million today. Furthermore, these figures do not include investors who have an equity interest in publicly held corporations via mutual funds, trusts, pensions, and profit-sharing plans.

Such a spectacular increase in the number of shareholders is partly due to the new fashions in the world of financing. Traditionally, corporations in need of finances have issued as little common stock as possible and have relied on internal cash and the bond market. There is a valid reason for this. The interest on a bond is tax deductible to the borrower, while common stock dividends paid by a corporation with fully-taxed dollars are taxable to the receiver. Consequently, pension funds and insurance companies are eager to put their money into bonds, whereas they are reluctant to assume the risks involved in buying common stock. Between 1961 and 1969, U.S. corporations raised $96.3 billion in net new cash in the bond market and only $8.6 billion in the stock market.

But the bull market of 1967–69 changed all that. A sustained rise in stock prices led most investors to believe that stocks at any price were better investments than bonds at any yield, and they absorbed billions of dollars worth of corporate stocks. Many investors were forced into thinking that by buying common stocks they would make a lot of money in a short time; others bought stocks as a hedge against inflation. A 5 percent bond looked attractive in the mid-1960's, but it was less than attractive in 1966 when the rate climbed to 6 percent. And a 6 percent bond looked poor compared with a 9.10 percent AAA-rated utility bond in 1969. So in

1969 and during the following year, big and small investors alike turned increasingly to equity. Furthermore, there does not appear to be any development that will reverse the trend.

Too Much in the Hands of Too Few

"Powerful on Wall Street, mutual funds and other institutions are also powerhouses in corporate affairs." With these words *Business Week* began its special report, "Why the Big Traders Worry Industry."[92] The report echoed the sentiment of many people on the subject of institutional investors. People seem to feel that most institutional investors and big traders are crooks, that they bounce the prices of their favorite stocks up and down in order to further their own interests, and that they are the root cause of financial doom for small investors.

This "confidence" in the power that institutional investors seemingly possess may be misplaced. However, no one can dispute the fact that the character of trading on Wall Street has changed significantly, owing to the phenomenal growth of big traders in recent years.

How important the pension funds, mutual funds, and life insurance companies have become is clearly illustrated in Figure 21–2. The big surge in block trading, indicating the growth of big traders relative to their small counterparts, is shown in Figure 21–3.

FIGURE 21–2

On the Buy Side: Net Purchases of Common Stock by Institutions

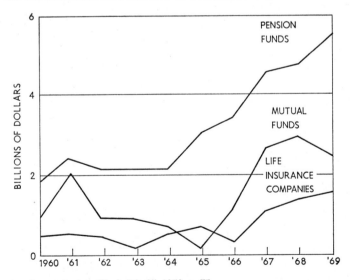

Source: *Business Week*, July 25, 1970, p. 57.

FIGURE 21–3

THE BIG SURGE IN BLOCK TRADING

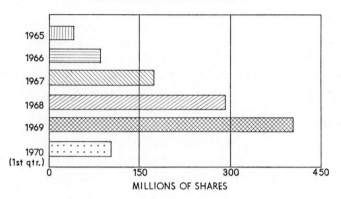

MILLIONS OF SHARES

Source: *Business Week*, July 25, 1970, p. 57.

Several factors are responsible for the spectacular growth of institutional investors. First, the economics of portfolio management has progressively become so complicated that it is no longer possible for an investor to succeed in the market without a sophisticated approach to investment. The successful investment team today consists of a financial analyst, a portfolio manager, and a trader. Only institutional investors can afford to hire such a team.

Second, as the market is deluged with billions of dollars worth of stocks, small investors have found it more and more difficult to select those stocks that are likely to serve their purpose. In order to cope with modern, active, volatile institutional investment policies, many large institutional investment groups have been established which have developed new trading techniques.

Third, the recent wave of brokerage-house failures has dramatized the financial problems created by numerous small traders. The Big Board has now proposed higher commissions on small trades and lower commissions on large trades, in order to buttress ailing brokerage firms and encourage institutional investors.

Finally, institutional investors offer many advantages to the millions of investors as well as to the ever-growing corporate community. As *Business Week* explains:

They draw the public's small sums into brawny packages, thereby tapping financial resources that would otherwise be inaccessible. They keep money moving, presumably into more promising investment areas. By expanding the economy's equity base, they make it easier for new enterprises to raise money.[93]

It is clear that the trend toward more institutionalization of stock market activities is likely to continue in the years ahead.

While institutional traders and investors do offer several advantages to the investment community, they are by no means universally admired. Government officials have been increasingly concerned over the growing participation of institutions in the market, and public outcries against the evils emanating from institutional investment have become frequent.

Not all of the criticisms directed against institutional investors are justified. For instance, it is often said that in recent years institutional investors have gained significant control over large corporations. This is a partial truth, as can be seen from Table 21–2. For instance, in July, 1970, 73 funds owned 25.2 percent of Northwest Airlines, whereas 30.5 percent of Philip Morris stock was owned by as many as 39 funds. It would be erroneous to conclude from these and related statistics that large numbers of funds are able successfully to join together and influence the operations of large corporations.

TABLE 21–2
THE BIG FAVORITES OF THE MUTUAL FUNDS

Company	Percent Owned by Funds	Number of Funds
Philip Morris	30.5%	39
Parke, Davis & Co.	28.1	40
Raytheon Co.	26.8	35
Fairchild Camera	26.1	35
Pittston Co.	25.7	53
Gimbel Bros.	25.7	24
Northwest Airlines	25.2	73
Norton Simon	24.0	32
Ampex Corp.	23.6	44
Otis Elevator	21.6	33
Delta Air Lines	19.8	43
Motorola	18.5	58
Union Camp Corp.	17.9	36
Johns-Manville Corp.	17.8	33
Household Finance Corp.	17.3	38
Newmont Mining Corp.	16.2	40
AMP	15.9	33
Kerr-McGee Corp.	15.9	29
Burroughs Corp.	15.8	98
C.I.T. Financial Corp.	15.8	45

Source: *Business Week*, July 25, 1970, p. 55.

Whatever the status of institutional investors, two things seem perfectly clear. In years to come, the influence of these investors on the financial scene will grow. It is also clear that the administration would want to curb their influence. In fact, some far-reaching reforms are already under way. Note the following:

A mutual fund bill which passed the Senate last year is now in the House Commerce Committee. By imposing stricter standards of fiduciary responsibility on fund managers and directors, the bill would make it easier for shareholders to sue over fees and sales charges.

The House panel is also busy with the insurance brokerage bill, which may give the SEC greater powers to police brokers' capital structure.

The SEC is holding hearings on the Big Board's latest commission rate proposals.

A bill introduced by Senators Wallace F. Bennett (R–Utah) and John Sparkman (D–Ala.) would forbid institutions to join the major exchanges.

Representative Wright Patman (D–Tex.) has intensified his scrutiny of bank trust departments, their concentrations of holdings, and possible manipulations.

The one-bank holding company bill should reach the Senate floor late this month. A version already passed by the House would sharply restrict banks from entering non-banking fields. . . .

[The SEC has sponsored the] Institutional Investor Study, headed by Donald Farrar, a Columbia University economics professor. [The outcome of this study may be very significant.]94

It appears safe to conclude that, while their powers might be curbed, the growth of institutional investors will not be stunted.

Hogs, Oats, and Modern Art

Another interesting change in investors' outlook has been brought about by the long bear market of 1969 and 1970. Millions of small investors who had piled up speculative stocks during the post-1966 bull market were totally disillusioned by the poor performance of their favorite stocks. While most were resigned to holding the depressed stocks, or were wiped out, some switched to the more unconventional investment forms, such as hogs, oats, modern art, and real estate. In more sophisticated language, many investors and brokers switched their tradings to commodity futures from stocks simply because there was a lack of speculative action in stocks and a great deal of action in commodity futures.

In addition to commodity futures, many investors and big corporations moved into real estate. For instance, in April, 1970 Texas Eastern Transmission Corporation, a $1.6 billion gas and oil company, acquired about 32 blocks of downtown Houston. Similarly, Lear Siegler, Inc., a fast-growing, diversified West Coast electronics company, slowly moved into the business of building homes and apartments, shopping centers, mobile home parks, and even entire communities. Large investors who ran into blind alleys in the stock market were also attracted to real estate, where the demand seemed virtually unlimited.

Many investors have also been induced to speculate in art, as the following comment indicates:

Demand for art works depicting the cowboy-and-Indian days is strong and growing, and Western art pieces have doubled in the last few years. . . . The big jump in prices has come just in the last few years. A Texas collector paid $6,000 for a Russell in the 1930's and sold it a year ago for $60,000. Shortly after, it was resold for $150,000. Twenty-One's collection—26 black-and-white oils and five bronzes—was acquired for $150,000 over a 35-year period. It is insured today for $1 million.[95]

I could go on and on, but this will suffice. Modern-day investors have learned that common stocks provide them with only one of many forms of investment. This development is comparatively recent, and you should be aware of it.

Caveats in Computerized Investment Activity

I should like to discuss briefly the role which computers have begun to play in the investment decision-making process in the seventies. Over the past few years, computers have invaded Wall Street to the extent that it is no longer possible to avoid them in developing a reasonably sophisticated plan of investment. Currently, computers are used to (1) eliminate companies of marginal interest; (2) compare the P/E ratios of selected companies; (3) compute market averages; (4) analyze financial variables; and (5) make investment decisions, given a set of preferences and constraints. As the investment world becomes more complicated, computers are likely to be used even more frequently.

While it is easy to be enamored by computer power, do not lose sight of its limitations. The computer is a superservant. It performs its tasks efficiently, faithfully, and with lightning speed. However, the user should recognize that the input must be accurate, the data base must be complete, and the desired output must be clearly specified. If these requirements are met, and if we are careful in using the computer, it will make our investment task more rational and efficient than would otherwise be possible.

Back to You, Finally

While all generalizations are hazardous, it is important to draw a general investment profile of the seventies. We have observed the change and turmoil on Wall Street. We mentioned that as the war decelerates, the economy in transition has been experiencing deep recession. However, the impact of the war on the economy appears to be diminishing noticeably. The government, with its proposed revenue-sharing plans and a full-employment budget, is reaffirming its faith in the Employment Act of 1946 and is expressing its conviction that a peacetime economy is viable. The latest Census Bureau survey indicates that consumer buying plans are strengthening and that the rate of inflation is slowing down. On April

19, 1971, the Dow Jones Industrial Average entered the "new" territory of 948, a climb of 317 points from the low of 631 reached 11 months ago.

On the other side of the balance sheet, wage increases and the possibility of further strikes suggest that there might be more price inflation and less growth than would otherwise be achievable. The rate of unemployment may continue to be higher than acceptable. Social evils will continue to plague the economy, and redeployment of national resources and priorities will make the task of national policy makers more intricate. In short, the recovery from the recession will be tortoise-like and the voyage long and bumpy.

So much for the immediate future. How will the U.S. economy look 10 years from today? Such forecasting is fraught with great dangers, since during this period far-reaching changes are likely to occur in every sector of the economy. However, one prediction can be made with relative certainty. If a Rip Van Winkle skilled in the methods and techniques of investment today were to return to the scene in 10 years, he would find his knowledge seriously outdated. This means that today's investors will have to develop a *flexible* frame of mind if they expect to achieve a measure of success.

What does this mean to you? It means that in making your selections of stocks which will be pacesetters in the years ahead, you need to concentrate on those stocks with something special going for them: stocks of expanding industries, of favorite "concepts," of corporations producing new products, of corporations with good marketing positions to capitalize on growing spending by business and consumers. I hasten to add that you must not take a rigid attitude toward a portfolio which you develop today. Change is the password for success in the investment world of the seventies, and you must change with the times. While the ability to change does not of itself assure success, no success is possible without it. Let me close with the fervent hope that you will experience a happier decade in the seventies.

Yesterday's World of Tomorrow has become to-day's reality; and yesterday's opportunities are gone forever.

—STANDARD & POOR'S CORPORATION

22

Food for Thought
and Thought for Food

THE INVESTMENT WORLD IN TRANSITION

At the end of the year One Thousand Nine Hundred and Seventy, the U.S. economy added another digit to the estimated size of its gross national product, reaching an annual rate of $1 trillion. Of course, this figure is not adjusted for inflation. Even so, the full implications of the economy's reaching the $1 trillion level are beyond the imagination of most of us. Similarly, there are many things about investing in the decade of the 1970's that no one can imagine today. But one thing we can be sure of: it is going to be different.

In an earlier chapter I discussed the salient features of the U.S. economy in transition and the possible changes in the investment climate in the coming decade. In another chapter I emphasized the fact that, just as every good architect carefully prepares a blueprint before erecting a building, every investor must carefully administer a balanced portfolio if he wishes to assure himself of success in the stock market. In this concluding chapter I would like to propose three investment resolutions for your adoption. I will close by pointing out to you the 10 most common mistakes to avoid; also there are 10 common sense rules which you should attempt to follow at all times.

257

The Three Resolutions

Recently I came across a David L. Babson & Company, Inc., staff letter, "Three New Year's Resolutions," which discussed the basis for the three investment resolutions I mentioned.[96] This is the finest essay I have ever read on the subject, and I will summarize it below (with minor changes).

One investment myth which never dies is that stock market swings can be accurately predicted. It is amazing that so much energy is expended on what is nothing more than a guessing game. In recent weeks the financial pages have been full of forecasts of the trend of stock prices in 1970. Whenever we hear someone remark that "so-and-so says the DJIA will end the year at 1100" or "such-and-such analyst or economist is looking for a big decline," we wonder why anyone reads this nonsense. The accuracy of previous predictions can hardly be the reason. This is obvious to those who have made a point of noting the market forecasts made at the beginning of any of the past 5, 10, or even 25 years. The fact is that these annual prognostications are so quickly forgotten that "market seers" can make them year after year without risking their reputations.

The only type of market prediction that people seem to remember is a bearish one made prior to a market decline. In contrast, few people recall bullish forecasts or check to see whether or not such forecasts later proved to be correct. For example, it is now almost forgotten that in mid-1929 Bernard Baruch urged the purchase of common stocks because "the economic condition of the world seems on the verge of a great forward movement." What must be emphasized, though, is not the fact that Mr. Baruch should have known better; throughout his lifetime this talented financier had a much greater insight into the future than all but a handful of his peers. Rather, the point is that *no one can accurately and consistently predict the stock market.*

I have previously observed that the most successful investors have been those who pay the least attention to short-term forecasts. On the other hand, investors who consistently try to outguess the market nearly always end up with a long string of unnecessary losses and missed opportunities. Many learn from bitter experience; others never do. They remain confirmed addicts by developing their investment objectives on the basis of whichever way they think stocks are temporarily headed. Accordingly, I suggest as Investment Resolution Number One:

> *I resolve to pay no attention to my own or anyone else's predictions as to what the stock market is going to do over the next few weeks or months.*

Another reason why some investors have unsatisfactory results is their failure to establish a long-range program. Having a sound plan and holding to it is just as essential to building a list of suitable investments as it is to constructing a good house. Yet only a small percentage of people ever draw up a financial plan and adhere to it faithfully through recurrent periods of optimism and pessimism. Too many investors buy stocks on the basis of tips, rumors, or the casual comments of friends. Their portfolios become illogical mixtures of securities, scattered at random among industries. Only relatively few shareowners have a clear idea of their investment objectives. Even those who do have a definite goal frequently abandon it somewhere along the line, often because they are lured into speculating in unseasoned issues totally alien to their needs; others panic and sell their holdings at a considerable loss. The trouble lies in the difficulty of setting up and adhering to a basic plan. A great amount of self-discipline is required to stick to the original guidelines under all conditions, and doing this calls for a more cold-blooded, unemotional attitude toward one's capital than most people can maintain.

Some investors also allow their judgment to be swayed from time to time by over-concern with future uncertainties. Yet this obstacle can be avoided if the major economic and investment trends which can be predicted are weighed against those which cannot. A reasonably complete balance sheet is the following:

The Unpredictables

1. What stock prices will do next week, next month, or next year.
2. How and when investor moods will change from optimism to pessimism, or vice versa.
3. Which group(s) of stock will become the next fad.
4. Whether international developments will bring war or peace.
5. How the political winds will blow.
6. When business activity will swing up or down.

The Predictables

1. The population of the United States and the rest of the world will keep on growing.
2. More people will need more goods and services.
3. Research will develop new products and new methods, creating more demand and greater productivity.
4. The burden of taxation will become even heavier.
5. The dollar's buying power will continue to decline.
6. Well-managed corporations will maintain their long-term process of earnings and dividends.

The list above could have been drawn up at any time during the last two decades. Yet throughout this period, the *predictables* have had a far greater impact on investment than the *unpredictables*. For this reason I submit as Investment Resolution Number Two:

> *I resolve to adhere faithfully to the long-term investment plan which I have drawn up on the basis of predictable rather than unpredictable trends.*

A third misconception is the widely held belief that the only way to have good investment results is to concentrate on making immediate and large profits. This is accompanied by a philosophy that places short-term profits above longer-term appreciation and encourages taking large risks to accomplish quick results. This approach—as old as the stock market itself—has lately become more popular than ever due to the publicity given to "performance investing" (a modern euphemism for short-term trading). The current scramble for "instant results" has fostered the idea that common stocks are just pieces of paper to be bought and sold like commodities. Consequently, many investors today consider the in-and-out approach synonymous with having an "aggressive" policy. And with this goes the notion that the higher a portfolio's turnover rate (the faster its holdings are churned), the more likely it is to do well.

Unfortunately, the new emphasis on trading is misleading the public as to what investing is really about. It lures those least able to afford losses into thinking that the "performance" cultists have some new technique at their command when they are only doing what in-and-outers have done for decades. It is also responsible for the dangerous appraisal levels to which many lower-quality stocks have lately been pushed.

A large number of today's new investors have been drawn into speculation because they think that the performance approach is the only way to build up their capital. In previous chapters I advocated an aggressive investment policy that is much more *certain* and far less *risky*. Briefly, the better course is to invest in those industries and companies which—because of the nature of their business, the capability of their management, their emphasis on research and other favorable characteristics—are almost certain *as a group* to achieve strong future growth of earnings and dividends. The investor in such stocks should adopt the same attitude as that held by the typical owner of a private business. The latter commits his capital to an enterprise he believes will do well over a long period. If sales and earnings should run into temporary difficulties, he sees no reason to rush out and sell the business. It is because of this attitude that many investors today own shares of Eastman Kodak, Merck, Minnesota Mining, IBM, Texaco, Honeywell, Corning Glass, or similar companies, at a cost basis of only a small fraction of current market value. And they are now receiving annual dividends equal to 10, 15, even 25 percent on their original investment. In contrast, a much larger number of investors have never owned shares of these or other comparably successful companies. Throughout the past 15 years, for example, IBM has been the one stock which nearly everyone has known he ought to own. Yet during this period, only 1 out of every 80 stockholders has actually added it to his portfolio.

Others may have owned IBM or similar outstanding issues in the past, but they later sold out because of their own or someone else's concern over short-term developments. Therefore, I put forth as Investment Resolution Number Three:

I resolve to think of myself as a part owner of the companies in which I invest and not as a buyer of pieces of paper that I count on selling within a short time for large profits.

THE FINAL WORD

It is time for me to bid you good-bye. I have enjoyed writing this book, and I hope you have had fun reading it. Let me close by summarizing the 10 most common mistakes in investing (untouchables) which you should scrupulously avoid and the 10 most important common sense rules (commandments) for successful investing.

The Ten Untouchables

As far as possible, do not:

1. Try to strike it rich quickly.
2. Aim at buying at the lowest and selling at the highest price.
3. Use hunches and tips for trading in the market.
4. Decide against building a balanced portfolio because you have a small amount to invest.
5. Fail to define your investment goals clearly and objectively.
6. Become enamored by high-performance stocks without further investigation.
7. Attempt to use esoteric market tools (such as puts and calls, shorting, etc.) without using extreme caution.
8. Neglect to take into account both fundamental and technical factors before buying a stock.
9. Buy a stock on the basis of its past and present performance rather than on its future.
10. Fail periodically to review your portfolio vis-à-vis your investment objectives.

The Ten Commandments

It makes good sense to follow, as consistently as possible, the following rules:

1. Invest in stocks only if you are psychologically, emotionally, and financially suited to playing the investment game.
2. Investigate before you invest.
3. Invest within, or even up to, but never beyond your means.
4. Make a realistic estimate of the return which you should expect on your investment.
5. Prepare yourself for short-term losses and disappointments.
6. Orient yourself to modifying your objectives systematically.
7. Learn to draw your own conclusions on the basis of what you read and hear.
8. Fit your program to your objectives.
9. Buy values, for in the long run only values count.
10. Be prepared to withdraw from the market if you feel strongly that you should be out of it.

See you in the market arena. SOON!

YIPD

Your Investment Personality Detector

Before you began reading my book *Inside Wall Street* I suggested that you take a quiz in order to determine your investment personality. Assuming that you did so, it might be fun to find out whether your investment personality has changed since reading the book.

The quiz is again reproduced below for your convenience. Please answer questions A through Z.

A. I consider myself the following kind of investor:
    1. cautious
    2. subjective
    3. action-oriented (that is, anxious to buy and sell frequently)
    4. sound
    5. objective

B. I like to think of the stock market as a place:
    1. where I can make a lot of money within a relatively short time
    2. where I can build a sound investment portfolio
    3. where I can invest all my savings safely
    4. where I can gamble
    5. which is a never-never land

C. I am a person who:
   1. likes action in the market
   2. takes a cautious but optimistic approach to investing
   3. acts on intuition in the market
   4. feels comfortable when I blindly carry out my broker's recommendations
   5. knows so little about the market that I should not operate in it

D. I would consider myself a successful investor if I were to:
   1. make money every time I sell a stock
   2. realize a *net* gain from my investment every year
   3. double my money every two years
   4. make 25 percent on my investment every year
   5. gain on an average 10–15 percent a year in the long run (that is, over 5-to-10 year period).

E. If my past investment record were a shameful one, this would suggest that:
   1. I had a very bad broker
   2. I failed to do my investment homework properly
   3. I lost money only because the market in general was bad
   4. big traders fixed the prices and made money at my expense
   5. I should have sold my losing stocks and switched to some that were getting ready for major moves

F. If I ever need information about a stock, I would obtain it:
   1. from a broker
   2. from a successful investor
   3. from a number of reliable sources
   4. from the company
   5. from an advisory service

G. When I look at the price of a stock, I like to think of this price as being:
   1. synonymous with the value of that stock
   2. somehow related to the value of the stock but not necessarily equal to it
   3. too low, too high, or just right, depending upon the amount of money I have
   4. an index of popularity of the stock
   5. of little consequence, since the ruling price can be totally out of line with what it should be

H. I would consider a stock worth buying if:
   1. its price has been going up consistently
   2. it is low-priced
   3. I had read something good about the company that issued the stock
   4. some advisory service has recommended it
   5. some of my successful investor friends own the stock

I. Before making a decision to buy or sell a stock, I would like to:
   1. investigate the stock as long as possible because I am never in a hurry to buy stocks
   2. spend very little time for fear I might lose the buying opportunity forever
   3. get as many views on the stock as possible

    4. re-evaluate my investment objectives

    5. first decide whether the market situation is ideal for making such a move

J. If my broker recommends I sell a stock I am holding, I should:
1. ignore his recommendation on the grounds that he is trying to make money for himself
2. investigate his reasons for giving me this advice
3. find out whether or not I could put my money in a better stock before deciding whether or not I should sell my stock
4. sell the stock right away
5. sell it if I could make a profit, but hold it if I would have to take a loss

K. If I were forced to take a loss in the stock market, I would:
1. consider my misfortune as part of the game
2. get terribly upset
3. check to see if I have made any profits in the recent past to offset the loss
4. make a serious attempt to learn from my misfortune
5. try to take my loss philosophically

L. If my broker were to call up and recommend that I buy a certain stock, I should:
1. buy the stock without delay
2. ask the broker if he has his interest or mine at heart
3. request the broker to send me all the relevant information he has on the stock
4. tell the broker I am going to think about his recommendation so as not to hurt his feelings and then do nothing about it
5. examine all the facts dispassionately and then make a decision

M. If the price of a stock were to decline sharply after I purchased it, I should:
1. be critical of myself for failing to get rid of the stock earlier
2. sell the stock at a loss and charge the loss to my bad luck
3. hold the stock until its price goes up so I may recover my loss
4. buy more of that stock to bring my average purchase price down
5. investigate the stock thoroughly before making another move

N. Buying at the low and selling at the high:
1. is the only way to invest in the stock market
2. is the best investment objective
3. is a worthwhile goal to pursue
4. can rarely be attained
5. should always be seriously attempted, even if it is difficult

O. If a stock I didn't own were to make a major move, I would:
1. not touch it with a 10-foot pole
2. grab it before the price advances even further
3. investigate the company which issued the stock before buying the stock
4. watch the stock closely
5. try to buy it on a short-term dip

P. I prefer to treat the past performance of a stock as:
1. of no consequence

2. of some importance
3. of utmost importance in a bull (rising) market, but of little importance in a bear (falling) market
4. only one factor to consider
5. of significance when the price of that stock is declining

Q. If the price of a stock I had purchased were to go up substantially, I would:
   1. sell it
   2. hold it in the hope I might make more money
   3. buy more shares of it hoping the price would continue to rise
   4. watch the price action on it carefully for a while
   5. investigate the company thoroughly before making up my mind about selling the stock

R. I consider the study of some leading stock market averages (for instance, the Dow Jones Industrial Average):
   1. to be of little value
   2. of great importance in making investment decisions
   3. of importance only for the chartists (those who graph fluctuations in market averages)
   4. useless, because what good is it to know where the market has been
   5. important only for buying and selling stocks but not for holding them

S. If the price of a stock I had purchased were to go down substantially, I should:
   1. buy more of it to average my buying price
   2. sell it immediately
   3. switch to a stock that is performing better
   4. ask my broker for advice
   5. hold that stock for my children

T. If I were to meet someone who boasted of his great success in the stock market, I would:
   1. take his story with a grain of salt
   2. ask him what his secret of success is and try to follow his method religiously
   3. compare his method with mine in the hope of benefiting from the comparison
   4. give his broker my business
   5. tell the successful investor my story and ask for his suggestions

U. I believe that a successful winner in the stock market, however defined, concentrates on:
   1. acting defensively
   2. outperforming the market
   3. learning new and better market techniques and perfecting the ones he already has
   4. trading, that is, buying and selling stocks frequently
   5. putting all his eggs into one basket and watching that basket carefully

V. The words "puts" and "calls":
   1. mean nothing to me

    2. say something about how to make lots of money cheaply
    3. are something too technical for me to comprehend
    4. are concepts I know I must understand before I can act intelligently
    5. are terms used by big professionals

W. During the 1969–70 bear market when stock prices declined sharply, I:
    1. took substantial losses
    2. did nothing thereby losing most of investment values
    3. bought several stocks very cheaply and came out a winner
    4. stayed away from the market completely
    5. got out of the market with huge losses and then got back into it when prices of most stocks had already reached their recent highs

X. Investing in the market is good for those who:
    1. want to make a lot of money in a short time
    2. wish to play the game defensively
    3. like to have a fixed monthly income
    4. have lots of money to play with
    5. possess technical knowledge about the market

Y. I have heard that every investor should attempt to buy different kinds (such as speculative, income, growth) of stocks so that his twin objectives of safety and appreciation in investment are simultaneously met. I think that this idea:
    1. is a sound one
    2. is basically bad
    3. should not be treated as a universal investment concept since each investor must buy stocks according to his own needs
    4. is an excellent one only for those who are wealthy and can purchase lots of stocks
    5. can work successfully in a bull (rising) market but not in a bear (falling) market

Z. During the next three years or so, I expect to:
    1. make a lot of money on the stock market
    2. become a professional investor
    3. stay in the market and try to break even
    4. do better than the average investor
    5. learn a lot about the market and become an intelligent investor

Now that you've finished taking the quiz, you may grade yourself by following the procedure outlined on page 268.

Now, tell me, did your investment personality change?

No?

Yes?

Maybe?

Whatever may be your answer, I wish you great success in your ventures.

Answers to Investment Personality Detector Quiz

QUESTIONS

ALTERNATIVES	A	B	C	D	E	F	G	H	I	J	K	L	M
1	3	1	1	1	2	4	2	3	2	2	3	1	1
2	2	5	5	2	5	1	5	1	1	5	1	1	1
3	1	2	1	1	3	5	1	5	5	2	1	5	1
4	4	1	1	2	1	3	3	4	2	1	5	1	2
5	5	3	2	5	1	3	1	1	3	1	3	4	5

ALTERNATIVES	N	O	P	Q	R	S	T	U	V	W	X	Y	Z
1	1	3	1	1	2	2	1	5	1	1	1	2	1
2	1	1	3	1	5	1	2	2	2	3	5	1	1
3	2	5	2	2	1	1	5	4	3	5	2	5	2
4	5	4	5	4	1	5	1	1	5	2	1	1	4
5	3	1	1	5	2	1	4	1	3	1	3	2	5

Total Grade	Your Investment Personality
26–51	Aggressive and speculative
52–91	Cautious and uncertain
92–130	Sound and confident

Footnotes

[1] "The Consumer: Behind the Nine Ball," *Time*, December 19, 1969, p. 69. Reprinted by permission from *Time, The Weekly Magazine*; Copyright Time Inc., 1969.

[2] Board of Governors of the Federal Reserve System, *The Federal Reserve System: Its Purposes and Functions* (Washington, D.C.: USGPD, 1947), p. 41.

[3] New York Stock Exchange, *Fact Book* (New York, 1970).

[4] McConville, J. A., "A Fundamental Approach," Investment Research Department, E. F. Hutton & Company, Inc., November 24, 1969.

[5] Burgess, Robert S., "Specialized Investment Services," *Library Journal*, March 1, 1970, p. 868.

[6] Leasco Systems & Research Corporation, *Now You Can Get the Corporate Reports You Use Regularly—Without a Hassle*, Report No. DB2 (Chicago: 1970), p. 1.

[7] Day, John D., "An Uncommon View of 'learned' Economic Reports," *Business Management*, October, 1969, p. 27.

[8] *Ibid.*, pp. 28, 32.

[9] Levin, Jesse, "Prophetic Leaders," *Financial Analysts Journal*, July–August 1970, pp. 87–90.

[10] Rolo, Charles, "The Folklore of P/E Ratios," *Forbes*, March 15, 1970, p. 76.

[11] *Loc. cit.*

[12] Stern, Joel, "The Case Against Maximizing Earnings Per Share," *Financial Analysts Journal*, September–October 1970, pp. 107–12.

[13] Thomas, Dana L., *The Plungers and the Peacocks* (New York: G. P. Putnam's Sons, 1967), p. 81.

[14] Puff, Robert C., Jr., "The 'Averages': What Do They Tell Investors?" *Weekly Staff Letter*, David L. Babson & Company, Inc., September 24, 1970, pp. 1–4.

[15] Gaumnitz, Jack E., and Carlos A. Salabar, "The Barron's Confidence Index," *Financial Analysts Journal*, September–October 1969, pp. 16–17, 70.

[16] Palmer, Michael, "Money Supply, Portfolio Adjustments and Stock Prices," *Financial Analysts Journal*, July–August 1970, pp. 19–22.

[17] Barnett, Stephen H., "The Monetary Indicators at Turning Points," *Financial Analysts Journal*, September–October 1970, pp. 29–32.

[18] Eiteman, Wilford, Charles A. Dice, and David K. Eiteman, *The Stock Market* (New York: McGraw-Hill Book Company, 1966), p. 403.

[19] Godfrey, M. D., C. W. J. Granger, and Oscar Morgenstern, "The Random Walk Hypothesis of Stock Market Behavior," *Kyklos*, XVII, 1964, pp. 1–30.

[20] Crouch, Robert, "The Volume of Transactions and the Price Changes on the New York Stock Exchange," *Financial Analysts Journal*, July–August 1970, pp. 104–9.

[21] Gould, Edson, "Daily Trading Barometer: It Signals a Market Rally," *Barron's*, February 16, 1970, pp. 23, 26.

[22] Keynes, John M., *General Theory of Employment, Interest, Money* (New York: Harcourt, Brace and Company, 1936), p. 156.

[23] Further details on charting: both vertical line; and point and figure, will be found in Harvey A. Krow, *Stock Market Behavior: The Technical Approach to Understanding Wall Street* (New York: Random House, 1969), pp. 159–215.

[24] Collins, Charles, "Market Ebb Tide," *Barron's*, April 27, 1970, pp. 5, 20, 22.

[25] Markstein, David, "Charting: A Quick Review," *Banking*, Vol. 59, No. 6, 1966, pp. 8, 10.

[26] Lerro, Anthony J., and Charles B. Swayne, *Selection of Securities* (Braintree, Mass.: D. H. Mark Publishing Company, 1970), pp. 65–70.

[27] Markstein, *op. cit.*, p. 8.

[28] Shepherd, William, "A Cynical Look at Men Who Make the Market," *Business Week*, July 4, 1970, p. 6.

[29] Thomas, Dana L., "Throwing Out the Book?" *Barron's*, July 6, 1970, p. 10.

[30] The following discussion borrows heavily from *Now About the Specialist*, New York Stock Exchange, New York, July 1968, pp. 12–14.

[31] Thomas, Dana L., *op. cit.*, p. 10.

[32] Ney, Richard, *The Wall Street Jungle* (New York: Grove Press, 1970), pp. 16, 18. Copyright © 1970 by Richard Ney. Reprinted by permission of Grove Press, Inc.

[33] Anonymous, *Wiped Out: How I Lost a Fortune in the Stock Market While the Averages Were Making New Highs* (New York: Simon & Schuster, Inc., 1966), pp. 10–115.

[34] Kennedy, David M., in the *Wall Street Journal*, February 9, 1970, p. 16.

[35] Eiteman, et al., *The Stock Market*, pp. 539–40.

[36] Cohen, Jerome, and Edward Zinbarg, *Investment Analysis and Portfolio Management* (Homewood, Ill.: Richard D. Irwin, Inc., 1967), p. 11.

[37] Hooper, L. O., "Time to Look at Cyclical Stocks," *Forbes*, January 15, 1961, p. 36.

[38] Greeley, John, and John Doherty, as quoted in Martin, Richard, "Heard on the Street," *Wall Street Journal*, March 30, 1970, p. 19.

[39] *Ibid.*

[40] "Opposites Attract a Following," *Business Week*, October 11, 1969, pp. 128–29.

[41] Durgin, James, "Cautiously Bullish," *Barron's*, November 9, 1970, pp. 3, 16.

[42] Molodovsky, Nicholas, "Recent Studies of P/E Ratios," *Financial Analysts Journal*, May–June 1967, pp. 101–8.

[43] Hammel, John, and Daniel Hodes, "Factors Influencing Price-Earnings Multiples," *Financial Analysts Journal*, January–February 1967, pp. 90–92.

[44] Levy, Robert, and Spero Kripotos, "Earnings Growth, P/E's and Relative Price Strength," *Financial Analysts Journal*, November–December 1969, pp. 60–67.

[45] Murphy, Joseph E., "Return on Equity Capital, Dividend Payout and Growth of Earnings Per Share," *Financial Analysts Journal*, May–June 1967, pp. 91–93.

[46] Gould, Alex, and Maurice Buchsbaum, "A Filter Approach Using Earnings Relatives," *Financial Analysts Journal*, November–December 1969, p. 61.

[47] "Calling the Shots with Higher Math," *Business Week*, July 20, 1968, pp. 89–94.

[48] "What Went Wrong With the Go-Go Funds," *Business Week*, May 30, 1970, p. 86.

[49] Friend, Irwin, Marshall Blume, and Jean Crockett, *Mutual Funds and Other Institutional Investors* (New York: McGraw-Hill Book Company, 1970), pp. 50–68.

[50] Seligman, Daniel, "A Cold Eye on Mutual Funds," *Fortune*, October 1970, p. 172. Courtesy of *Fortune* Magazine.

[51] "The Toughest Kid in Block Trading," *Business Week*, October 4, 1969, pp. 114–16.

[52] Arthur Wiesenberger Services, *Investment Companies* (New York, 1969), pp. 50–51.

[53] "Fund Analysis Finds Its Freud," *Business Week*, September 13, 1969, p. 128.

[54] Merrill Lynch, Pierce, Fenner & Smith, Inc., *Leisure* (New York, 1968), p. 4.

[55] "Putting Cash to Work," *Fortune*, February 1970, p. 181.

[56] Soldofsky, Robert, and Craig Johnson, "Rights Timing," *Financial Analysts Journal*, July–August 1967, pp. 101–4.

[57] Martin, Richard, "Looking for Losers," *Wall Street Journal*, January 23, 1970, pp. 1, 13.

[58] Thomas, Conrad, "Primer for Shorts," *Barron's*, November 2, 1970, pp. 15, 16.

[59] McEnally, Richard, and Edward Dyl, "The Risk of Selling Short," *Financial Analysts Journal*, November–December 1969, p. 76.

[60] Turov, Daniel, "Stock or Warrant?" *Barron's*, March 9, 1970, p. 9.

[61] Reilly, Frank, and Kenneth Hatfield, "Investor Experience with New Stock Issues," *Financial Analysts Journal*, September–October 1969, p. 80.

[62] Bank Administrative Institute, *Measuring the Investment Performance of Pension Funds* (Park Ridge, Ill., 1968), p. 14.

[63] Richardson, Lemont, "Do High Risks Lead to High Returns," *Financial Analysts Journal*, March–April 1970, pp. 88–99.

[64] Hoffland, David, "The Folklore of Wall Street," *Financial Analysts Journal*, May–June 1967, p. 85.

[65] Biggs, Barton, "Dubious Guide," *Barron's*, May 18, 1970, pp. 9, 19.

[66] "Wrong Again?" *Wall Street Journal*, June 17, 1970, p. 1.

[67] Granger, C. W., "What the Random Walk Model Does NOT Say," *Financial Analysts Journal*, May–June 1970, p. 91.

[68] Shelton, J. P., "The Value Line Contest: A Test of Predictability of Stock Market Changes," *Journal of Business*, July 1967, pp. 258–69.

[69] Eiteman, Wilford J., and Dean S. Eiteman, *Common Stock Values and Yields, 1950–1961* (Ann Arbor: University of Michigan, Bureau of Business Research, 1962). Mimeographed.

[70] Lorie, James, "Some Comments on Recent Quantitative and Formal Research on the Stock Market," *Security Prices: A Supplement, Journal of Business*, 1966, p. 110.

[71] McClintick, David, "Securities Trade Called Outmoded, Tangled by Saul," *Wall Street Journal*, November 16, 1970, p. 3.

[72] "The Gambling Game That Wall Street Plays," *Business Week*, October 31, 1970, pp. 58–61, 64.

[73] Weinberg, Eli, "For Eliminating the Stock Certificate," *Wall Street Journal*, September 24, 1970, p. 12.

[74] Loomis, Carol, "The Capital Mess on Wall Street," *Fortune*, July 1970, p. 143.

[75] "Wall Street Leaders Plan a United Front to Oppose SEC Commission-Rate Position," *Wall Street Journal*, November 11, 1970, p. 2.

[76] Davant, James (Managing Partner, Paine, Webber, Jackson & Curtis), "A Letter to All Our Customers," November 1, 1970, p. 1.

[77] Loomis, Carol, "They're Tearing Up Wall Street," *Fortune*, August 1, 1969, p. 88.

[78] "A Computer to Bypass the Broker," *Business Week*, March 8, 1969, pp. 96–97.

[79] Lawson, Herbert, "Limiting Liability," *Wall Street Journal*, November 9, 1970, p. 26.

[80] *Ibid.*

[81] This discussion is based upon "Billion-Dollar Rumor Factory," *Business Week*, August 9, 1969, pp. 26–27.

[82] Donnelly, Richard, "Inside Out?" *Barron's*, September 21, 1970, p. 3.

[83] *Ibid.*

[84] Editors of *The Wall Street Journal*, *The New Millionaires and How They Made Their Fortunes*, Macfadden-Bartell Corporation, New York, 1966, p. 9.

[85] Fisher, Lawrence, and James Lorie, "Rates of Return on Investments in Common Stock: The Year-by-Year Record, 1926–65," *Journal of Business*, July, 1968, pp. 291–95.

[86] "How Much Should My Portfolio Grow Each Year?" *Weekly Staff Letter*, David L. Babson & Company, Inc., Boston. Reprinted by Paine, Webber, Jackson & Curtis, Bulletin No. 187, December 1969, pp. 1–4.

[87] *Ibid.*, p. 2.

[88] Shackle, G. L. S., *A Scheme of Economic Theory*, Cambridge University Press, New York, 1965, p. 1.

[89] Homer, Sidney, *Structural Changes in the American Bond Market*. Speech delivered in Bellagio, Italy, on June 3, 1970. Mimeographed.

[90] "The Trillion-Dollar Economy," *Business Week*, October 17, 1970, pp. 65–66.

[91] Silberman, Charles E., "The U.S. Economy in an Age of Uncertainty," *Fortune*, January 1971, p. 75.

[92] "Why the Big Traders Worry Industry," *Business Week*, July 25, 1970, pp. 53–57.

[93] *Ibid.*, p. 53.

[94] *Ibid.*, p. 61.

[95] "The Bull Market in Western Art," *Business Week*, June 13, 1970, p. 92.

[96] "Three New Year's Resolutions," *Weekly Staff Letter*, David L. Babson & Company, Inc., Boston. Reproduced by Paine, Webber, Jackson & Curtis, Bulletin No. 13, January 1969, pp. 1–4.

Glossary

Asset Value—per Common Share—company's net resources at market value (after deduction of all liabilities, preferred stocks' liquidating value, and accrued dividends, if any), divided by the number of common shares outstanding.

Asset Value—per Preferred Share—company's net resourcres at market value (after deduction of all liabilities, any prior preferred stocks' liquidating value, and accrued dividends, if any), divided by the number of preferred shares outstanding.

Balanced Fund—An investment company that at all times holds bonds and/or preferred stocks, in varying ratios to its holdings of common stocks, in order to maintain relatively greater stability of both capital and income.

Balance Sheet—A condensed statement showing the nature and amount of a company's assets, liabilities, and capital on a given date.

Bear—Someone who believes the market will decline.

Bear Market—A declining market.

Big Board—A popular term for the New York Stock Exchange.

Blue Chip—The common stock of a large, well-known corporation with a relatively stable record of earnings and dividend payments over a period of many years.

Bond—A security representing debt—a loan from the bondholder to the corporation.

Broker—A person in the business of effecting transactions in securities for the accounts of others who receives a commission for his services. Closed-end investment company shares are usually bought and sold through brokers.

Bull—One who believes the market will rise.

Bull Market—An advancing market.

Call—An option contract that gives the holder the right to purchase a particular security from another person at a specified price during the term of the option, which may be any period of time but is rarely longer than six months and ten days. May be used either for speculative or "hedging" purposes.

Capital—The assets of a business. Forms of asset capital include plant and equipment, inventories, cash receivables, etc. The term refers also to the claims on the corporation's assets represented by its outstanding securities.

Capital Gains—Long-Term—profits realized from sale of securities held for more than six months.

Capital Gains—Short-Term—profits realized from sale of securities held six months or less.

Captial Gains Distribution—A distribution to investment company shareholders from net long-term capital gains realized by a "regulated investment company" on the sale of portfolio securities.

Closed-End Investment Company—An investment company with a relatively fixed amount of capital whose securities are traded on a securities exchange or in the over-the-counter market, as are the securities of operating business corporations.

Common Stock—A security representing ownership of a corporation's assets. The right of common stock to dividends and assets ranks after the requirements of bonds, debentures, and preferred stocks. Generally, shares of common stock carry voting rights.

Conglomerate—Company whose operations embrace those of several diversified industries under one corporate name.

Current Assets—Those assets of a company which are reasonably expected to be realized in cash, or sold, or consumed during the normal operating cycle of the business.

Current Liabilities—Obligations due within a period of a year or less.

Debenture—A bond secured only by the general credit of the corporation.

Dividend—A payment from income on a share of common or preferred stock.

Dollar Cost Averaging—An automatic capital accumulation method that provides for regular purchases of equal dollar amounts of securities and results in an average cost per share lower than the average price at which purchases are made.

Earnings—per Common Share—net income after deducting all charges, including preferred dividend requirements, divided by the number of common shares outstanding. Net income does not include profits from the sale of securities.

Earnings Report—A statement—also called an income statement—issued by a company showing its earnings or losses over a given period.

Equity—The residue of value for the owner of an asset remaining after deducting prior claims. The equity of a corporation may be divided into common shares alone or may include preferred shares as well. In calculating the equity of a common stock, preferred stock as well as debt must be deducted from total assets.

Good 'Til Cancelled Order (GTC) or Open Order—An order to buy or sell which remains in effect until it is either executed or cancelled.

Growth Stock—A stock that has shown better-than-average growth in earnings and is expected to continue to do so through discoveries of additional resources, development of new products or expanding markets.

Hedge—To offset. Also, a security that has offsetting qualities. Thus, one attempts to "hedge" against inflation by the purchase of securities whose values should respond to inflationary developments. Securities having these qualities are "inflation hedges."

Hypothecation—The pledging of securities as collateral for a loan.

Income—Gross—Total amount of dividends, interest, etc. (but not capital gains), received from company's investments before deduction of any expenses.

Income—Net—Balance of gross income after payment of expenses, fixed charges, and taxes. Also referred to as net investment income.

Inflation—A persistent upward movement in the general price level of goods and services which results in a decline in the purchasing power of money.

Investment Company—A corporation or trust through which investors pool their money to obtain supervision and diversification of their investments.

Margin Call—A demand upon a customer to put up money or securities with the broker. The call is made when a purchase is made; also when a customer's equity in a margin account declines below a minimum standard set by the Exchange or by the firm.

Monthly Investment Plan—An arrangement for regular purchases of stocks listed on the New York Stock Exchange, possible through member firms.

Mutual Fund—Same as Open-End Investment Company.

Net Assets—By common usage, total resources at market value less current liabilities, but strictly accurate only for single-capital-structure companies.

Odd Lot—Less than a round lot, which is usually 100 shares. On securities exchanges, buying and selling costs may be somewhat higher on odd lots than on round lots. Not applicable to open-end investment companies.

Open-End Investment Company—An investment company whose shares are redeemable at any time at approximate asset value. In most cases, new shares are offered for sale continuously.

Par Value—The amount fixed by the issuer of a security as the capital represented by that security. A corporation which issues a $10 par stock and receives $15 for each share allocates only $10 to capital and the remainder to "unearned surplus."

Preferred Stock—An equity security (generally carrying a fixed dividend) whose claim to earnings and assets must be paid before common stock is entitled to share.

Put—An option contract that gives the holder the right to sell a particular security to another person at a specified price during the term of the option, which may be any period of time but is rarely longer than six months and ten days. May be used either for speculative or "hedging" purposes.

Round Lot—A fixed unit of trading (usually 100 shares) to which standard commission rates on a securities exchange will apply.

Short Sale—The sale of a security which is not owned, in the hope that the price will go down so that it can be repurchased at a profit. The person making a short sale borrows stock in order to make delivery to the buyer and must eventually purchase the stock for return to the lender.

Special Situation—Usually describes venture capital type of investment, but may also refer to a conservative but relatively unknown investment or to heavy commitments in investments that, in the opinion of the management, are temporarily undervalued by the market.

Stop Order—A stop order to buy becomes a market order when a transaction in the security occurs at or above the stop price after the order is represented in the Trading Crowd. A stop order to sell becomes a market order when a transaction in the security occurs at or below the stop price after the order is represented in the Trading Crowd.

Thin Market—A market in which there are comparatively few bids to buy or offers to sell or both. The phrase may apply to a single security or to the entire stock market.

Up Tick—A term used to designate a transaction made at a price higher than the preceding transaction.

Warrant—An option to buy a specified number of shares of the issuing company's stock at a specified price. The warrant may be valid for a limited period of time only, or it may be valid permanently.

Yield—Income received from investments, usually expressed as a percentage of market price; also referred to as return.

Selected Bibliography

Chapter 3

How Over-the-Counter Securities Are Traded, Merrill Lynch, Pierce, Fenner & Smith, Inc., New York, June 1968.

Market for Millions, American Stock Exchange, New York, 1969.

Martin, Richard. "Market Hot Spot," *Wall Street Journal*, May 6, 1970, pp. 1, 8.

Thomas, Dana L. *The Plungers and the Peacocks*, G. P. Putnam's Sons, New York, 1967.

Understanding the New York Stock Exchange, New York Stock Exchange, New York, July 1968.

Chapter 4

Sands, Edith. "Sources of Information for Economic Forecasting," *Financial Analysts Journal*, July–August 1969, pp. 17–18, 34, 68–70.

Weintrob, Harry. "Financial Information on Microfiche and Microfilm," *Financial Analysts Journal*, November–December 1969, pp. 17–19, 68–70.

Chapter 5

Doody, Francis S. *Introduction to the Use of Economic Indicators*, Random House, New York, 1965.

"When Figures Are Stranger than Fiction," *Business Week*, October 4, 1969, pp. 42–44.

Note: No selected bibliography for Chapters 1, 2, 6, 13, and 14.

Chapter 7

How to Read a Financial Report, Merrill Lynch, Pierce, Fenner & Smith, Inc., New York, March 1967.

Newell, Gale. "Is Quarterly Financial Data Adequate for Investment Decision Making," *Financial Analysts Journal*, November–December 1969, pp. 37–43.

Radar, Lawrence A. "A Stock Is a Company Is People," *Financial Analysts Journal*, September–October 1969, pp. 105–7.

Understanding the New York Stock Exchange, New York Stock Exchange, New York, July 1968.

Chapter 8

Milne, Robert D. "The Dow-Jones Industrial Average Re-examined," *Financial Analysts Journal*, November–December 1966, pp. 83–88.

West, Stan, and Norman Miller. "Why the New NYSE Common Stock Indexes?" *Financial Analysts Journal*, May–June 1967, pp. 49–54.

Chapter 9

Barnett, Stephen H. "The Monetary Indicators at Turning Points," *Financial Analysts Journal*, September–October 1970, pp. 29–32.

Mittra, S. *Money and Banking: Theory, Analysis, and Policy*, Random House, New York, 1970.

Sprinkel, Beryl W. *Money and Stock Prices*, Richard D. Irwin, Inc., Homewood, Ill., 1968.

Chapter 10

Crouch, Robert. "The Volume of Transactions and the Price Changes on the New York Stock Exchange," *Financial Analysts Journal*, July–August 1970, pp. 104–9.

Godfrey, M. D., C. W. J. Granger and Oscar Morgenstern. "The Random Walk Hypothesis of Stock Market Behavior," *Kyklos*, XVII, 1964, pp. 1–30.

O'Brien, John. "How Market Theory Can Help Investors Set Goals, Select Investment Managers and Appraise Investment Performance," *Financial Analysts Journal*, July–August 1970, pp. 91–103.

Tabell, Edmund, and Anthony Tabell. "The Case for Technical Analysis," *Financial Analysts Journal*, March–April 1964, pp. 67–76.

Chapter 11

Jiler, William. *How Charts Can Help You in the Stock Market*, Commodity Research Publications, New York, 1962.

"The Stock Chartist Tries to Pierce the Foggy Trend," *Business Week*, July 5, 1969, pp. 66–67.

Wheelan, Alexander. *Study Helps in Point and Figure Technique*, Morgan, Rogers & Roberts, Inc., New York, 1954.

Chapter 12

Now, About the Specialist, New York Stock Exchange, New York, July 1968.

Chapter 15

"Calling the Shots with Higher Math," *Business Week*, July 20, 1968, pp. 89–94.

Durgin, James H.   "Cautiously Bullish," *Barron's*, November 9, 1970, pp. 3, 16.

Hayes, Douglas.   "The Undervalued Issue Strategy," *Financial Analysts Journal*, May–June 1967, pp. 121–27.

Molodovsky, Nicholas.   "Recent Studies of P/E Ratios," *Financial Analysts Journal*, May–June 1967, pp. 101–8.

"Opposites Attract a Following," *Business Week*, October 11, 1969, pp. 128–129.

Whitbeck, Volkert, and Manown Kisor, Jr.   "A New Tool in Investment Decision-Making," *Financial Analysts Journal*, May–June 1963, pp. 2–8.

Chapter 16

"A Fund Wizard Builds an Empire," *Business Week*, May 3, 1969, pp. 76–78.

Bogle, John.   "Mutual Fund Performance Evaluation," *Financial Analysts Journal*, November–December, 1970, pp. 25–33, 124.

"Turn for the Better?" *Barron's*, November 30, 1970, pp. 3, 16.

Chapter 17

Thomas, Conrad.   *Hedgemanship: How to Make Money in Bear Markets, Bull Markets, and Chicken Markets While Confounding Professional Money Managers and Attracting a Better Class of Women*, Dow Jones–Irwin, Inc., Homewood, Illinois, 1970.

Chapter 18

Eiteman, Wilford, and Dean Eiteman.   *Common Stock Values and Yields, 1950–1961*, University of Michigan Business Research, 1962. Mimeographed.

Murphy, John.   "The Value Line Contest: 1969," *Financial Analysts Journal*, May–June 1970, pp. 94–100.

Chapter 19

"A Computer to Bypass the Broker," *Business Week*, March 8, 1969, pp. 96–97.

"Big Board Tries a New Price Plan," *Business Week*, February 21, 1970, p. 36.

Schreiner, John.   "Stock Fees: Debating the Big Board," *Wall Street Journal*, June 11, 1970, p. 11.

"The Gambling Game That Wall Street Plays," *Business Week*, October 31, 1970, pp. 58–61, 64.

Chapter 20

"Do You Own a Portfolio or Just a Stock?" *Business Management*, September 1969, p. 20.

Chapter 21

"1971: Economic Outlook: The Economy in Transition," Federal Reserve Bank of Kansas City, *Monthly Review*, January 1971, pp. 3–12.

Packer, Stephen. "New Era for the Capital Markets in the 1970's?" *Financial Analysts Journal*, July–August 1970, pp. 10–16.
"The Seventies," *Business Week*, December 6, 1969, pp. 77–144.

Chapter 22

"10 Common Mistakes in Investing," Francis I. du Pont & Company, New York, pp. 1–6.
"Three New Year's Resolutions," *Weekly Staff Letter*, David L. Babson & Company, Inc., Boston. Reproduced by Paine, Webber, Jackson & Curtis, Bulletin No. 13, January 1969, pp. 1–4.

Index

A

Accounts, voluntary, 171
Actions, defensive and offensive, 143–44
Advances and declines, as market indicator, 49, 87–88
Advisory services, 31, 34–36
Aggregate indebtedness, 215
American Stock Exchange
  Index, 67
  nature of, 26–27
  versus NYSE, 27
Approach
  filter, 149–50
  quick-act, 135
  quick-dip, 135–36
  technical, 150–52
Assets
  current, 15
  definition, 15
  fixed, 15
Autex system, 225
Automatic trading of stocks, 210–11
Averages, market, 48

B

Balance of payments, as economic indicator, 43
Balance sheet
  Britts Company, 16
  definition, 15

Balanced funds, 169
Balanced portfolio, 236
  concept of, 236–38
Bank Administration Institute, 193
Bank letters, 34
Bargain stocks, 136–37
Barnett, Stephen H., 83
Barometer, Daily Trading, 95
Barron's Confidence Index, 69–70, 97
Big Board system, 224–25
Big traders, on Wall Street, 251–54
Biggs, Barton, 204
Bill, mutual fund, 254
Block trading, 168
Blue chip stock, 19
Bond
  bearer, 14
  callable, 14
  collateral-trust, 14
  convertible, 14
  debenture, 14
  definition, 14
  income or adjustment, 14
  mortgage, 14
  municipal, 175
  as source of fund, 15
Book value, of a stock, 54
Broker
  bypass, 224–25
  charges by, 26, 217–20
  data from, 31, 37–38
  problems of, 213–16

281

68.

2H273